CHARLES IVES REMEMBERED

Charles Ives Remembered

AN ORAL HISTORY

BY VIVIAN PERLIS

NEW HAVEN AND LONDON, YALE UNIVERSITY PRESS, 1974

Published with assistance from the foundation
established in memory of Philip William McMillan
of the Class of 1894, Yale College.

International standard book number: 0–300–01758–8
Library of Congress catalog card number: 74–75288

Designed by Sally Sullivan
and set in Times Roman type.
Printed in the United States of America by
Halliday Lithograph Corp., West Hanover, Mass.

Published in Great Britain, Europe, and Africa by
Yale University Press, Ltd., London.
Distributed in Latin America by Kaiman & Polon,
Inc., New York City; in Australasia and Southeast
Asia by John Wiley & Sons Australasia Pty. Ltd.,
Sydney; in India by UBS Publishers' Distributors Pvt.,
Ltd., Delhi; in Japan by John Weatherhill, Inc., Tokyo.

CONTENTS

MUSIC

LIST OF ILLUSTRATIONS

*Courtesy of the John Herrick Jackson Music Library, Yale University.
†Copyright © 1974 The National Institute of Arts and Letters
 Used by Permission
Other sources are indicated in parentheses.

FOREWORD

Forty years ago, in 1934, I published an article in the magazine *Modern Music* on the music of Charles Ives, based on a first acquaintance with the remarkable collection of his *114 Songs* that he himself had published and had sent to me. The essay began: "It will be a long time before we take the full measure of Charles Ives." In the intervening forty years, the music he produced in comparative obscurity has found a world audience, and the American musical community has discovered its first composer of major significance.

It is gratifying to realize that only America could have produced a Charles Ives. Or, to be more specific, only New England in the last quarter of the nineteenth century. In mid-nineteenth century, when our literature could boast such writers as Whitman and Thoreau, Emerson and Emily Dickinson, we had no comparable figure in the field of serious music. As everyone knows, in its more cultivated forms, music is the last of the arts to develop. Not until the advent of this greatly gifted New Englander were we able to point to a comparable figure in the world of symphonic literature.

In listening to the music of Ives, I have sometimes puzzled over what it is that makes his work, at its best, so *humanly* moving. I am thinking, for example, of the extraordinary first movement of his *Harvest Home Chorales,* written in 1897, and set for double chorus, organ, and brass instruments. In those few pages, Ives reflects a richness of human experience rarely met with in music of that or any other period.

Ives, when he composed, was incredibly daring: no one before him had ever ventured so close to setting down on paper sheer musical chaos. The marvel is that he got away with it. I well remember showing pages to musicians—good musicians—most of whom thought it very remarkable, but complained that it was so "confused"—if only he could clean it up a bit. It's ironical to think that it is this very "confusion" that now makes for the special excitement in Ives's music. Even some very broad-minded and forward-looking musicians who had every reason to be interested in music that was new and different had the same response. Serge Koussevitzky, at that time conductor of the Boston Symphony, was definitely intrigued, but I got that same reaction from him: You can't play it; it's too confused. Can't he straighten it out?

As the full musical stature of Ives the composer became apparent, the basic tragedy of his situation came to preoccupy my mind. How, I wondered, does a man of such gifts manage to go on creating in a vacuum, with no audience at all. As I look back, I was really concerned not so much with Ives alone, but with the thought of the many American composers who were writing their music without sufficient contact with an audience, and I thought of Ives as the prime example. It began with a preoccupation of my own: how does one get an audience, and what happens to a composer who does not have an audience? In that respect, Ives is a very American phenomenon. One can hardly imagine such a man in Europe. To write all that music and not hear it one would have to have the courage of a lion.

It is never easy for a writer to pin down the essence of a composer's work. This is particularly true for the music of Ives, so many-faceted, so rich in textures, and so various in content, from the simplest to the most complex pages. This becomes all the more remarkable when one realizes that he rarely, if ever, heard adequate performances of his more ambitious works during the period of his active creative life.

The upsurge of interest in the music of Ives in recent years, both at home and abroad, has greatly enhanced the position of the American composer on both sides of the Atlantic. This is especially true of the international music scene, where our serious composers have been particularly slow to make their mark. The Ives centennial year (1974) is certain to increase the worldwide interest in his work.

I append to this brief foreword a letter Ives sent me in 1932. Perhaps I should explain that it was written after a premiere performance of seven of his songs at the first Yaddo Festival in Saratoga Springs, New York, on May 1, 1932 [see p. 164]. The festival was followed by a symposium on music critics and criticism, to which the second paragraph of his letter refers:

Low-Wood
Windermere
July 21, 1932

Dear Mr. Copland:

I want to write you, if just a line, to tell you that I appreciated greatly your playing some of my songs. If they went well, it was due to the way you and Mr. Linscott handled them. I am grateful to you both. Please thank Mr. Linscott for me.

But the way you stood up in "congress", and had your say from "within out" gave added substance to the whole festival. Not exactly all critics are "lily pads"—but too many are.

With appreciation and best wishes

Yours sincerely,
Charles E. Ives

When we get back we are looking forward to the pleasure of meeting you personally—and I hope then to be able to be of some help in the work in any way I can.

AARON COPLAND

PREFACE

In our desire for certainty in an uncertain world we would like to have all the answers to the perplexing questions about Ives's music. But the way a composer translates his experience into the work created is elusive, and the relationships between Ives's life and his music are intricate, subtle, and complex. The interviews presented in this book, with those who knew and worked with Charles Ives, cannot explain his music. They can, however, give a clearer picture of this extraordinary man and bring into focus the place and time in which he lived. They help to point out the complexities of Ives's life and career, retaining contradictions and ambiguities, which may deter the myth builders and those who must have the answers. I daresay, if Ives were here himself, he would not know the hows and whys of his compositions. He did not want to be categorized, dissected, pigeonholed. When you have caught his music one way, he turns it into something else before you can finish your analytic sentence. His personality was like this too—full of paradoxes—making it almost impossible to define what he was really like. The paradoxes and questions remain, partly because of Ives's desire for privacy and his belief in a continuing, unexplained spirit. Even more, one can feel his sense of fun. One can almost hear him say, "You can't catch me!" Once, while studying an Ives manuscript with awe and respect, I turned a page to see that Ives had drawn an eye winking up from inside a treble clef. And I recall his nephew Chester Ives saying, "If you'd ever get too serious, Uncle Charlie would let you walk in front of him, then he'd trip you up!"

Charles Ives, with his paradoxes, complexities, and eccentricities, was an ideal choice as the subject of an oral history project. He was not conventional and did not choose conventional people as his friends and associates. As a result, those interviewed are interesting, sometimes extraordinary people in their own right. The Ives Project consists of fifty-eight transcribed interviews, and it is the only extensive biographical oral history of an American composer. The first twenty-five interviews were supported by Yale University and the CBS/Records Group. The National Endowment for the Humanities funded a grant in 1970–71 for completion of the project. In 1971 the National Institute of Arts and Letters presented an award in recognition of the research and for aid toward its publication. The tapes and transcripts are part of the Ives Collection at the Yale Music Library, which houses Ives's music manuscripts and papers placed there by Harmony Ives soon after her husband's death in 1954. They are available in their entirety, with few restrictions, as source material for Ives scholars, students, and others interested in American music.

The idea for the project was formulated while working with the Ives Collection in 1968. I became aware that there were a number of people still living who had known and worked with the composer, and that an effort should be made to collect and preserve their memories of him. Mrs. Ives was already too ill to be approached. Julian Myrick, Ives's insurance partner and friend, was in his eighties and also ill, but it was possible to interview him. Mr. Myrick's hearing was weak, and I was too timid to raise my voice. But we soon got used to each other, and Mr. Myrick thoroughly enjoyed having the undivided attention of someone familiar with people and places no one else remembered. When this fine gentleman died a few weeks after our last interview, I realized that an emergency situation existed, and, together with a colleague, Martha Maas,* I decided to search out and talk to everyone of importance in Ives's life while this was still possible. We did not consider then that we were doing something called "oral history," a term more commonly associated with political figures and presidential archives.

Those who knew Ives felt the magnetism of his personality and knew that their lives had been touched in some special way. For this reason, almost everyone agreed readily to an interview, while a few took years of patient coaxing, and only one never consented. Distance, age, fear of the tape recorder, and sometimes plain old New England reticence were occasional obstacles. Once in a while it was necessary to pay a call first or come to tea and hope that the tape recorder might come along the next time. But from New York to Texas, and many places in between, it was the feeling of warmth and generosity that was predominant from Charles Ives's friends, family, and colleagues as they shared their memories of him. Many contributed correspondence, photographs, and other memorabilia to the Ives Collection. For all this I am grateful, and for permission to publish these interviews.

The interviews presented in this book are edited, some considerably, in order to minimize repetition. Since one of the major hazards of oral history is the fallibility of memory, changes have been made to correct factual errors. A few of the interviewees themselves made changes in their transcripts in

---

*Now Assistant Professor of Music at Ohio State University, Martha Maas conducted the following interviews in 1969: Lewis Bronson, Charles Buesing, George Hofmann, Charles Kauffman, Ely Ryder, George Roberts, Gertrude Sanford, John S. Thompson.

preparation for publication. In at least one case (Elliott Carter) this resulted in substantial differentiation between the published material and the original interview.

Librarians and historians rallied to Wiley Hitchcock's call to arms when he wrote: "Let's wake up to the fact that we live in the electronic age. Let's put films and microphones and tapes to work for us as scholars and historians. Let us not consider them as audio-visual *aids,* secondary means, but as potential *sources,* primary means. . . . No culture before ours had had such a fantastic variety of means for *creating,* not just preserving, the raw materials from which history is written."* To him and to many other colleagues I am grateful for enthusiastic support of the Ives Project and for their recognition of oral history as a valid method of research. I appreciate the help of Eugene Becker, Leonard Bernstein, Sidney Cowell, Oliver Daniel, Alfred Knopf, Jr., Alfred B. Kuhn, Goddard Lieberson, Norman Lloyd, Martha Maas, Sam Parkins, Harold Samuel, Brooks Shepard, Jr., and Richard Warren. I am indebted to the Yale University Library, the Yale School of Music and its dean, Philip Nelson, the CBS/Records Group, the Mutual of New York Library, the National Endowment for the Humanities. The National Institute of Arts and Letters has given its support and granted permission to use visual and quoted material from the estate of Charles Ives. Aaron Copland has graciously contributed his thoughts about Ives and for this I thank him. Frank Rossiter deserves special acknowledgment for generously giving of his time and knowledge. Claudia Anderson and Amy Catlin went far beyond their typing duties with advice and assistance. Jim Sinclair, Elizabeth and Ken Singleton contributed helpful suggestions. I am grateful to Robin Bledsoe and Judy Yogman, editors, for their expertise and encouragement.

The following valuable literary sources are cited frequently throughout this book: Howard Boatwright (editor), *Essays Before a Sonata and Other Writings* (New York: W. W. Norton & Co., 1961); Henry and Sidney Cowell, *Charles Ives and His Music* (New York: Oxford University Press, 1955); John Kirkpatrick, *A Temporary Mimeographed Catalogue of the Music Manuscripts . . . of Charles Edward Ives* (1960); John Kirkpatrick (editor), *Charles E. Ives Memos* (New York: W. W. Norton & Co., 1972). Hereafter, I have taken the liberty of referring to them as: Boatwright, *Essays;* Cowell, *Ives;* Kirkpatrick, *Catalogue;* and Kirkpatrick, *Memos.*

I am more than grateful to a few individuals: my husband, Sandy, followed the Ives Project and the book preparation from beginning to end with unfailing enthusiasm and devotion; my assistant, Caitriona Bolster, pre-

*H. Wiley Hitchcock, "A Monumenta Americana?", *Notes 25* (1968): 11.

pared the index and contributed in so many ways, big and small, with extraordinary patience and dedication; John Kirkpatrick, with characteristic Ivesian generosity, creativity, and humor, inspired me with the spirit of Charles Ives and with the joy of his music.

VIVIAN PERLIS
New Haven, Connecticut

YOUTH AND YALE YEARS

Birthplace of Charles Ives. The following inscription is on the reverse side of the photograph:
The old Ives family household over 115 years old
The old Ives family waggon over 100 years old
The old family horse "Belmont" 34 years old (1895)

Compliments of Isaac Ives -95

Charles Ives was born in the old "Ives house" on Main Street in Danbury, Connecticut, on October 20, 1874. The primary source of information about the generations of Iveses who lived in that house is AMELIA VAN WYCK,* whose father was Charles Ives's first cousin. Amelia was born in 1884. She was an artist, and before her marriage she had her own studio in Greenwich Village. Her strong spirit of independence, which must have appealed to her cousin Charlie, was still evident at the time of these interviews, which took place first in her apartment in Norwalk, and later in a little house in Westport, Connecticut.† An extensive collection of Ives memorabilia surrounded her—family paintings were on the walls; old toys were on the shelves; and boxes of letters, pictures, and account books from Ives ancestors were everywhere. Amelia Van Wyck shared samples of these as she spoke with pride and affection about the family.

William Ives was a ship's captain.‡ The *Truelove,* his ship, brought settlers from England to Boston in 1635 and then the first settlers to New Haven in 1638. The story is that he didn't stay on the first trip, because his wife wasn't well enough to come with him. On the next trip he went back and brought her, and settled. Then the family spread out northward to Wallingford, Meriden, and Middletown.

Isaac's family was in Meriden.§ Isaac moved to Danbury expecting to practice law. He boarded with a man named Benedict, and he married a Benedict daughter. She died, and a couple of years later he married Sarah Amelia White. Isaac was in several businesses which didn't work out well in Danbury. For a brief time he joined a tanning business, and then he went to New York before 1800 where he had a wholesale grocery business. It wasn't until he started a hat business in Danbury that he was successful. Isaac was active in the New York branch. Most of the time when he was in New York, his wife stayed with her father in Danbury, and their son George‖ lived in Danbury with some of the family. He was sent to school at Mr. Thomas Tucker's. Mr. Tucker was a retired New York merchant who thought Danbury should have a school, so he opened one for the

---

*Mrs. Henry Van Wyck, née Amelia Merritt Ives.
†November 7 and 21, 1968; March 31, 1969.
‡William Ives (ca. 1607–ca. 1647), first American ancestor of Charles Ives.
§Isaac Ives (1764–1845) was Charles Ives's great-grandfather.
‖George White Ives (1798–1862) was Charles Ives's grandfather.

children of his friends and charged a dollar a year for their school books and materials. It was this Mr. Tucker from whom Isaac bought the Ives house in 1829 [see p. 1].

The family all hoped that the house would stay in the family forever after. It meant a great deal to them. Isaac was very much interested in his gardens. He had a rose garden on one side of the house, a little fountain, and then of course they had their vegetable gardens. The flower garden was between the house and the barn. There were double Russian violets and loads of lily-of-the-valley, and all around the border of the house little star-of-Bethlehem flowers, and syringas over the side porch. The house always smelled of beeswax and fruit, and sometimes of the white Madonna lilies they used to have loads of. Yes, the house meant a great deal to all the family, and the children all lived there. There was the barn behind the house and then the land farther up the hill where Isaac owned property. A brook runs through, and that is where Isaac dammed up the brook and made a pond, and then piped the water down to the house. He had the first bathroom in Fairfield County. People came from miles around to see it.

When Isaac died, Sarah was very worried, because she believed that when you went to heaven, you progressed. She was worried for fear it would take her so long to catch up with him. Isaac's son George kept on with his father's business and it flourished. George became a prominent man in Danbury.

George felt that Danbury should have a savings bank, and the bank started at the house. First he had a wooden chest in the dining room, and then as the business got larger, he moved it to a desk. And he would take deposits along the street. Somebody would come along and say, "Oh, Mr. Ives, I want to put this money in." So George would put it in his pocket and then put it in the bank. When he was out and people wanted to make deposits, his wife Sarah* took care of it. The bank grew and acquired other offices and moved to a little building next to the house. And then it built its first real building.

The George White Iveses had five children: Joseph, Isaac, Amelia [Sarah Amelia], Sarane, and George,† who was Charlie's father.

George was a small boy when the house was a bank building. He didn't go into business like his father. His interest was music. All properly brought up young people in those days had to have not only French and Latin les-

---

*Née Sarah Hotchkiss Wilcox (1808–99), Charles Ives's grandmother.
†George Edward Ives (1845–94).

1866   1852   1849   1909

This photograph, taken about the time of World War I, shows all four homes of the bank standing side by side. The date under each building indicates the year that it was first occupied by the bank.

sons, but drawing, painting, and music. So Joseph and Isaac and Amelia all had music lessons, and all of them were bored with it. It was just a waste of time and money, so George was not offered any music lessons. And then one day, the family was going on a Fourth of July picnic and George said, "If you don't mind, I'd rather stay home and pick cherries to earn some money to buy a flute." When his talent and his interest seemed to grow, his father found him the best music teacher possible in New York in 1860, a German master, Carl Foeppl. He lived in Morrisania in The Bronx, and George went there to study with him. Then, when George was seventeen, he became the leader of a Civil War band [the First Connecticut Heavy Artillery]. The band was connected with his cousin Col. Nelson White's regiment, and it was supposed to be one of the finest bands in the Civil War. When George returned to Danbury, he brought home with him a little colored boy who had done odd jobs around the camp, and he was sent to school in Danbury. His name was Anderson Brooks [ca. 1855–1906?], and he lived at the house.

George became the bandmaster. Of course Danbury thought that that was just kind of foolishness. Music and art were not things that you really worked at. They were entertainment, but George really worked at it. He played piano, violin, and organ and he had a cornet band. Still, I don't think it was a very affluent business, so he had to work also in his father's bank. A band in a town like Danbury would not bring you a very large fortune. George taught music too. He gave me lessons for a while, George did. One time a visiting orchestra came to Danbury to give a concert, and something happened to the conductor, so George took over and conducted the strange orchestra, much to the nervousness of the family. They wondered how it would go, but it went very well. George was more capable than Danbury expected him to be. He had very little recognition from his home town. And I think Charlie really got very little recognition from his home town.

When George married, he and Mollie* lived in the house in the large bedroom over the south parlor. My great-grandmother [Sarah Hotchkiss Wilcox Ives] lived in the bedroom over the dining room, which was a very fine place for her to live, as she was in charge of the house, and it had stairs down to the kitchen and down to the front of the house. They all got along beautifully, and the children had a wonderful time. And of course they had visiting children. When people went visiting at that time, it wasn't just a weekend, because transportation was something. So they stayed two or three weeks or a month. It would be a very full household. I was always fascinated with one of the little rooms that looked out on Chapel Place. It had the most wonderful wallpaper of children in boats, rowing around and among the rushes. That was there for goodness knows how many years.

It was always a very open house. One night, a horse and buggy drove up with two strangers in it. The woman came up and said that her husband was very sick, and she couldn't take care of him, and they didn't know where to go. So they stayed at the Iveses until the man was better and they could go back to their farm. I'm not sure which family they were, but I have an idea that they were the parents of two young women who afterward worked for the Iveses. Another time, the time of the wagon trains going through to the West, one wagon train spent the night in Danbury. And a little girl in the train was too sick to go on. They just left her with the Ives family until her other friends could come along and pick her up. She left a little blue and white plate behind, and that always stayed in the corner cupboard in the south parlor. It was known as "the little girl's

*Mary Elizabeth Parmelee became Mrs. George E. Ives (1849–1929) on January 1, 1874.

Joseph Moss Ives, one year; Charles Edward Ives, three years.

plate." I have it. And of course there were plenty of friends and cousins who stayed off and on. It seemed to be an expandable house.

Charlie and Moss* were born in the house. When Moss was coming, Mollie didn't want too much confusion, so George had to go up to the barn to practice the violin. Charlie, who was under two, was sent along where he sat happily in Uncle Joe's buggy playing with the whip while his father practiced. So Charlie's introduction to music began at an early age. In 1879, Aunt Amelia wanted to come back to the Ives house to live, and what Aunt Amelia wanted, she usually got. So George and Mollie with

---

*Joseph Moss Ives (1876–1939) was called Moss. He signed himself, "J. Moss Ives."

Charlie and Moss, moved out to Stevens Street to a home of their own. A few years later, they moved to the house on Chapel Place, which was made over out of the barn of the old house. So when Charlie practiced piano when he was growing up, it was in the same place where he'd sat in the buggy and raised his whip some years before.

The Iveses were looked up to in the town. There were a few families that *were* the town—the Whites and the Iveses and the Tweedys—and then other families moved in. The church was next door to the house—it was built on what used to be our vegetable garden. I can remember, when I was quite small, people stopping by after church at Great-grandmother's. They used to call it having Sunday school over there. They discussed what was going on in the world, men and books and so forth, until it was time to pick up the children from their Sunday school class and go home to Sunday dinner.

In the summers the whole family took turns being down in Westbrook, Connecticut, at my father's* house for several weeks at a time. Charlie and Moss were there almost every summer. And Great-grandmother was

*Howard Merritt Ives (1860–94), Charles Ives's "Cousin Howdie."

Charlie Ives, age eight, with cousin Sarane Seeley, Westbrook, Connecticut, 1882.

*Three generations of Iveses photographed outside the Danbury house ca. 1887: center,
Ives's grandmother Sarah Hotchkiss Wilcox Ives (1808-99); far left, Charlie's "Cousin
Howdie," Mrs. Van Wyck's father, Howard Merritt Ives (1860-94); far right, Mrs. Van
Wyck's mother, Anna Wood Miner Ives (1857-1942) holding baby Harry; standing left rear
Charlie's brother Joseph Moss Ives (1876-1939); standing right rear, Charlie at about age
thirteen; front, Amelia Merritt Ives later Mrs. Van Wyck. On viewing this picture recently,
Amelia Van Wyck commented on the fact that she was given a boy's style haircut, since her
parents had wanted her to be a son, while her younger brother was allowed to have curls.*

there, and Aunt Amelia and Uncle Lyman,* and some of the Seeleys, the
other cousins. It was a whole row of family. We called it "Cousins' Beach."
It was quite a closed corporation.

My first definite memory of Charlie is the time he came to a party at our
house in Balmforth Avenue in Danbury with the grown people. I was four,
and he was fourteen. The grown-ups were all talking in the front and back
parlors, and Charlie and I were bored, so we wandered into the dining
room, where the table was all ready. There was a large platter of lobster

*Lyman Denison Brewster (1832–1904) married Ives's Aunt Amelia in 1868. He was a
prominent lawyer and judge in Danbury.

salad, and the cat was having a happy time with it. So Charlie and I put the cat outdoors, smoothed over the salad, and nobody knew anything about it. Then when I was thirteen or fourteen, he took me to the Yale-Harvard regatta at New London. That was when he was in college, and it was pretty decent of an undergraduate to take a small cousin. And Harvard won. That was a bitter blow.

After that I didn't see very much of Charlie until he was married. I did see him once when he was living in one of the "Poverty Flats,"* the one on Central Park West, and I had my first studio on West 67th Street. I was studying at the Art Students League. Charlie brought Bart Yung, one of his classmates who shared the Poverty Flat, over one evening. Charlie had just started in the insurance business then and was with Mutual Life. The Mutual Life was in a way a family business, because two of the cousins were officers—Granville White and Robert Granniss. That was how Charlie happened to go into Mutual Life when he decided he wanted a business life.

I saw Harmony and Charles at their 11th Street apartment, and then in the 22nd Street house. The 11th Street apartment was their first place. It was way over toward Sixth Avenue, and there was a little Jewish cemetery on the corner, and their windows looked out on that, which gave them light and air. And they had a fireplace. It was here that was the only time I ever saw anyone stand up to Aunt Amelia. She was visiting Harmony and Charles, and I was over there for dinner. Charlie started to put another log on the fire, and Aunt Amelia said, "Don't. There's enough on it, Charlie." Charlie hesitated, and Harmony said, "Put on what you want to, Charlie." So Charlie put the log on, and the skies didn't fall. I expected them to, but they didn't. Aunt Amelia was a dominating person.

There was always a piano wherever Charlie lived. In the 11th Street apartment Charlie used to try some of his music out on me. It was at the time when all the hurdy-gurdies were playing *The Merry Widow Waltz*. And people said, "Amelia knows two tunes. One is *The Merry Widow* and one isn't, but she doesn't know which is which." So Charlie would sit down and play something, and he'd say, "What is that?" I remember once I said, "It sounds like Sunday in the country." And he said, "That's just what it is." It was part of the *Concord Sonata,* I think. To another one I said, "That sounds like a storm at sea." And he said, "No, it's in the mountains." When they were having some of Charlie's music played in the 22nd Street

---

*Poverty Flat was the name given to two apartments on the fourth floor of 317 West 58th Street by a group of Yale graduates. Later, Poverty Flat moved to 65 Central Park West.

house, I was always invited. I went twice to hear it. I made a drawing of Charlie at the piano in the 22nd Street house. That was an upright against the wall, upstairs in the study. And I don't know whatever became of that. I made a couple of little sketches of their daughter Edie,* which I think they liked, and then I made a little drawing of the old house for them at a time when they couldn't get up there.

Charlie didn't discuss music very much with me, but we used to have knock-down-and-drag-out fights over his political ideas†—his "People's

*Edith Osborne was born in 1914. The Iveses adopted her the following year.

†In 1918 Charles Ives formulated a plan for peace negotiations. In a short article for which there are several drafts in the Ives Collection, he wrote: "A People's World Union (or call it the United States of the World), under whose constitution each country will be free to live its own life, no country shall try by force to capture another country—no more sneak-thieving by mediaeval-minded dictators. . . . A People's World Union Army or police force . . . analogous to that of the usual town and city police in most countries today—who get the horse thieves." Ives included in his plan an international voting age of eighteen and wrote several versions of the article, the last toward the beginning of World War II, headed, "The World's Only Hope!". See Boatwright, *Essays*, pp. 225–31.

Amelia Van Wyck's drawing (ca. 1919) of the Ives house from the rear, showing the old pear tree around which the house was built, and which Mrs. Van Wyck says, "was like a member of the family."

World Union" and his belief that the people should vote on important issues directly and not turn things over to the politicians. Charlie liked to talk to me. He said that being an artist made me the other oddball in the family.

Edie was four when they were in the 22nd Street house, and the first serious heart attack of Charlie's was when they lived there. It was 1918 and he was working on a committee to establish and sell Liberty Bonds. Charlie thought that there ought to be a small fifty-dollar bond so that everybody could contribute and be part of it. Franklin Roosevelt, who was the chairman of the committee (by virtue of his name, I suppose), scorned the idea of anything so useless as a fifty-dollar bond. Charlie had an argument with him* and Charlie won, but he had a heart attack either during or directly after the meeting which was in the Manhattan Hotel on 42nd Street on the opposite corner from the Grand Central Station at Vanderbilt Avenue. It was so bad that they couldn't move him from the hotel. Harmony had to go up there. He was really very sick for a long time. Finally he was moved home to 22nd Street again. Eventually Harmony had a breakdown from the strain. I saw them a great deal during that time. I was living nearby, and I was just married. I used to go down and spend the day there to keep Edie amused.

I'll never forget the drive when they were well enough to go back to Redding. Henry† and I drove them, and since our own car didn't have but two seats, we borrowed my brother's car. So with Harmony and Charlie in the back, and Edie between them (she was dropped off in Scarsdale to stay with Harmony's sister Louise) we started for Redding. I had a bottle of spirits of ammonia in one pocket and a bottle of brandy in the other, and I'd look around every once in a while to see if either were needed, because they were both so frail. When we got to Wilton, a tire blew. There was nothing in the car to fix the tire, so I had to get out and walk down the road till I came to a house where I could borrow a jack. The car eventually got there, and oh, they were so happy to be back in Redding!

---

*Harmony Ives's diary dates this Liberty Bond meeting as October 1, 1918. Franklin Roosevelt had pneumonia at that time and canceled all engagements. Ives may have had this argument with a representative of Roosevelt.
†Henry Van Wyck, Amelia's husband.

❧

There were not many people left in Danbury who remembered Charles Ives as a boy. One was ELY RYDER (1876–1972), interviewed July 29, 1969, at his summer home in Brewster, New York.

Charles Ives and I were teen-agers of about the same age. One day I went up on the hill to the Ives house to visit Charlie, and I found him playing a piano. I was astonished to find that he played it with his feet as well as with his hands. All expert piano players use their feet to affect the piano, but I just learned it that day!

Another personal memory of Charlie Ives relates to playing tennis. On West Street in Danbury there was a Rider family house (no relation to our family) with tennis courts back of it, and we teen-agers all played there. There'd been some effort to fix up the surface, to kill weeds by salt. One day I was down there, and Charlie was there. I heard him introduced to a young lady, and the result is very typical of Ives as a young man. When he was introduced to this young lady, he hemmed and hawed, and he said, "Look at the salt on the tennis court," and then he turned abruptly and ran away. He was a very timid young man.

*Charles Ives
at age fourteen.*

When PHILIP SUNDERLAND (1871–1972), a Danbury architect, was interviewed on November 29, 1968, it was a surprise to find that not only did he remember Charles Ives as a boy in Danbury, but he had vivid memories of George Ives as well. Philip Sunderland was three years older than Charles Ives. He lived to the age of one hundred and one. He was responsible for moving the old Ives house in 1923 when the Danbury National Bank (now the Fairfield County Trust Company) acquired the site on Main Street for its building. Ives insisted that the house be moved uphill on Chapel Place rather than be razed. The house was moved again in 1966 to fourteen acres of land adjoining Rogers Park, Danbury.

At the time Charles Ives was born, Danbury was about 11,000 inhabitants. Originally it was just a little country town. It achieved fame in the Revolution when the British came up and burned a lot of houses and marched back through Ridgefield where they shot General Wooster. We used to be considered the hat town of the United States. And then gradually, as hats were more or less abandoned, they've given it up. I don't think there's a real hat factory in Danbury now.

As a contemporary, I knew Charles Ives, boy and man. When he appeared in a public capacity as organist of the Baptist Church here, I marveled at that very much. He was kind of a boy prodigy. But as a young boy I knew him only slightly. Not very intimately at all. And I feel as though I have missed a great deal in not knowing him better. I had some thoughts of my own. I was very much interested in Thoreau, always, myself.

When Charles Ives went to New York in that insurance business right after college, he disappeared from my acquaintance. The way I became acquainted with him again, finally, was when we were moving the Ives house in order to build the Danbury National Bank, of which I was the architect. Charles Ives's mother lived in the house while it was being moved. And he came up to see me and tell me he hoped I'd look after her. Incidentally, he gave me a check for $2,500 to pay the bills. I didn't think of such a thing as suggesting payment—he just did this on his own, and we never used it all up. I established a joint account in the bank, in Charles Ives's and my own name, and when the balance was left, all he had to do was put his own check in for it. Mother Ives stayed in the house while it was being moved, at great inconvenience. We did the best we could for

Amusements.

The feature of the evening, in the musical line, was the rendition of the "Holiday Quickstep," composed and arranged for an orchestra by Charlie Ives, a thirteen-year-old son of George E. Ives. Master Ives is certainly a musical genius, being an accomplished performer on several instruments, as well as a composer and arranger. The "Holiday Quickstep" is worthy a place with productions of much older heads, and Master Charlie should be encouraged to further efforts in this line. We shall expect more from this talented youngster in the future.

From The Evening News, *Danbury, January 17, 1888.*

Concert in Baptist Church,

FOR THE

BENEFIT OF NEW CHURCH FUND,

Friday Evening, May 8th, 1891.

MISS ISABELLA FAYERWEATHER,
Contralto.

MISS SARAH L. TREADWELL,
Violinist.

CARROLL D. RYDER, EDWIN S. GRIFFETH,
J. WESLEY O'CONNOR, JOHN C. DICKENS,
Male Quartette.

MASTER CHARLES E. IVES,
Organist.

✱PROGRAMME✱

1. OBERON, Overture. } . . . . *C. M. Von Weber*
   March, in D. }

2. VIOLIN SOLO, "Cavatina" . . . . *Raff*

3. ADAGIO, Pianoforte Sonata, Op. 2, Arr. by Best . *Beethoven*

4. QUARTETTE, "O, for the Swords of Former Times". *Holden*

5. PRELUDE AND FUGUE, No. 1, Op. 37 . . . . *Mendelssohn*

6. CONTRALTO SOLO, "My Redeemer and My Lord". *D. Buck*
   (From Golden Legend.)

7. *a.* TANNHAUSER, "Song to the Evening Star." } . . *Wagner*
   b. LOHENGRIN, "Elsa's Song," . . . . }

8. VIOLIN SOLO, "Fantaisie Pastorale," Op. 56 . . . . . . *Singelee*

9. FANTAISIE, "The Storm," (E minor) . . . . *Lemmens*

10. QUARTETTE, "Serenade" . . . . *Pfeil*

11. CONTRALTO SOLO, Aria, "Rest in the Lord," from Elijah,
    Mendelssohn

12. NATIONAL AIRS FOR VIOLIN AND ORGAN . . . .
    (Arr. with Pedal Variations.)

Danbury News Print

Baptist Church program, May 8, 1891.

her. After it was on its foundation and reestablished, she had changes made in the house. The bank had me look after that. That was 1924. We moved the house up the hill on Chapel Place, not very far. Now it's been moved again down to Rogers Park. Ives came before we moved the house, and while we were moving it, and he came while we were altering it. He used to come to see his mother. He seemed to be very careful of her and wanted everybody to realize that she was to be treated well.

I knew Charlie's father, George. After all, I was older than Charlie. I used to see George Ives in an office [hat business] where he worked for Mr. Merritt, the uncle of Howard Ives, a nephew of George Ives on the other side. Howard Ives was the head bookkeeper and financial man of the business, and George was his assistant as a clerk. George Ives was a kind of original creature. I remember him looking out of the window of Mr. Merritt's office. Mr. Merritt was always looking after everything. They were building a bridge across the stream, and George Ives looked out one morning and saw Mr. Merritt out there. George said, "There you are, you damned old monopolist, you have to tell them how to build a bridge!" Now that's the kind of fellow he was—talking under his breath in this office, which would be heresy, if anybody heard it.

George Ives was the bandleader. He was the organizer of it and led the band with his cornet. He was a great cornet player. He used to play his cornet on the march while he led the whole kaboodle. I don't remember how large the band was, but it was a full-fledged band. I think they had appointments outside of Danbury as well. He used to march right up by here. They'd be going one way with the band, with another band going the other way 'round the park here, and the two would clash—that interested him very much, but people in Danbury didn't think it was very interesting to see the two bands blending and playing different tunes. They didn't take George Ives very seriously. He was only the bandleader.

George Edward Ives, ca. 1890.

George Ives was involved in a wide range of musical activities,* in which his son joined him from an early age. In addition, George Ives's extraordinary interests in sound experimentation stimulated the boy's imagination. Charles Ives was educated in the Danbury schools and the Danbury Academy, followed by one year at Hopkins Grammar School. He had a solid academic musical education from his father, combined with firsthand, daily experience in almost every aspect of practical music making. George and Charles Ives were colleagues and friends as well as father and son. It is no wonder that the death of George Ives in 1894 before his fiftieth year, in his son's freshman year at Yale, was a particularly heavy blow to the young Ives.

Enthusiasm and support for Ives's music was not to come from Horatio Parker† or from any other teachers at Yale, but from Dr. John Cornelius Griggs (1865–1932), choirmaster and baritone soloist at Center Church on the green in New Haven where Ives got a job as organist while he was at Yale. Some years later, Ives wrote to Griggs:

> *I don't know as you remember, but when I came to Center Church, under and with you, my father had just died. I went around looking and looking for some man to sort of help fill up that awful vacuum I was carrying around with me—the men among my classmates—the tutors program, etc.—and a kind of idea that Parker might—but he didn't—I think he made it worse—his mind and his heart were never around together. You didn't try to superimpose any law on me, or admonish me, or advise me, or boss me, or say very much—but there you were, and there you are now. I didn't show how or what I felt—I never seem to know how—except some[times] when I get sort of mad. I long to see you again and so does Mrs. Ives.‡*

---

*A sampling from programs in which George Ives performed shows the diversity of his musical activities: 1869—Ives conducted a "chorus of forty voices with orchestra"; 1876—"Ives Celebrated Band to play on the steamer Arrowsmith to and from New York and Brooklyn to South Norwalk"; 1879—"George Ives with the Swedish Lady Vocal Quartette" playing cornet solos.

†Horatio Parker (1863–1919) was a composer, organist, and teacher. He studied in Germany, and after his return to the United States, continued to compose in the prevailing Germanic style of the nineteenth century. His works include orchestral music, chamber works, two operas, and a great number of choral works, the most well known being an oratorio, *Hora Novissima.* Parker was professor of music at Yale University from 1894 until his death.

‡From a sketch of a letter written early in January 1930, quoted in Kirkpatrick, *Memos,* pp. 257–58.

In the same year that Ives entered Yale College, Horatio Parker became the new Battell Professor of the theory of music. He reorganized the music program into seven courses: harmony, counterpoint, history of music, strict composition (fugue, canon, triple and quadruple counterpoint), instrumentation, free composition (part-songs, glees, piano pieces, sonatas), practical music. The music courses were electives open for credit only to upperclassmen, but there is evidence that Ives and other qualified underclassmen were welcomed by Parker as auditors. Ives may have given more attention to his audited music courses than to the required curriculum—the Yale College gradebooks from 1894-98 show that his grades were barely passing except for the music courses for which he had credit as an upperclassman. Ives studied organ with Dudley Buck and Harry Rowe Shelley. A gauge of his ability as organist can be taken from the fact that his predecessor at Center Church in New Haven was Harry Jepson, instructor of organ at Yale. Ives stepped into that position as a freshman and retained it until commencement four years later.

Mandeville Mullally (1874–1957) was Ives's roommate at 76 South Middle all four years at Yale. Ives had other friends and an active social life. If he was somewhat casual about his required studies, he was serious about what he wanted to do in music. By the time he graduated from Yale, he had been composing for some eleven years, and he had some substantial works completed or under way.* Most of these (certainly the pieces Ives considered best) were written outside of the classroom. When Ives wrote his Memos some years later, he had this to say about his experiences with music at Yale:

> If more ear stretching had gone on, if the ears and minds had been used more and harder, there might have been less "arrested development" among nice Yale graduates—less soft-headed ears running the opera and symphony societies in this country—and less emasculated art making money for the commercialists controlling the movies, tabloids, and most of the radio programs.
>
> In the music courses at Yale . . . things or ideas of this nature, or approaching them, were not so much suppressed as ignored. Parker, at the beginning of Freshman year, asked me not to bring any more things like these into the classroom, and I kept pretty steadily to the regular

---

*The *First Symphony*, the *First String Quartet*, several organ pieces including the *Thanksgiving Prelude and Postlude* for organ, which became the *Thanksgiving* movement of the *Holidays Symphony*, some overtures and marches for piano and orchestra or band, several fugues, some of *The Celestial Country*, anthems and part-songs, about fifty songs, and music for fraternity (Delta Kappa Epsilon) shows.

*classroom work, occasionally trying things on the side. . . . With Parker
I went over the . . . same harmony and counterpoint and classroom text-
books and I think I got a little fed up on too much counterpoint and
classroom exercises (maybe because, somehow, counterpoint gradually
became so much associated in my mind as a kind of exercise on paper,
instead of on the mountains). [Kirkpatrick, Memos, pp. 41, 48-49]*

*Inquiries were sent to the surviving members of the Yale classes from
1897 through 1900. Three people were found who knew Ives at Yale.
Two were from his own class of 1898*—Dr. Charles Farr and Harry A.
Hatch. Another, Lewis Bronson, was Yale 1901. Although these men were
not close to Ives, they remembered him. They had courses with some of the
same professors, and their reminiscences describe Yale and New Haven
as they were during Ives's college years.*

*LEWIS BRONSON (1881–1969) was a tenor who studied composition
with Horatio Parker at Yale and sang under Dr. Griggs at Center Church.
He was interviewed at his home in New Haven on July 28, 1969.*

I came down to New Haven in '96, as my father's business was in New
Haven, and entered Yale College in '97. I was interested in music, and
almost from the beginning I went to the four o'clock service in Center
Church which, at that time, had the best church quartet that I knew about.
It was made up of Mrs. [Max] Robbins [soprano], the wife of a French
professor [Fred O. Robbins] at the university; Miss Margaret Roberts
[contralto]; Mr. [Wallace] Moyle, who was, from my standpoint, the finest
tenor that New Haven has ever produced; and Dr. Griggs, who was head of
the music department at Vassar and came over to Center Church to be the
baritone and the leader of the choir. It was quite a trip for Griggs. He had
to go from Poughkeepsie to New York City and then up to New Haven.
But we had good trains in those days.

At first, they simply had the quartet at the morning service and the four
o'clock service on Sundays. Then Griggs made up his mind that he wanted
to do a little broader work, and he decided to get in a small chorus which

---

*The Yale classbook for 1898 erroneously lists Ives's birthdate as 1876, and there are
several "personal history" forms in the Yale alumni archives which give his birthdate as
1875. These variances caused a birth certificate search which verified the 1874 birthdate. The
errors in Yale's records may have something to do with the fact that Ives was twenty when
he entered Yale, two years older than most of his classmates.

he was able to pull together by offering vocal lessons. The organist was Charles Ives. I can still see him sitting up on the old organ stool. He was thin and tall and dynamic in his handling of the organ—he was all over the thing.

The chorus sang only at the four o'clock service, but we had choir rehearsals and gave some fairly substantial pieces with Mr. Ives playing the organ and the quartet and chorus directed by Dr. Griggs. We had a rehearsal every week, and the members of the chorus received lessons in return. We had a good quartet, so that we could really do some pretty elaborate pieces.

None of us knew anything about Mr. Ives then. You wouldn't expect me, as a youngster of sixteen or seventeen, to forecast what the big people didn't forecast about Ives, so I didn't think much about him and he didn't make the kind of impression at the time that that quartet made on me. Ives left here and nobody heard anything more about him for years. But Dr. Griggs thought very highly of him.

After Yale graduation, DR. CHARLES FARR (1875–1972) entered Yale Medical School. He practiced in New York City for many years. Ives's good friend, the composer Carl Ruggles, was a patient of his. When Dr. Farr was interviewed on September 19, 1970, in a rest home in New York, he remembered Mullally (Ives's roommate), Dave Twichell (Ives's friend and Harmony's brother), and Ives himself.

Ives was a better-educated man than I was. I had made high school in only three years, and I had to work like a dog my first year in college. I studied so hard that I shared the freshman prize in mathematics. Ives had much more social life,* and he was a man of prominence. He liked sports, as I did myself, and we had the same freshman courses of Greek, Latin, mathematics, and English literature. We all had Billy Phelps and loved him.†

---

*Ives belonged to the club HéBoulé, to Wolf's Head, and to Delta Kappa Epsilon.

†William Lyon Phelps. Ives studied English literature with Phelps in his freshman and sophomore years and took a course in American literature with him in his senior year.

"HELLS BELLS,"

—OR—

The Fight that Yaled.

For the last time the '98 extravaganza company presents the rib-fracturing phantasy of which the headlines appear above. This mammoth production over which no time and expense have been wasted, brings to a culminating climax the apex of our efforts. The favorable notices we have received may be summed up in the words of Mr. Blakeslee of the Grand, who remarked at a dress rehearsal: "Be jes, you're all right. It's the heaviest thing that ever came down the line." Owing to the long run (and back) which the piece has had at rehearsals, the management (which is us), has decided to make this souvenir night. Tasteful memoirs of the event will be distributed from the stage at the close of the first act. The front row will be especially reserved for Pfingst, Coffin, Munger, Miller, J., Pierce and Flannel Meade.

And now, making our debut backwards, we can only say "We're not for you; ain't you for us?"

CAST-OFF* CHARACTERS.

DUNCAN COGG, the man with a wheel,	-	DAVE BURRELL.
HIRAM BUNCTIOUS, of the yacht Dickey Quart, brother ship to the steamer Richard Peck,	-	HORSEMAN BORDEN
WILLIE CONNECT, a Yale man up to date,		DRINKUS BURNETT
NOEY WONT, warped out of line,	-	CULLY KERNOCHAN
MRS. MOSSY GRAVES, not so often, but once in a while,	- - - - -	JULE RIPLEY
MAY WINYEW, ask her,	- - - -	MART DODGE
IDA KNOUGH, another Herald personal,	-	C. I. O. W.† BETTS

SUCCUP DREGS,	} Harvard {		BILLY WILCOX
CAMBRIDGE BACHLOTZ,	{ Stoodents }		MYSTERIOUS CLARK

Two sordid fellows of the baser sort.

SANDY BANKS, a half-rater steward,	-	FINGER JIM WADSWORTH
BRIDGET RUSSELL,	{ No relation to Lillian, } but first cousin to the { Russell Brothers.	PILLBOX WINTHROP

STUDENTS,	- - - - -	ERNIE HOWE KID NEAL RIGO TERRY HANK WRIGHT

MOTORMAN,	} Both from Brooklyn, {	BROM BAYLISS
CONDUCTOR, -		BILL RAY
FARMER DAVIS,	{ No allusion to Wirt, but just { as windy,	BOB CALLENDER
LEHMAN,	{ The real thing from the { old world,	JACK LIVERMORE

*The printers error.
†"Come in out of the wet." ST. MARK'S STORIES.

Program of Hells Bells, *a Delta Kappa Epsilon show. On the right-hand page, above "Hail to Phi," Mr. C. E. Ives is credited with furnishing "much original music for this play."*

SAILORS,   -   -   -   .   - { INKY LEWIS
DARRY PECK
TWISTER TURNBULL
MORRIS ELY

Bags, valises, and Saratoga drunks.

Mr. FRANKLIN LORD will run the calcium.

The best part of this show is the scenery, which we exhibit in the following order:

ACT I.

SCENE I.   Moonlight on the deck of the Dickey Quart.

SCENE II.   Cabin of the yacht.

ACT II.

Yale Corinthian Yacht Club, showing Winthrop's half-rater displaying signal " owner lunching."

ACT III.

Near the race at Poughkeepsie, showing one cantilever of the longest unsupported span in the world.

The scenery is written by Blakeslee and Thomas, and the word-painting of the show is by Hinsdale, Kennedy and Wadsworth. In regard to the yacht, the audience are getting the long end of it.

The electrical displays and devices are furnished by The Connecticut Electrical Co., of 25 Center St.

Messrs. Blakesley & Thomas will manipulate the scenery and mechanical properties.

The man who planned the stage will be lynched if found.

Mr. C. E. Ives has furnished much original music for this play; his latest masterpiece will be sung at the close of the 3rd Act. The words were written by F. G. Hinsdale. You are all requested to join in the chorus, but kindly wait until it sounds familiar.

HAIL TO PHI.

All of our labors over now,
  Times of parting come to all ;
Come they must,
  Strengthen here the vow,
Phi the brotherhood,
  Altar of our faith and trust ;
Some of our brothers moving on,
  Forth to face the restless world
Life's stern fight,
  All their sorrows, cares and troubles gone ;
Gone, alas ! their days in Phi so bright.

Hail to Phi, its blaze of glory,
  Never will grow cold,
Dear to all thy children's hearts,
  Ever faithful as of old,
All our days we'll love thee, never fail,
  When we feel in after life
Chill fortune round us fold,
  Then we'll hasten back to Phi and Yale.
Hail to Phi ! Hail to Phi !
  Strong the bond. Strong the bond,
Likewise Yale the Alma Mater.

PLAY COMMITTEE.

HINSDALE.   BORDEN.   IVES.

KENNEDY.   SIMMONS.   WADSWORTH.

This play was written by Hinsdale, Kennedy, Wadsworth.

VALE.

HAROLD A. HATCH, Yale class of 1898, was interviewed on September 10, 1970, at his home in Sharon, Connecticut.

The class of 1898 started 350 strong, and we graduated 300. We were small enough so that the members of the class knew each other by name by the end of the first term. We freshmen met each other almost at once, the occasion being a wrestling match with the sophomore class, and I met practically all the class in the next few days, including Charlie Ives and his roommate, Mullally. I remember Ives as a very pleasant classmate, deeply interested in music. The class was homogeneous and friendly right through the four years.

The freshman year was mostly prescribed courses. After that you had more selection. George Trumbull Ladd taught philosophy, and practically everybody attended his class. He had a tradition of not reading any of the examination papers and passing everyone with excellent marks. Those that required marks were very careful to take his course. And everyone studied with Billy Phelps. He attended all our reunions, and was probably the most popular professor in our day. My studies were interesting and very helpful later in life, but what I remember most about Yale is my friendship with my classmates, who were a delightful group of men.

Mandeville Mullally and Charles Ives in their room, 76 South Middle, Yale, ca. 1895.

THIRTY-THIRD

ANNUAL SPRING CONCERT

OF THE

YALE

GLEE AND BANJO CLUBS

HYPERION

TUESDAY EVENING, JUNE 27, 1899

PART III

1. **MEDLEY**   *Arranged by Austin*

   MANDOLIN CLUB

2. **BELLS OF YALE**   *Mason, '99 and Ives, '98*

   MR. SCHNEELOCH AND CLUBS

3. **SON OF A GAMBOLIER**   *Carmen-Yalense*

4. **PSYCHOLOGY**   *Carmen-Yalense*

   MR. SHEEHAN AND CLUB

5. **BRIGHT COLLEGE YEARS**   *Durant, '81*

Bright college years, with pleasure rife,	In after years should troubles rise
The shortest, gladdest years of life :	To cloud the blue of sunny skies,
How swiftly are ye gliding by,	How bright will seem thro' Memory's haze,
Oh why doth time so quickly fly ?	Those happy, golden, by-gone days.
The seasons come, the seasons go,	Oh, let us strive that ever we
The earth is green, or white with snow ;	May let these words our watch-cry be,
But time and change shall naught'avail,	Where'er upon life's sea we sail,
To break the friendships formed at Yale.	" For God, for Country, and for Yale."

Yale Glee Club Program, June 27, 1899.

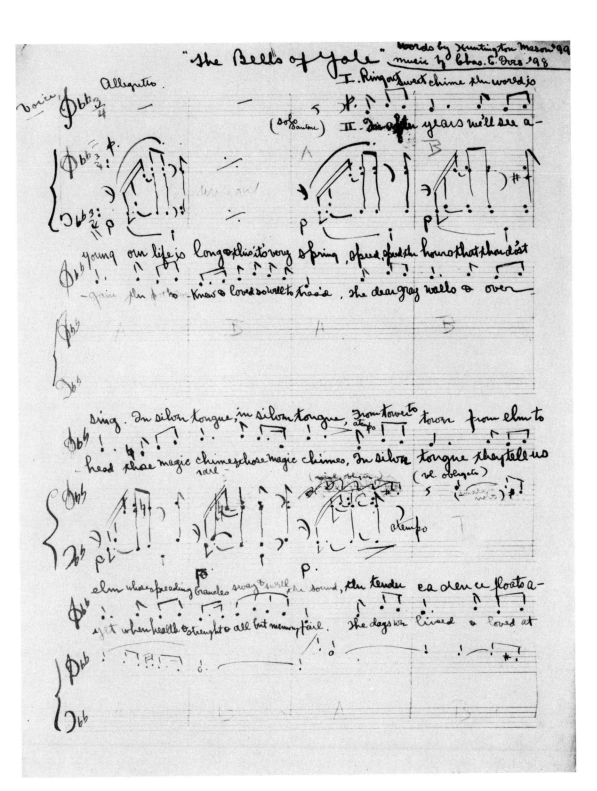

Autograph page, The Bells of Yale.

INSURANCE

Ives & Myrick Co.

Where $15,000,000 Was Paid For Last Year

The picture shown above is of the corner of the building at Nassau and Liberty Streets, New York City, where more life insurance was written last year than in any other general agency office in New York. Just above the entrance are the offices of IVES & MYRICK, managers of the MUTUAL LIFE, who paid for more than $15,000,000.

The decision to go into business instead of trying to make a living from music did not come to Ives suddenly upon graduation from Yale. He had seen at close range the difficulties of his father's chosen profession. More-over, he knew that he wanted to be a composer and that there are far fewer opportunities for composers than performers. At Yale, Ives had seen un-favorable reactions from musicians such as Horatio Parker to the mildest kind of deviation from the established musical norm. What could he expect for his kind of music? Ives knew that there would be no way he could make a living with it.

Life insurance was an exciting and challenging new business based on idealistic concepts. It gave Ives an outlet for serving his humanistic ideals while searching for financial independence. He took a job with the Mutual Life Insurance Company in their actuarial department at a salary of five dollars per week and moved into Poverty Flat. Ives continued his work as organist and choir director—at the First Presbyterian Church in Bloom-field, New Jersey, for one year, and then, from 1899 to 1902, at Central Presbyterian Church on West 57th Street in New York City.

Ives was good-looking, outgoing, and well liked during these years at Poverty Flat. The demands on his time were enormous, even for an athletic young man with Ives's energy. He found time to go to night school to learn something about the law, and to pitch on his agency's baseball team. And somehow, Ives found time to compose, even in the midst of what must have been somewhat less than private and quiet surroundings at home.

Whether Ives himself requested a transfer out of the actuarial depart-ment of Mutual Life, or the decision was made for him, is not known. We do know that in the spring of 1899 Ives moved to Charles H. Raymond & Co., general agents for Mutual Life. This was where Ives met the man who was to become his business partner and lifelong friend, Julian S. Myrick.

JULIAN SOUTHALL MYRICK (1880–1969) and Charles Ives had an extraordinary relationship, particularly in light of the fact that they were such different personalities. These differences have often been pointed out, with astonishment at the strength and duration of the relationship. Actually, the widely divergent interests of the two men made it possible for them to function together as well as they did. Neither man had any desire to encroach upon the other's domain. Ives could be the writer-educator-

Concert

And Presentation of a New Cantata,

"The Celestial Country!"

WORDS BY HENRY ALFORD.   MUSIC BY CHARLES E. IVES.
(Latin Text from St. Bernard.)

For Solo, Quartet, Octet, Chorus, Organ and String Orchestra.

MISS ANNIE WILSON . . . . . . Soprano
MISS EMMA WILLIAMS . . . . . Contralto
MR. E. ELLSWORTH GILES . . . . . Tenor
MR. GEORGE A. FLEMING . . . . Baritone

The Kaltenborn String Quartet :

MR. FRANZ KALTENBORN . . . . . First Violin
MR. WILLIAM ROWELL . . . Second Violin
MR. GUSTAVE BACH . . . . . Viola
MR. LOUIS HEINE . . . . . 'Cello

MR. CHARLES E. IVES . . . . . Organist

Assisted By

MRS. SPRINGER,   MISS MARY GROUT,
MRS. DULANY,   MISS MANSFIELD,
MISS CAROLINE ANDRESEN,   [Mezzo-Soprano.]
MISS MARTHA SNEAD,   MISS SARAH EDWARDS,
MISS CHARLOTTE SNELL,   MISS MINA ANDRESEN,
   [Soprano.]   MISS DOLORES REEDY,
                     [Contralto.]
MR. JOHN W. CATCHPOLE,   MR. A. C. EADIE,
      MR. HARRY B. MOOK.
     [Tenor.]
MR. EDWIN F. FULTON,   MR. HERMAN TROST,
MR. FREDERICK BALLANTYNE, MR. THOMAS.
     [Basso.]

Horns : In B flat (Euphonium) . . MR. W. S. PHASEY
      In A . . . . . (Player to be Announced)

Central Presbyterian Church,
New York

Friday,
April 18, 1902.

The Celestial Country, *program of its first performance at Central Presbyterian Church, New York, April 18, 1902.*

CHARLES E. IVES' CONCERT

And New Cantata, "The Celestial Country."

AT the Central Presbyterian Church last Friday night the organist, Charles E. Ives, a Yale graduate and pupil in music of Professor Parker, gave an invitation concert which had for its principal number a new cantata by Ives, "The Celestial Country," words by Henry Alford, for solo, quartet, chorus, organ and string orchestra, augmented by two horns.

The work shows undoubted earnestness in study and talent for composition, and was fairly creditably done, the thirty singers and players entering into the spirit of the thing with enthusiasm.

Beginning with a prelude, trio and chorus, with soft, long-drawn chords of mysterious meaning, picturing the far country, the music swells to a fine climax, various themes being heard, used later on. Indeed, throughout the work there is homogeneity, coming from the interweaving of appropriate themes. Following the opening chorus there is a bass solo, sung on this occasion by the alto, however, Miss Emma Williams; it is lyric and full of grace, in B flat, and the low F's at the close came out finely.

There follows a quartet in D minor, difficult, with chromatic harmonies, and in the trio with alternating 3-4 and 4-4 time measures. It comes to a pianissimo close on the words "Until the eve be light" most effectively. The Intermezzo for strings alone, con sordini, is song-like, with the first violin and later the viola singing the melody, and this, too, comes to a close in softest tones. This Intermezzo the Kaltenborn Quartet will find useful for their concerts. It is full of unusual harmonies and pleasing throughout.

The a capella octet which follows has interwoven the principal theme of the quartet, followed by the tenor solo, one of the effective numbers of the cantata. This is in G major, well suited to a lyric tenor voice, with a graceful running figure in the accompaniment, the climax coming on the words "Till our faith be sight" on a high A, which rang out clear and true, sung by Tenor E. Ellsworth Giles.

The finale is composed of a chorus, chorale and fugue. This shows some original ideas, many complex rhythms and effective part writing, the chorale in 4-2 time, the fugue built on the theme of the chorale. With an obligato soprano on the high C, all voices fortissimo, the work comes to a triumphant close.

Those who shared in the first presentation of this work were Miss Anne S. Wilson, soprano; Miss Emma Williams, alto; E. Ellsworth Giles, tenor; and Geo. A. Flem-

A review of The Celestial Country *with Ives's opinion of the review scribbled over it.*

philosopher, excusing himself from all problems of office discipline and social engagements which would have been distasteful to him; Myrick could turn his talents to the day-to-day workings of the agency and its contacts with the home office and elsewhere.

Both men sought accomplishment outside the insurance business. Myrick's interest was in tennis, and by 1915, the same year that he became president of the Life Underwriters' Association, he was elected president of the West Side Tennis Club. The fact that each partner had an engrossing interest outside of the insurance business, albeit in distinctly different directions, must have intensified the bond between them. Julian Myrick always had great respect for Ives's musical work. He sensed that here was a man of genius. It is to Myrick's credit that he always tried to do what he could for Ives's music even while admitting his own inability to comprehend it.

Julian Myrick was interviewed at his apartment in New York on October 14, 1968; November 4, 1968; and December 11, 1968. The last visit was made shortly before Mr. Myrick's death, January 8, 1969.

I first met Charles Ives in 1899 at Charles H. Raymond & Company which was located at 32 Liberty Street. My father got me my job there, and I started in March 1898 about three months before Charlie. I was an applications clerk, and he came in to relieve me. I'd been doing a poor job, but his handwriting was so bad that they preferred mine, so I got the job back, and he went out to handle the agents. That's just the way it happened. Charlie and I became fast friends from then on. We divided the work that way not only in the Raymond Agency but later on. I handled the financial part of the business, and Charlie handled the agents.

The Raymond Agency was dissolved in 1906, and Charlie and I started our own business in 1907. We called it Ives & Company [51 Liberty Street], and it had nothing to do witl the Mutual Life.* Later we became Ives & Myrick when we came back to Mutual Life in 1909. They opened an agency for us after we'd accomplished a great deal on our own. We had a good plan, and it worked out satisfactorily, so we were successful from the start. We got our business from general insurance brokers and got them to put in life insurance departments, and as a result they sold a great deal of life insurance, which they placed through our agency. Charlie used a for-

*Ives & Co. was an agency of the Washington Life Insurance Company. They had a successful start but the agency was canceled when the parent organization was sold to another company.

Two pages from the insurance booklet, The Amount to Carry, showing Ives's formula for "measuring a prospect."

The Relation Which the Cost of Adequate Life Insurance, Scientifically Determined, Bears to the Income-Schedule on the Opposite Side and the "Formula" by Which Life Insurance Can be More Accurately Comprehended, Will be Explained Upon Request.

The root of all social progress is in what man can do rather than in what he does. The financial success of many a man to-day is to a great extent retarded because he thinks too much of what his neighbor thinks of him superficially. He does things because his neighbor does them. He refuses to think for himself, and if he does he is afraid to follow out his convictions. Living up to the neighbor's income rather than one's own is a national tendency. A big six-cylinder car where there ought to be a Ford and a Ford where there ought to be no car is a symptom of this. Thrift requires moral courage, together with a mental effort which every man can make if he will. Statisticians tell us that we waste $8,000,000,000 yearly. Experts in such matters have figured out that 10% of our food is wasted by housekeepers.

That people are beginning to think seriously about this phase of modern living is evidenced by the fact that Universities are establishing domestic science courses and in some of the larger Cities, Municipal Departments are collecting information and statistics along these lines. The schedules submitted were prepared from papers by economists, authoritative articles and exhibits from various sources and from personal investigation, observation and experience. They contain no amount where the limit is unreasonable. If conformity to any column seems impracticable one can be sure that some one in a similar position is conforming to it and prospering. The average man can spend and save in such a way that he can get ahead instead of behind, if he only knows how. To admit that he cannot is to admit that he is not as efficient in buying as he is in earning; that he doesn't realize that conservation is as important as production. Living fixedly under a definite plan is not necessarily an irksome procedure, nor does it mean that a man cannot do his duty to society as well as to his family. The more intelligently thrifty a man is, the more generous he can be, and the more generous he is, the more he can enjoy life.

A sub-division under the various heads will be found profitable. The amounts in column B2 for financial development are in most cases more than is required to carry a normal amount of insurance. There is a popular misconception that an insurance premium is all cost. This is not so. Only a part is expense and a large part of all premiums on standard forms (except Term) can be charged to investment for future funds. If a man does the right thing by his family by carrying adequate insurance, even on the Ordinary Life plan, he is simultaneously building up a future income for himself at a time when most men wish to ease up in their active business careers. A demonstration of this will incur no obligation on your part.

(OVER)

IVES & MYRICK
Managers

The Mutual Life Insurance Company of New York

38 NASSAU STREET   TELEPHONE JOHN 3632   NEW YORK

CLASSIFICATION—(A) Living Expenses *(for maintenance).*   (B) Savings *(for development).*

(Family of two adults and two children.)

Income....	$780	$1,000	$1,200	$1,500.00	$2,000	$2,500	$3,000	$3,500.00	$4,000	$4,500.00	$5,000	$7,500	$10,000	
FOR MAINTENANCE:														
(1) Rent	$180	$ 240	$ 276	$ 315.00	$ 400	$ 475	$ 510	$ 600.00	$ 700	$ 810.00	$ 900	$1,350	$ 1,750	(1)
(2) Food	304	320	360	435.00	540	600	690	752.50	760	765.00	800	1,050	1,200	(2)
(3) Clothes ...	101	115	150	195.00	280	325	390	455.00	520	540.00	625	825	975	(3)
(4) General Household Items	113	135	162	202.50	250	325	450	577.50	640	720.00	775	975	1,125	(4)
(5) Medical ...	10	10	12	15.00	20	25	30	35.00	40	45.00	50	75	100	(5)
	708	820	960	1,162.50	1,490	1,750	2,070	2,420.00	2,660	2,880.00	3,150	4,275	5,150	
FOR DEVELOPMENT:														
(1) General ...	32	80	108	142.50	210	350	420	437.50	540	650.00	725	1,125	1,500	(1)
(2) Financial ..	40	100	132	195.00	300	400	510	642.50	800	969.50	1,125	2,100	3,350	(2)
	$72	$180	$240	$337.50	$510	$750	$930	$1,080.00	$1,340	$1,620.00	$1,850	$3,225	$4,850	

ILLUSTRATION

A (4) Fuel — Heating — Lighting — Household Supplies — Laundry — Carfare — Ice — Furniture — Telephone — Postage — Newspapers — Repairs — Interest Payments — Servant's Wages — Fire Insurance — Taxes (except those on residence), etc.

A (5) This is the only column which will vary to any great extent, as it can be controlled only indirectly. It is difficult to find any statistics to base the average on, so a nominal amount is taken. Any amount exceeding the above must be charged to B-1.

B (1) Anything pertaining to the mental, moral and physical development—Extra School Tuition, Books, Magazines, Music, Art Lessons, Etc.—Lectures, Church Contributions, Charity, Concerts, Social Clubs,—Amusements, Vacation,—Athletics, Gymnasium, Travel (Automobile Expenses)—Medicine, Doctor's and Dentist's Bills, in amount over A-5,—Etc.

B (2) Savings for Life Insurance and Investments (Savings Bank, Real Estate, Stocks and Bonds, Business Capital, Etc.); also personal accident and health insurance.

Notes:—If there are more or less than two children, columns A-2 and A-3 should be increased or decreased, and the balance credited or charged to Column B-1, or between B-1 and B-2 proportionately.

If insured lives out of the city and commutes, Commutation cost should be put in A-4 and the difference, if any, between A-1 and suburban rent plus commutation, in Column B-2.

If insured owns residence, taxes are put in A-1, repairs and upkeep in A-4, and difference in B-2. (If there is a mortgage on the property, interest charges go in A-4. Insured must decide whether extra insurance be taken, or whether the family shall shoulder the debt.)

(OVER)

mula for the amount of insurance to carry and how to carry it. It was so successful, nearly everyone in the business used it eventually.*

Ives never did direct selling, but he was a very good trainer of agents and taught them how to sell. I joined all of the organizations and did the outside contact work of the agency. Charlie worked primarily with the agents, training them and giving them selling ideas, which were always very good. Charlie belonged to all of the social groups, but he took no active interest. That's the reason that, generally speaking, I'm better known in the business.

In spite of his shy and gentle nature, Charlie was a very firm, positive man, and when he got on a job or project, there was nothing that he neglected. He had a great conception of the life insurance business and what it could and should do, and he had a very powerful way of expressing it. He did a great deal of writing, much of it published and widely used. Charlie was responsible for the material that went to make up the classes, more so than I was. More and more education came into the business, not only led by ourselves but by the whole industry, so we had constant improvement. Our agency was the first to have a school for insurance agents. We built our business up by degrees. We had one man start with us, Verplanck,† but later there were many employees. Ives's contribution to the business was very great, and he worked continuously to improve it. He felt that the protection of the family and the home was a great mission.

Charlie came to the insurance business straight from college and lived with a group of Yale men in a good-sized apartment called Poverty Flat. They had about seven or eight men living there together at one time. It was a group of boys that were just starting in business and by degrees they'd become engaged, get married, and move out. It was a pretty lively place. I dropped in very often, and when it was finally reduced to about three, I joined them for a few years. That was after Charlie was married.

Ives had something like a heart attack as early as 1906, I believe. Apparently he had had something there for a long time, and I think it was diagnosed then. We had a medical department in Mutual Life, and he used to go to them. They recommended that he go for a rest, and he decided to go to Old Point Comfort, Virginia. The manager of the main office asked me to go with him, and we stayed there over the Christmas holidays.

---

*Ives wrote this "formula" in a pamphlet *The Amount to Carry and How to Carry It,* published in 1912. It was revised as *The Amount to Carry; Measuring the Prospect* and reprinted several times. Ives wrote many other booklets which were available on request to interested parties. Some of these: *Life Insurance with Relation to Inheritance Tax,* 1918; *Work or Fight,* 1918; *Spanish Influenza,* 1919; *How to Read the Rate Book,* 1920; *Life Insurance Scientifically Determined,* 1923; *Policies for Children,* 1924.
†William S. Verplanck, pp. 47–49.

Soon after we formed our partnership, Ives was married [June 9, 1908]. Harmony was from Hartford, and Charlie was a classmate of her brother Dave Twichell at Yale and got to know her through him. She had trained as a nurse in Hartford. Harmony was a beautiful girl, and lots of men were chasing her. Ives had a lot of competition.

Harmony Twichell, ca. 1902, in nurse's uniform, at about the time she and Charles Ives met.

The wedding of Harmony Twichell and Charles Ives, June 9, 1908, Hartford, Connecticut. The bride's father, Reverend Joseph Twichell, officiated.

Ives was writing music all the time when I first knew him. There was a piano at Poverty Flat. His friends joked about it, and he just took that good-naturedly. But Harmony encouraged him all the time in his writing. He worked very hard at it. But people couldn't understand it. Charlie's music never interfered with his business. He would take his music home with him and work on it over the weekends. I hardly ever heard anything about it. Once when we were moving from one place to another, we had a little safe. Charlie had one part, and I had another. He'd cleaned out his part, and I went to clean out my part, and there was a stack of music. And I said, "Charlie, you want me to throw this away?" And he looked and said, "Why, Mike! God, that's the best thing I've written!" And it was *The Fourth of July* about to be thrown away. That was dedicated to me, and his wife was responsible for that.

Ives left the business in 1930 because of illness, but he always retained an interest in the firm, not a financial interest, but he was always appreciative of knowing what was going on, and every now and then he made a suggestion. I lived up at 79th Street and I used to go down to 74th Street most every Sunday to talk over ideas, and so I was able to keep him in touch with what was going on in the agency that way. His suggestions were very helpful, and we used them.*

I got some man to go up and interview him, and it was tape-recorded. It was Ives speaking about his views on everything. But the tape was lost—what's happened to it nobody knows.† And I finally convinced Charlie to let a photographer take some pictures. I got one of the best there is—Mr. Eugene Smith of *Life* magazine.

---

*Myrick retired as manager of the agency in 1941 when he became second vice-president of the Mutual Life Insurance Company of New York.

†This tape has never been found.

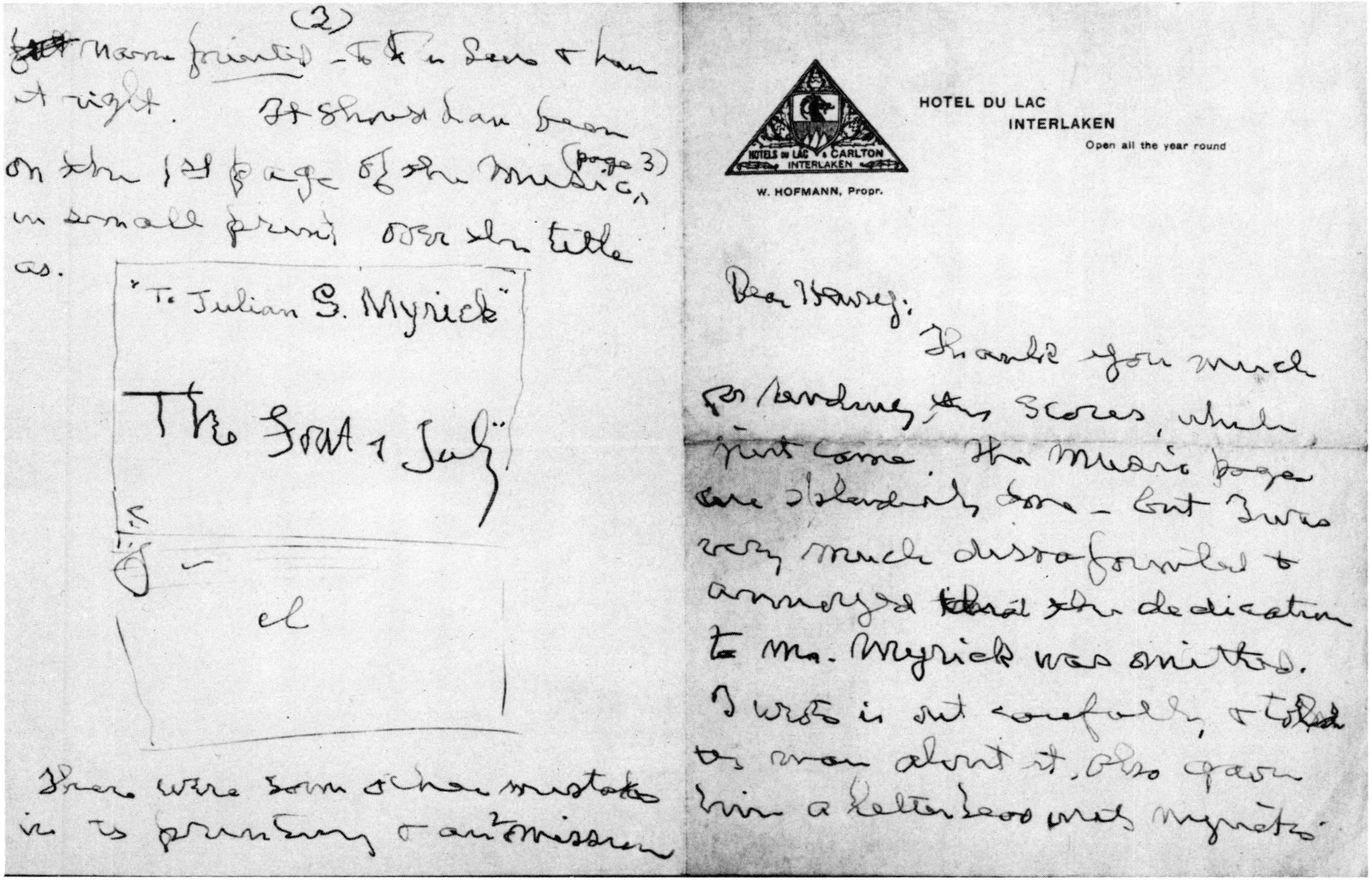

HOTEL DU LAC
INTERLAKEN
Open all the year round

HOTELS DU LAC & CARLTON INTERLAKEN

W. HOFMANN, Propr.

Dear Henry:
Thank you much for sending the scores, which just came. The music pages are splendidly done — but I was very much disappointed & annoyed that the dedication to Mr. Myrick was omitted. I wrote it out carefully, & told the man about it, also gave him a letterhead with Myrick's

(2)
name printed — to be in same & have it right. It should have been on the 1st page of the music (page 3), in small print over the title as.

"To Julian S. Myrick"

The Fourth of July"

There were some other mistakes in the printing & an omission

The first two pages of a letter from Ives to Henry Cowell, who was responsible for the publication of The Fourth of July, *concerning the dedication to Julian Myrick.*

On the upper left margin of the first page of the manuscript for The Fourth of July, *Ives wrote to his copyist:*
Mr. Price: Please don't try to make things nice! All the wrong notes are right.
Just copy as I have. I want it that way. CEI

What the Business Owes to Charles E. Ives

When Charles E. Ives retired from active participation in the Ives & Myrick agency of the Mutual Life a few months ago the insurance fraternity of Greater New York lost contact with a guiding spirit whose impress upon his fellows was stimulating, uplifting and of untold value to life insurance production. His creative mind, great breadth of culture, intensive sympathies and keen understanding of the economic as well as of the material needs of the community made it possible for him to evolve literature which paved the way for additional sales of life insurance and helped straighten out complications which confront the underwriter in his daily path through life. This remarkable student, seated in his Connecticut home with pen in hand, has loved to concentrate upon and to analyze the problems of insurance and of finance, and to solve or readjust those problems with a master mind. Always shall I be proud and happy in the recollection of our partnership of twenty years' standing, not only because of its intimate nature but no one had a better opportunity than was mine of knowing how great was his contribution to the cause of life insurance progress. In my opinion that contribution has never been properly assayed or acknowledged. The passing years will demonstrate that his philosophy will ever hold good.

> Julian S. Myrick, Manager,
> The Mutual Life Insurance Co.,
> Wadsworth Building, 57 William Street,
>   New York City.
> ("The Ives & Myrick Agency")

When Ives retired from the insurance business, Julian Myrick placed this dedication in The Eastern Underwriter *of September 19, 1930, somewhat to Ives's embarrassment.*

W. EUGENE SMITH, photographer, was interviewed on July 6, 1973. Although one of the Smith photographs of Ives is well known and widely used, the others, which include the only known pictures of Ives and Myrick together, had never been seen, not even by Julian Myrick during his lifetime. Attempts over many years to secure these photographs were in vain. Finally, thanks to Mr. Smith, they have been made available.

In all of my years and experience of making photographs I have never seen anyone more terrified of the camera than Charles Ives. The only comparable reaction I have seen is that of the so-called uncivilized native who feels that the camera takes away something of his soul. It was not that he was not friendly, but he was plainly terrified. He had a real paranoia about cameras and photography.

It was Julian Myrick who got together with Gene Cook of *Life* magazine to set the thing up. On the way over to Ives's town house Myrick explained to me that although he really did not understand what Ives was doing, he

The only known photograph of Charles Ives with Julian Myrick, ca. 1947. Photo W. Eugene Smith.

Ives, ca. 1947. Photo W. Eugene Smith.

realized his genius, and he wanted these photographs made of Ives. Myrick explained that Ives agreed to the session only because I was presented to him as a fellow artist.

Ives was semicordial when we met, and Mrs. Ives was very sweet. The house on 74th Street was dimly lit which disturbed me, but I began to make some pictures. Suddenly Ives got terribly upset and threw himself down on the couch. I thought I had killed him. He was panting and palpitating. After a while he sat up and recited a poem for me that he wrote. I wish I could remember it, and I hope someone has found it.* It was all about Beethoven and Beecham and a put-down of musical society with a long list of musical greats, particularly conductors. By now he was sitting in the wicker chair and had put his left arm way out which would have made it look chopped off in a picture. Ives leaned forward and glowered at me but his left hand was still up. So I asked him to bring his arm in next to his body. He said, "No!" very angrily, but then a twinkle came into his eyes and he pulled his arm in and put it on the cane. He leaned forward and I took a terribly long exposure. And that's the best picture—the one everyone knows and uses.

*This "poem" has not been found.

Ives, ca. 1947. Photo W. Eugene Smith.

Ives met WATSON WASHBURN through Julian Myrick who married Washburn's sister Marion in 1910. Ives was best man at the wedding. Washburn, a tax lawyer, handled the tax business for Ives & Myrick and the personal tax affairs of both partners. When he was interviewed in his New York office on April 18, 1969, Washburn talked about the friendship between Julian Myrick and Charles Ives: "They were such close friends that I don't think they needed any legal advice when they separated. I think Charlie continued to be a full partner for a couple of years while he was sick, in the hope that he would recover and be able to go on as before. I know that he had a reasonable amount of money all the rest of his life. He and Mike arranged it between themselves on a most friendly basis." When asked about Ives's music, Washburn admitted that he preferred "the old classical airs rather than Charlie's modern music. Charlie would occasionally remark jokingly that he was trying to wake people up a little and he didn't think they should spend their lives just having their ears constantly massaged with the same old music."

Ives liked one battered brown felt hat which he wore for many years. But figuratively speaking, he wore at least two hats, one very different from the other. Those who knew Ives in one role did not often catch a glimpse of him in another. Ives's daily activities until his retirement revolved around the downtown New York business world. His family and his associates thought of him as a successful insurance man, obviously capable and very intelligent, with perhaps a slightly artistic bent. Rarely did anyone in the insurance business consider that Ives had more than an avocational interest in music. Ives was not merely playing a role—he was sincerely dedicated to insurance work. But he knew that his few musician friends were not really interested in the insurance business, and that his business associates could not understand his music. Ives respected privacy far too much to push his work on anyone. If he agonized over his composing, he did so alone. Certainly no one in his business or family life, except his wife Harmony, paid much attention to it.

The results of Ives's efforts in both insurance and music, these two widely divergent fields, came from the same mind—a mind of extraordinary creativity and imagination. Underlying all of Ives's efforts was his incredible idealism. He believed that men should communicate directly with each other on a personal basis, one to one. In his music, one finds this sense of immediacy, of communicating almost tangible experiences; his political beliefs depended on getting rid of the politician's standing between people; his insurance teachings were based on the insurance salesman's determining the right kind of policy for each client's individual needs. This idealism extended to a deep concern for the common man—Ives devised policies small enough so that insurance would be available for the workingman and his family.

Ives was an innovator in business as well as in music. Insurance was a hard-hitting, competitive trade, especially during World War I and the Depression. Many of Ives's ideas which were initiated during those years have now become basic in the life insurance business, including the training school for agents and the concept of "estate planning." The success of Ives & Myrick Co. was due to the originality of Ives's ideas and to the confidence and daring with which both partners applied those ideas to the selling of life insurance.

The Ives & Myrick agency began in 1909. Five years later its volume had increased from $1 million of paid-for insurance annually to $6 million. In that year of 1914 they moved from their first offices at 37–39 Liberty Street to the Mutual Life Building at 38 Nassau Street. Ives & Myrick began to be recognized as leaders in advanced methods of insurance service. By 1919, they had sixty men working for them full-time, and they were the second-ranking agency in the country, with only Mutual's Chicago office doing a larger volume of business. Evidently neither Ives nor Myrick saw the necessity for modeling their agency on the established type of insurance office. Ives always believed that "just because something is always done one way is no reason to keep doing it that way." An article of September 25, 1919, in the National Underwriter *was headed "Ives & Myrick of New York have built up a unique agency organization." The article continues:*

> *Naturally the atmosphere is somewhat different than that found elsewhere. No agency meetings are held. There are no weekly, monthly or yearly get-together gatherings. For an agency doing so large a business there are an unusually small number of men having offices in their location. A number of the agency's best producers have offices at some other location even though they are giving all of their time to Mutual Life. In fact, a number of the rules that other agencies regard as vital are not observed by Ives & Myrick, although their production records have not suffered as a result of it. Ives & Myrick are following a course of action laid out by themselves and are keenly aware of the value of adapting*

themselves to the conditions that confront them and have produced a life insurance organization which is unusual and successful.

In the twenties, Ives & Myrick became "the largest agency office without exclusive territory in the United States." On May 1, 1923, the agency moved to 46 Cedar Street, and then again in 1926 to larger quarters in the Wadsworth Building on Cedar and William Streets. Economic expansion in the United States made conditions favorable for tremendous growth in the insurance business. Ives & Myrick were there to handle this, and they did extremely well—in 1927 the agency doubled its business volume over 1926, and they continued to thrive, even during the Depression years.

There was a strong feeling of loyalty at Ives & Myrick. Many of the staff and employees stayed with the company for long periods of time, as was the custom in those days. The fondness which the staff as a whole felt for Ives is obvious when one looks at the Ives & Myrick scrapbook at the Mutual of New York Library and sees such items as: a letter sent during the holiday season of 1932, two years after Ives's retirement, signed by twenty-nine of the "office girls," thanking Ives for his "kind remembrance and the beautiful flowers you sent to each of us at our annual Christmas party"; a telegram in 1933: "Tender regards from us all. The Family"; another in 1936: "You are still an inspiration for those of us who knew you and vicariously for those who did not."

In the main, the employees at Ives & Myrick seemed to have great respect for both partners. It must be remembered that Ives could assume the position of teacher and spiritual leader, and he did not have to be tough with anyone about bringing in the business. It is a simple fact that some preferred Myrick, others preferred Ives, and that these preferences would show themselves in the interviews.

Directly below the names of Charles E. Ives and Julian S. Myrick on all agency announcements was the name of William S. Verplanck (1883–1942), associate manager. The other associate managers and the supervisors were listed below Verplanck, who, as Myrick pointed out, was the one man who had started with the agency.

In 1971 Verplanck's son, WILLIAM S. VERPLANCK, professor of psychology at the University of Tennessee, advised that a trip to Knoxville might be in vain, since his mother, Kathryn Verplanck, would not agree to an interview. He held out the hope, however, that a talk with her might be arranged after a preliminary social visit. Professor Verplanck was interviewed in his office at the University on March 25, 1971.

The Verplanck family used to own part of Dutchess County, New York. My grandfather retired in 1880 to become a gentleman farmer, which meant essentially that he just sat up there in Fishkill and did nothing. And none of the boys went to college. They just went through the schools in Fishkill and then went down to the big city as soon as they were old enough to get a job. My father William Verplanck started to work in the late nineties fresh out of Fishkill. The only job he ever had was with Ives & Myrick. He was a kind of protégé of Mr. Ives and worked very closely with him all through those years. Father always looked on Mr. Ives as a sort of father, and he really worshiped him.

Father and Myrick never did get along, and when Mr. Ives retired my father worried about it, but everything went fine for him with Mr. Myrick till 1936 when Father became a very ardent Roosevelt fan and actually wore a Roosevelt badge. The net result for Father was that the period between 1936 and the time of his death in 1941 (he died of complications following stomach ulcers) was associated with a cut in his income from Ives & Myrick. Roughly they had him cut down about thirty-three percent of what he was used to, and it was financially disastrous to him. But he wouldn't keep his mouth shut, and all those Republicans around there really gave him hell.* Ives and Myrick were an odd combination. I remember Mr. Myrick always looking like the most distinguished man in eighteen countries, with a great affinity for the lawn tennis club and so forth. Whereas old Charlie Ives didn't care a hoot about any of those things.

After Professor Verplanck's interview, a social call was made to his home which finally (late that same evening) resulted in an interview with KATHRYN VERPLANCK, who worked at Ives & Myrick as Ives's personal secretary for a few years before she and William Verplanck were married in 1912.

Mr. Ives felt that he could trust me. I took care of his and Mrs. Ives's personal bank accounts, and I knew what was going on between Mr. Ives and Edith's family. Mr. Ives was so generous to them. They were a very poor family, and they didn't have any money. After the Iveses took Edith, her family bothered him to death for more money, and he kept giving to

---

*Ives was a Wilsonian Democrat.

them. Edith was only a little girl when this was happening. The Iveses would never give her up because they loved her dearly. I don't know how, but Mr. Ives settled the thing. I know that later he felt free and clear about having Edith as his child.

The office of Ives & Myrick at 38 Nassau was a great, big area, and one part of it was the cashier's place, where Bill Verplanck always sat with several stenographers. Mr. Ives had a good-sized private room, and whenever he wanted anything personal done he always called for me, and he always kept the door closed. My husband's title at Ives & Myrick was cashier, but he was really a kind of partner there. Mr. Ives called him "Willy," and his word had to go in on everything. Mr. Ives wanted my husband's name on the letterhead up top there over Myrick, but Myrick wouldn't stand for that. At first, when Bill and I started going together, Mr. Ives didn't approve, but later on he did. After we were married, and my daughter was born, we asked Mr. Ives to be her godfather. He came to visit us in Ramsey, New Jersey, and he was there for the christening.

Ives & Myrick office, 38 Nassau Street in the old Mutual Life Building. At the far left, Julian Myrick; William Verplanck to his right.

I was aware of Mr. Ives writing music, although others weren't. I used to go up and visit him at his New York apartment, and sometimes he'd just leave us on the spur of the moment to go up and compose something. And at work sometimes Mr. Ives would be dictating a letter, and all of a sudden something in the music line would come up in his head, and he'd cut off the letter and go into the music. I think that music was on his mind all the time.

I can't say enough nice things about Mr. Ives. He was loved by everybody and kind of feared, too, because he was so superior to everybody, and because he was a very independent person. He didn't care what anybody said. He had his own opinion, and that was it.

The only contemporary colleague of Ives still alive at the time of these interviews was Julian Myrick. JOHN S. THOMPSON (although only ten years younger than Ives) and the other agency men interviewed considered themselves of a younger generation. John Thompson started work as an actuary at Mutual Life in 1905. He was interviewed July 14, 1969, at his home in Providence, Rhode Island.

The profession of actuary deals with the theory of probability and the application of that theory to the mortality table. It's the application of that thought to everything a life insurance company does, whether it's selling insurance or annuities or adjusting from one plan to another. Most of the young men who want to be actuaries even now have to engage in about five to eight years of private study in order to become Fellows of the Actuarial Society and to get a sufficient grasp of the fundamentals of the business and make themselves useful to a life insurance company at a decent salary. One of the main features of an actuary's work is dealing with agents. Agents sell the business. They're the ones who make it go, and that's what Mr. Myrick and Mr. Ives recognized in organizing one of the most important agencies, not only of the Mutual but in the New York area. It was really a very remarkable selling organization. Ives and Myrick made it their business to teach and inspire agents. They didn't leave any stone unturned in order to make agents well informed, resourceful, and industrious. And that is much more of a problem than getting technicians like myself to understand the techniques of the business in the investment field.

I recall one time when Mr. Ives and Mr. Myrick visited the actuarial department of the home office—that was a device on their part to get the whole home office interested in the success of their agency. The actuarial department in which I worked for six or eight years before I went to the front office had about sixty people at two long rows of desks. Mr. Myrick went down one aisle and Mr. Ives down the other and they passed out cards saying they would like to have us contract with Ives & Myrick to handle any business we got. They defined their rate of commission and the general rules of the agency contract. They wanted us to be part-time agents for them, and occasionally they struck someone who wanted to work full-time. But the qualities of an agent are entirely different from those of the inside worker. There wasn't anything indirect or irregular about this procedure of Ives & Myrick. I took them in some business, and then I received a commission. I thought at the time I was lucky to be able to get any commission at all for doing nothing except just report that someone was interested in insurance. The agent they sent out to get the contract was the one who did the real footwork. I signed with them, and I stayed a member of the agency right up until I left the Mutual Life of New York in 1926.

When Ives & Myrick ran a little ad on the second page of the *New York Times,* I went to see Mr. Myrick and asked him all about it, and he told me that the ad said just exactly what Mr. Ives would have written down if he were talking to a young fellow about selling insurance. For example, if you write $100,000 you get $1,500 first-year commissions the year you do that. This ad started people thinking about the possibilities of making money in the life insurance business other than by getting a salaried position. Mr. Ives told me later that the ad cost about five hundred dollars. But if you get one hundred answers, it might easily be worth it. It was an eye-catcher.

Mr. Myrick was a powerful leader in any situation. Charlie was essentially an artist, and I think that the limited contact with the public was rather to his liking. Mr. Myrick had a quiet manner and never raised his voice. He had a breadth of development which was wholesome. Julian's big qualification was understanding of men, and he was able to inspire them with the thought that he knew what was good for them and what was good for the company, and usually what was good for those two was all right for Ives & Myrick.

Major influences on important creative artists are always a matter for discussion. In the case of Ives, the most powerful stimuli came not from musical sources (although he admired Brahms and Franck), but from men of literature. Emersonian transcendentalism and the ideas of the Concord group formed the core of Ives's philosophy. He lived as though Emerson were standing beside him, and this is reflected in his music and in his prose writings. In both, Ives quoted from his past experiences and favorite people. In his music, Ives might use an old hymn or the theme from Beethoven's Fifth Symphony, *while in his insurance writings he might include a Yale cheer or a saying from Mark Twain. Sometimes these quotations are found in surprising places—one does not expect to see a quotation from Emerson's* Self-Reliance *in an insurance advertisement.*

Ives enjoyed writing, and he liked to attempt various literary forms.* George Hofmann, one of the supervisors at Ives & Myrick, pointed out that writing was Ives's prime occupation and major contribution to the business. Ives tried short stories, essays, and plays, and he particularly liked to use dialogues between an imaginary agent and a prospect. Ives did a great deal of writing for Ives & Myrick—form letters, advertising copy, stories and articles for the monthly bulletin, The Estate-O-Graph, *which was published for many years. His writing has, even today, a quality of freshness and spontaneity hardly typical of the stilted, oratorical style of the day.*

GEORGE HOFMANN became a supervisor for Ives & Myrick agents in The Bronx. Ives, who was very much concerned with the education of agents whom he viewed as counselors rather than salesmen, directed Hofmann in teaching classes for new agents. Hofmann, in turn, gave directions to the other supervisors. When George Hofmann was interviewed in Hagaman, New York, on September 13, 1969, he talked of Charles Ives with a respect bordering on worship.

I became acquainted with Charles E. Ives at the age of sixteen [1904] during my summer vacation from high school, when I was appointed as office boy to one of the district agencies of Mutual Life, the Robert Hardy Agency. It was located at 125th Street and Seventh Avenue, and it was my

---

*See Boatwright, *Essays;* also, Kirkpatrick, *Memos,* app. 9, "George's Adventure" and "The Majority"; app. 10, "Broadway."

Ives & Myrick advertisements.

[Prospects' names, in reports on this factory is kept indexes in agency files, from occupational items, changes in relative position etc.

A short letter from the managers, precedes the agents call. (No inner office, prospect directly approachable)]

Agent: "I've called in accordance with the letter of my firm.

Prospect "Oh, you're that insurance man. Now I'm not interested. I won't take any more insurance, and I don't want to discuss insurance" etc.

A: "I'm rather glad to hear you say that."

P: (looks up, rather surprised) - "What's - that ?"

A: "If you hadn't, I'd been a little disconcerted"

P: (and then a smile) Mean an agent's disconcerted! - Not so, I see an insurance agent disconcerted, and they bother most every day"

A: "You wouldn't be bothered, if you'd asked them a certain question"

P: "What for instance?"

A: I'll tell you. It'll take just 12 minutes

P: Never mind. - I told you I didn't want to discuss "life insurance" (starting to rise. - agent keeps seat)

A: "Life insurance won't be mentioned during this 12 minutes — unless you bring it in — that is, by your own deductions." (Prospect makes no answer but turns over papers on his desk. Agent ignores this.

A: Now Mr. ————, in any kind of a business calculation, I assume you're willing to be governed by authoritative data? (pushing a pad towards him. Prospect hesitates.)

A. I'm morally certain you've never been shown this. Whether you buy from me or not this simple formula will be of practical help to you in all of your business and financial problems" (Hands him a pencil. This is the critical point in this kind of an interview. If prospect refuses to continue, an attempt to arouse further curiosity, and then to have a definite appointment for a demonstration of the plan.)

A. "Just jot down in percentages (you needn't show me the items), that part of your income which is certain to go on for at least 32 years." (many prospects ask why 32 years. This didn't)

P (hesitates - puts nothing down)

Left: Excerpt from Ives's handwritten draft for the insurance story, "Broadway."

Above: Cover page of an issue of the Estate-O-Graph, *a monthly magazine published by Ives & Myrick.*

duty to deliver the mail and applications produced by the agents to the main office on Nassau Street. The Raymond Agency office was in the same building as the home office of Mutual. This was where Charles Ives worked, and one day, when I went to deliver the mail, I met him and he invited me to sit down and talk to him. The information he imparted to me on that day has remained with me until this present date. He impressed me with the importance of using all that the good Lord had given to me in the way of brain power or, as he would say, "grey matter." The business of life insurance was simple in those days, and Ives made three points: first, the information that I imparted to clients was to be always accurate; second, that it was my responsibility to decide what would be best for each individual; third, that there was not a service that I could render to my fellow man that was more important than the business of life insurance, because it instilled in the soul and mind of my fellow man the responsibility of meeting his obligations. Charlie was a humanitarian from the bottom of his heart to his head, and I came away from the first meeting feeling that he was a great philosopher and moralist.

After high school I had two years of law and then took full-time employment with the Mutual Life Insurance Company. Eventually I became the supervising clerk of the medical department. In this department I was in close contact with both Charlie and Mr. Myrick, who by this time had become the managers of Ives & Myrick. About three years thereafter [1912], Mr. Ives asked me to consider joining their organization, and I became a supervisor working between their agency staff and the home office.

My duty as a supervisor was to introduce young college graduates to our business, to invite them to join our organization, and to instruct them. We gave lectures every Monday and every Friday. My particular field, assigned by Mr. Ives, was talking on the general values of life insurance. My basic premise, approved by Mr. Ives, was that in entering the business of life insurance, you would have to consider yourself as responsible as a theologian, a physician, a lawyer, and a financial adviser. I stressed to the new agents that insurance encompassed all of these fields. I asked the class to consider what I said for a minute or two, and if they felt they couldn't encompass that mental attitude, they'd better take their hats and coats and leave. Rarely did any of the students leave. I reviewed all my notes with Charlie before I entered the classroom to address my class of about thirty-five men.

The prospective agents, now known as counselors—that was Charlie's idea—would return on the Friday following the first lecture to hear the next one, which was on the application of the different services a life in-

THE Fall Terms (1928) of the Agency Instruction Courses of this office will continue in accordance with the following schedule of days and subjects.

The subject-matter presented is as comprehensive and as practical as is possible in the number of hours given. Agents are urged to attend the classes consecutively, completing a course of ten lessons. Although the courses are designed more for new agents, any agent who desires to review any particular subject is invited to attend. Many agents in the past have found these classes of material help in their work.

Classes begin at 4.45 P.M. and are held in the Reference Room—4th Floor—46 Cedar Street, New York City.

Sept. 28—Synopsis of Course—Essential Uses of Life Insurance (Program)
Structure, Salesmanship, Underwriting.

Oct. 1—Fundamental Actuarial Principles, Rate Book Analysis.
Oct. 5—Policy Contracts.
Oct. 8—Selling Plans (Family Protection, Incomes, Insurance Programs, etc.).
Oct. 15—Selling Plans (continued)—Salesmanship Essentials.
Oct. 19—Business Insurance.
Oct. 22—Estate Problems and Taxation.
Oct. 26—Insurance Trusts.
Oct. 29—Analysis of Actual Cases.
Nov. 2—Underwriting and Office Procedure.

Nov. 16—Synopsis of Course—Essential Uses of Life Insurance (Program)
Structure, Salesmanship, Underwriting.
Nov. 19—Fundamental Actuarial Principles, Rate Book Analysis.
Nov. 23—Policy Contracts.
Nov. 26—Selling Plans (Family Protection, Incomes, Insurance Programs, etc.).
Dec. 3—Selling Plans (continued)—Salesmanship Essentials.
Dec. 7—Business Insurance.
Dec. 10—Estate Problems and Taxation.
Dec. 14—Insurance Trusts.
Dec. 17—Analysis of Actual Cases.
Dec. 21—Underwriting and Office Procedure.

IVES & MYRICK, Managers

The Mutual Life Insurance Company of New York

57 WILLIAM STREET and 46 CEDAR STREET

Telephones, John 3662 - 3832

Life Insurance Courant (December, 1927).—"The Mutual Life dividends are big dividends and result in a very low net cost of insurance." . . . . "The Mutual Life occupies a very conspicuous position in the ranking of the low net cost companies."

New York Herald Tribune (January 23, 1928).—"The Ives & Myrick agency of the Mutual Life Insurance Company of New York has grown from $1,600,909 in 1909 to $38,097,000 in 1927 in paid-for business, a net gain of $4,145,000 over 1926. This is simply the result of hard work, progressive ideas and sound principles of organizing and underwriting. It is one of the great agencies of the country."

Secretary of the U. S. Treasury.—"Underlying conditions sound, living cost lower, deterrent factors disappearing, business progress expected to continue."

The above reflects three points of interest to prospective agents.

A schedule of Ives & Myrick insurance classes.

surance company could extend to the individual. In subsequent lectures, I talked on family trusts; business life insurance and its responsibilities, which included the liquidation of business assets; and also taxation. Classes went on for a month with eight meetings for me in a month. There were four of us teaching. I was in charge of the training meetings for the other three. I planned the program for them, but I always reviewed it with Charlie Ives. Mr. Ives never met with the other supervisors or addressed a class. Julian Myrick never appeared at these lectures either. Ives gave me the idea of an eight-stage teaching program, and I worked it out. Afterwards I had it published and copyrighted. It covered a client's lifetime, and took him from the inception of his career as a young man through his retirement age.

My office was right across the hall from Charlie's. I never had to knock —I just walked in, and I did so frequently. Charlie's office had two doors: one of solid wood that let him in from the elevator, which he'd lock after he came in; the other one, directly opposite my office, had smoked glass in it so you couldn't look into it. Mine and everybody else's was clear, even Myrick's. You couldn't tell who was in Charlie's office, and in fact, you wouldn't even know that it was part of our office.

Myrick called me in one day, and he said, "Charlie and I have been talking about taking you as an associate." And so I became an associate manager with the wholehearted approval of Charlie. We had what we call brokerage agents, who made up the largest part of our staff. I had 306 brokers to supervise. I wanted to be top man, and my production for these brokers would average around $18 million a year. I am talking about written business, not paid-for business. It wasn't our fault if a case was declined for physical, moral, or financial reasons. We wouldn't know about that. Our actual responsibility was to get the business.

Ives's job was to interpret the feeling of the agency field for increased production and to cultivate the thinking of the public mind toward the need for life insurance. And he got to the public through his literature. The first thing Charlie ever wrote to my knowledge was a pamphlet *Two for One*. I brought that idea to him, and I told him the whole story—it was about a man becoming a father. In a literary way Charlie was much more capable than I was. If anyone gave him literature to write, he'd pen it right off on his desk. Charlie didn't want anything to do with office discipline. Mike would do all that. To look at Charlie's desk you'd think he was the busiest man in the world, but if you asked him about anything, he'd pull a piece of paper out from under a pile that thick, and it was always the right thing.

I happened to know through his secretary that Charlie was quite generous when it came to charity. He never spoke of it and never said anything to me about it. He wanted to give as much to everybody of whatever God had ordained him with, and this included his thoughts. Charlie was a deep thinker. If he couldn't answer a question, he'd say, "George, let it go until tomorrow morning." The next morning he'd come to my office and say, "Come on, we'll talk it over now."

We had very pleasant visits in Redding. Charlie would be disturbed if I didn't bring the whole family. Mrs. Ives always took Mrs. Hofmann and the children outdoors. Charlie would play the piano for me, and when he got tired of playing and he'd see I was getting tired of listening to him, we'd go outside. We'd lie on the grass out there and Charlie wouldn't permit me to talk business. "Hold that until Monday, George." We'd talk about music, or about his career going through college, and politics. We talked about conditions in the country. If Charlie knew about the disturbed situation between the races in this country now, it would make him very unhappy. Our company never took colored applicants, but I employed a colored gentleman for accounting and he was also an attorney. He was the first colored man the Mutual Life ever insured. I wrote him for fifty thousand dollars, and the application came to the attention of our vice-president for underwriting. He called me down and said, "Don't you know the Book of Rules?" But I got that application through, and this opened the way for other colored applicants. When Ives heard about this, he gave me a little tap on the shoulder. "Good work." That's the only way he ever showed any outward affection.

During the Liberty Bond drive they used to have their meetings for bonds right down on our corner.* They had girls there selling them, and if you bought a bond, you got a kiss. Ives and I would go down together, and he

---

*War made Ives intensely unhappy, but he felt that everyone who could not be fighting should work as hard as possible to help the fighting men. Ives & Myrick asked their agents to give two days of their time in June 1917 to the selling of Liberty Loan Bonds. And for the Third Liberty Loan Campaign Ives wrote a circular which he had printed at his expense to be handed out in the streets and hung on buildings. It advised civilians on the essentials during wartime. About the automobile, Ives wrote: "A pleasure car is non-essential. The allies need your gasoline. Release your chauffeur for work in the army, factory, or farm. If you must have a chauffeur, get one over forty." Concerning amusements: "Twice a month is enough for anyone to go to the theater. Too many moving pictures dull the mind. Turn to the genius of Dickens, Thackeray, Hugo, Dumas, Hawthorne, Poe, etc. Or if the mind is strong enough you will find diversion and pleasure in Charles Lamb, Emerson, or Thoreau." Ives advised that everyone cut down to two meals a day, with only a bowl of milk for lunch and requested that "the soldiers have the smokes." Ives continued with advice about servants and travel, and with the admonishment to work in the garden instead of going on vacation. The circular concluded with, "The Soldier gives up everything. What are you giving up?"

would buy a hundred-dollar bond, and then push me over and I'd get two kisses.

Through our conversations Charles Ives inculcated into my system the basic things that man should do in life. Ives was like a second father to me —a kind of spiritual father. Somehow he taught me without saying everything explicitly. He had a magnetic personality—you could see the radiation from his eyes.

Ives, Battery Park, ca. 1917, at the height of his business career.

PETER M. FRASER, retired chairman of the board of the Connecticut Mutual Life Insurance Company, was interviewed at his office in Hartford, Connecticut, on November 21, 1969.

I started to work with Ives & Myrick as a supervisor in 1915 when they were at 38 Nassau Street. I had been in the home office of Mutual Life, and Ives & Myrick asked if I wouldn't like to become associated with them. I'd been selling insurance on the side after hours, and I think they thought that here's a fellow that wants to get ahead. Later on I left them to come with this company, Connecticut Mutual. I was with Ives & Myrick not more than three or four years.

Salaries were low, but Ives & Myrick had an incentive. If they exceeded the quota which was given them by the home office, the excess amount was divided among the supervisors. It was an original idea with Ives & Myrick. It wasn't much money, as I look back on it, but the incentive was there to go out and work as hard as you could. A good life insurance man doesn't think of hours.

Our setup then was not unlike what the banks have today, where we were all out in the open—we didn't have private offices. After a while, we'd get a little bit of a cubbyhole where we could take somebody in. After all, we worked mostly outside the office. I had charge of Brooklyn, and Mr. Hofmann had The Bronx, and Mr. Conroy [Thomas Conroy] had uptown. We were always out making contacts, trying to get them to represent the Mutual Life. When I came here to Connecticut Mutual they didn't have any brokerage business at all, but now we drive hard for it. The idea came from Ives & Myrick.

One time, I went to Myrick and showed him a picture of my future wife and I said, "I'd like to marry this girl." He took a look and said, "You better hurry up and do it and don't waste any time." I did, and then he gave me a raise. Mr. Myrick and I became very close friends, even though there was quite a disparity in our ages. When I became a competitor it had no effect on our friendship. After I left the firm, Mrs. Fraser and I saw quite a lot of the Myrick family. They had a daughter at Farmington School here in Hartford, and they would come up to see her and we would entertain them.

Once a year the agency would have a little party, and we'd go over to a bar and restaurant on Liberty Street. They might have a little champagne or something like that and a free lunch. At the yearly party they would give us a bonus for our production. In dollars it wasn't much—it was a dollar a thousand, but it was the incentive again. Only the supervisors and the office managers went to these dinners—it wouldn't be more than eight or nine people. Mr. Ives always left early.

If Ives and Myrick had been general agents instead of managers for Mutual Life, both men would have become immensely rich. As general agents, instead of being on a paid salary, it's your money and your business and you run it. But they were on salary. And I'm sure that as they grew the salaries went up. But they would have had a great fortune in deferred commissions that they never got. For example, when I retired, I received income for nine years. When Ives quit, he was through. He got a pension, certainly, but pensions were a mere pittance. No, they didn't make the money that a general agent could make, even though Mr. Myrick became nationally known as "Mr. Life Insurance," and he became head of the Life Underwriters' Association.

Four years after the Ives interviews began (and a year after the inter-viewing was thought to be finished), MRS. SAMUEL BERNERI of New York City was identified as the former Louise Garbarino, private secretary to Charles Ives at Ives & Myrick for the eight years between 1921–29. She was interviewed on March 23, 1972.

When I describe Mr. Ives to my children or my husband, I mention Abraham Lincoln. I think Mr. Ives looked like him. He was tall and gaunt, and he was very humble and quiet. He even stepped quietly. And money didn't mean much to him. Often he'd come in without money in his pocket. He didn't have a car in New York—he took the subway. And like Lincoln, Mr. Ives was a very shy person. He had a private entrance to his office. He didn't like to come through the main office. The funny thing was, these big brokers—and we had some pretty big ones—would come over to my desk and try to get an appointment to speak with Mr. Ives. They had to come through me first. But he'd usually refer them to either Mr. Myrick or one of the men out front. And yet he'd see a little printer, and he'd give him a long interview. Mr. Ives used his private exit when people would try to make a fuss over him. I saw him run out of his private office many times to avoid people. There was a couch for him in the office because he used to get these heart attacks. When he felt ill he'd lie down, or he'd put on his coat and rush home. But when he'd get a bad attack, he'd put one of those pills under his tongue and he'd lie down.

Mr. Myrick was a very fine man, and he was different from Mr. Ives. Mr. Ives would wear an ascot, I remember, at times, and he was not much interested in clothes. But Mr. Myrick was a real society clothes type. I do know that Mr. Myrick had a great deal of respect for Mr. Ives.

When I started working for Mr. Ives, I tried to be very tidy and neat, and I'd dust the desk and fix all the papers. You could make one hundred mistakes and Mr. Ives would never scold; he would teach. He'd throw papers all over the floor—very disorganized, I thought at the time. And he told me never to pick them up and never to touch them. He knew what he was doing. He never asked me to take a letter or do anything for him without being humble almost to a degree that's hard to describe. I never met anyone since like him. He'd almost be ashamed to ask you to do something for him. I remember one time when Ives & Myrick were insuring Bernarr Macfadden* for a million dollars. Helen Wills† was in the office at the time, and Mr. Myrick too, since he was the president of the tennis association. Mr. Ives had given me a lot of dictation, and he did something he never did. He came out and paced back and forth waiting for these letters. Macfadden or somebody was leaving on a boat, and there was a deadline we had to meet. I had a lot of moxie and I said, "Mr. Ives, if you're going to walk up and down in back of me, I'll never be able to have these letters ready." Well, he was so apologetic. Another boss might have told me to get off my high horse. But he apologized and went inside and then I was able to take care of it. That was the type of man he was—an understanding person.

Mr. Ives never became terribly personal with anybody, except when you had trouble. My mother was ill one time, and he called me in and he wanted to pay her expenses, and I told him that my dad was able to handle it. Mr. Ives told me to stay home until my mother was better.

One time I sent in my letter of resignation. I had had words with Mr. Verplanck. He called me Mussolini, and I resented it. Mr. Ives called me in the next day and asked me why I was leaving, and I told him that I didn't like Verplanck calling me Mussolini because I'm Italian. Mr. Ives sat me down and told me all about the culture of Italy and treated me like a child, which I was, and explained that I should never allow anybody to

*Bernarr Adolphus Macfadden (1868–1955), physical culturist, publisher.
†Helen Wills, Womens National Tennis Champion for six years in the twenties.

give me a complex. And he said, "We'd like you to stay with us. Would you be happy if you had nothing more to do with Mr. Verplanck?" And he saw to it that I never did another letter for Mr. Verplanck. Mr. Verplanck got his own private secretary out of it. In fact, I told this to Mr. Verplanck, when he said that my tears got me what I wanted. That day Mr. Ives rang for Mr. Verplanck to come into his office, and Ives slammed the door closed. They were yelling, both of them. And Mr. Ives was not supposed to get excited. He put his hat and coat on, slammed his door, and left the office.

When I first went to work for Mr. Ives, he asked me to remember that anything he ever dictated was purely personal and was not to be discussed with anybody in the office. He never stressed anything too strongly, but he did make a strong point of that. His concern was about Edith. He was afraid of somebody who was trying to reach him about this child, and he had said to me that if anyone should ever ask, I was not to ever say anything about her. I got the impression that there had been trouble, and that this was his reason for asking me not to allow anyone in his office who was not connected with insurance, unless they were announced.

I did a lot of clerical work for Mr. Ives. I used to keep every bit of correspondence that went out, any pamphlets or anything from the home office. Mr. Ives had a great big scrapbook, and I would take it from his big library table to my desk and work on it. It wasn't that heavy, but he'd warn me, "Don't lift it up yourself." He was fastidious about the scrapbook. When he dictated, he was very careful, too, about his words and the punctuation.

We worked Saturdays until noon, and from nine to five other days. Mr. Ives sometimes came in at ten or eleven, and he might leave at five, or at two. It would all depend on how he felt. Then he might not show up for a week. Sometimes he'd come through his private entrance, and I wouldn't even know he was there until he would buzz me for a letter. One day it was very embarrassing. I took his pillow to sit on, thinking he was out. And he came out looking for it.

I married in October of '29. Mr. Ives was ill and staying in West Redding. He wrote me to wish me well, and he enclosed a personal check. I went back to the office for visits—I was friendly with Mr. Myrick's secretary and with Mrs. Lord, the bookkeeper—but I never saw Charles Ives there again.

CHARLES J. BUESING was one of the younger men strongly affected by the writings and teachings of Charles Ives. He was a clerk in the home office of Mutual of New York in the mid-twenties, until he transferred to the Ives & Myrick agency in 1929. Mr. Buesing was interviewed in New York in September 1969.

From the very beginning, I could notice the marked difference between Mr. Myrick and Mr. Ives. Mr. Ives was a very shy, retiring man. His office was on the courtyard, way around the corner, completely out of sight from everyone. Mr. Myrick, on the other hand, was in a glass-enclosed office where he could see and be seen by everyone including those who stepped off of the elevator. Without any discredit to Mr. Myrick, I believe much of the success of the agency was due to Mr. Ives, not only his genius, his planning, his aid to the salesmen, his teaching, but also the kind, gentle soul that he was. I never saw him angry. I never heard him speak harshly to anyone. He was a very kindly person and people responded to him.

Mr. Ives was way ahead of his time in teaching young men like me and older established salesmen something about a more professional approach in the selling of life insurance, instead of just selling a policy just because a policy was a good thing to have. He came up with a plan. By measuring the economic value of a man to his wife and children, and translating that into an amount of insurance within the man's ability to pay, we got, at long last, away from policy pedlars into a science. It was the beginning, the glimmering of a profession, where, forgetting the love and affection aspect, one could diagnose a man's economic worth to his wife and family as a breadwinner in cold cash dollars. It was so simple, and yet it was so unique, and there is very little difference today, except that what is being done today is in much larger amounts of insurance. But there is not very much improvement on that early method.

I was so anxious to get out in the field that I would get into every teaching session that I could, whenever I could break away from my duties as a clerk. Mr. Ives gave us something to work with, and even though I was not selling at that time, when I began my selling in 1934 I used his techniques.

The first time I ever walked into Mr. Ives's office, his swivel chair was way back, his feet were up on the bottom drawer of his desk, and his desk was just a mass of papers. His eyes were closed, and for the moment, when I saw him like that I thought, "Well, I've caught the boss asleep." So I tiptoed into the office and put the paper down on his desk and never made a sound. As I turned to go, he said, "Charles, when you see me with my eyes closed, I am not asleep," and I turned around and he was in exactly the same position with his eyes still closed. He said, "Come in and sit down, young man." Never opened his eyes. And then he asked me about my family, my work, and my future plans. He encouraged me to stay in the business, to go out and do a better job than I was doing as a clerk, and to spread the benefits of life insurance to more people.

It's very hard to describe, but Mr. Ives made everyone feel important. He had the ability to make everyone with whom he was associated feel like a king. He would talk with anyone. I can remember meeting other executives of our company on the street. I would know them by seeing their photos in the paper, and I'd address them, but in those days, that was an affront. If we had not been formally introduced, they would just look and turn away. Remember, this was in the days when men came to work in limousines with high hats and striped pants. Charles Ives was not of that nature.

We worked a half-day on Saturdays. We would rarely see Mr. Myrick, but Mr. Ives would be there many Saturdays. One man came by me one Saturday afternoon, and he had tears in his eyes. As Mr. Ives went out the door, this fellow said, "There is a great man." And he told me this story. He had had the experience for the past few months of not making any sales at all. Since we were wholly on a commission basis, if you didn't sell, you just didn't eat. Charles Ives walked up to this man's desk and he thought he looked rather dejected so he said, "Charlie, (his name was Charlie too) do me a personal favor. Will you take out your wallet?" And he did. "Now," he said, "you open it." Then he said, "Will you point it toward me?" The wallet was empty. Charles Ives said, "I thought so. No one can ever make a sale of anything with an empty wallet. Now, I want you to take this as a business loan. I know you'll have so much confidence with what I am going to put in that wallet that you will pay me back, and I don't want any I.O.U. or anything else." And he put fifty dollars in there. It was after the crash, and this man had fifty dollars in his pocket. He hadn't seen that much income in the past couple of months. It made a big difference with him. This is the kind of man that Ives was.

During the Depression in the downtown Wall Street area we cast our eyes to the sidewalk, hoping to pick up a dime or a nickel, but we also cast our eyes skyward to avoid falling bodies. It was that desperate. I went home twice with the blood of suicides on my suit. Right on Cedar Street, while I was walking in the center of the street about two o'clock in the afternoon, a body came hurtling down from the top of the 120 Broadway building and killed a very close friend of mine who was just seven feet away from me. Another time, one of our associates was restrained by me from going out the window into the courtyard from an office right next to Charlie Ives's. Charlie was not in his office at that time. We were on the sixth floor, and I kept yelling until the cashier heard me and we pulled the man back. The times were desperate. We had sixteen million unemployed and everybody was afraid of losing his job. This was when Charles Ives made it his business to be concerned about people, and this made him very unusual.*

Julian Myrick's office had two and three times the photographs that I have here. Charlie Ives's had none. When *Time* magazine wrote their first article about Ives's music, a reporter came around to the office looking for a photograph of Charles Ives, and we searched all over. There were plenty of Julian Myrick, but not one of Charles Ives. They wrote that article while Ives was still living, and they went to his home and asked for a photograph but he refused to cooperate. He would give them no information and would give them no photographs. He just thought it was a lot of fuss, and he did not want any part of this. I took on the job of calling Mrs. Ives on the telephone and telling her what was required and pleading on behalf of *Time* magazine to get a photograph, and she finally conspired with me and agreed to get it. He chose one of himself sitting in an old chair with an old sweater on and an old battered hat on his head.

---

*Actually, Ives retired about six weeks after the crash and was not in the office much during those weeks. Mr. Buesing may remember these incidents from a slightly earlier time.

FAMILY, FRIENDS, AND NEIGHBORS

The Ives house in West Redding, Connecticut. Photo Lee Friedlander.

Joseph Moss Ives (1876–1939) was Charles Ives's only brother. He was a Danbury lawyer with six children, and Harmony and Charles Ives were devoted to all of them. When they chose a site for their country house, in 1912, it was in West Redding, not far from the family in Danbury. The nephews had many happy visits there, and their Uncle Charlie always had time for them, even in those particularly busy years before his illness and retirement. The family were pleased to talk about Uncle Charlie, since, aside from their obvious affection for him, and for their Aunt Harmony, they feel that the usual portraits, drawn from Ives's later years of old age and illness, do an injustice to the active, fun-loving personality they remember.

BREWSTER IVES, second oldest son of Joseph Moss Ives, was interviewed on January 24, 1969, at his home in New York City.

The children of Joseph Moss Ives (left to right): Moss, Bigelow, Richard, Brewster, Chester; (in front): Sarane.

I was born in Danbury, Connecticut, in 1903 before Uncle Charlie was married. Father and Uncle Charlie had a very intimate relationship with each other. Father never attempted to appreciate Uncle Charlie's music, because he recognized that it was the kind of music that would be foreign to his ears, but he respected him, knew of his innovations, and was interested in them in the same way that he knew of their own father's fascination and experiments with music. My father and Uncle Charlie were devoted to one another as boys and remained so throughout their lives. Father died about fifteen years before Uncle Charlie, and I remember that it had a marked effect upon Uncle Charlie as he missed him so much. Aunt Harmony was equally devoted to Father and they, too, had a wonderful relationship. Whenever Father came into New York, he would drop in on them unannounced. Uncle Charlie was an extremely sentimental person who was devoted to his family. He relived his boyhood in Danbury to a degree that was quite unusual. He remembered incidents of his childhood which he was constantly recalling in later years. This was always a surprise to the rest of us, as I doubt that our childhood memories were as clear.

Uncle Charlie was extremely fond of his mother, and there was a great bond between them. I hardly believe there was another mother that could have been prouder of her son than Grandmother Ives. She would constantly remind all of us of his genius. She convinced herself that he was one, and she thought of her husband in the same way. She'd usually start talking about Grandfather Ives and tell us how he pioneered in music and how impressed he was with Uncle Charlie's musical promise; how Uncle Charlie had stayed with his music, and how she was even more proud of that than of his business accomplishments.

On his visits with our family, Uncle Charlie would always joke with us boys. We were on a different basis with him than nephews might expect to be, and we really regarded him as another father. He used to play touch football with us and teach us how to punt and dropkick. We'd play football with Father on one side and Uncle Charlie on the other. He was a lot of fun for us as we grew up. We'd debate with him, and many times we had some pretty heated discussions. It was always stimulating when he was part of it.

My earliest recollection of Uncle Charlie's music was a concert that he took me to alone. I don't believe I was more than fifteen at the time. We went to the old Aeolian Hall on West 43rd Street, and we sat in the back row. His music wasn't played until toward the end of the concert. It was a violin sonata, and he had his music with him. It started with what sounded to most people like discords, and there were protests from the audience that you couldn't miss. There were one or two who just shouted "No, No"

AEOLIAN HALL 34 West 43rd Street
NEW YORK

Modernists

3
Sonata Recitals
for
Violin and Piano
JEROME GOLDSTEIN
Assisted by

HENRY HOLDEN HUSS

CLARENCE ADLER
LEROY SHIELD

Wednesday Evening, November 14, 1923, at Eight-fifteen

1. HENRY HOLDEN HUSS   Op. 14 A Minor
2. LEO ORNSTEIN   Op. 31
3. ERNEST BLOCH

Tuesday Morning, January 15, 1924, at Eleven

1. GERMAINE TAILLEFERRE
2. BÉLA BARTÓK   Iere Sonate
3. EUGENE GOOSSENS

Tuesday Morning, March 18, 1924, at Eleven

1. LOUIS GRUENBERG   Op. 9
2. CHARLES E. IVES
3. ILDEBRANDO PIZZETTI   Sonata in La

Management of POND BUREAU 25 West 43rd Street

Scale of Prices (Tax Extra)

Boxes seating 6 ....$15.00	For the series $40.00
Parquet A to P 2.00	For the series 5.00
Balance 1.50	For the series 3.00
Balcony A to C 1.00	For the series 2.50
Balcony D to E............... .75	For the series 1.50
Balance .... .50	For the series 1.15

BOX OFFICE:

Aeolian Hall, 34 West 43rd Street, New York City

Please enter my subscription for .... (subscription) (single) seats in

................for Mr. Goldstein's Recitals, for which I enclose my check for
LOCATION
.... dollars.

(Signed) ....

Aeolian Hall, March 18, 1924. Identified by Brewster Ives as the concert he attended with his Uncle Charlie, although a review indicates that the audience reaction to the Ives sonata was not unfavorable.

and got up and stalked out of the room. Others did the same thing, and there were boos and catcalls. Uncle Charlie turned, tapped me on the knee, folded up his music and said, "I think we'd better go home." It hurt him no end, but it didn't dim his enthusiasm one iota. He was right back at it the next day. But I think it did shake him.

I was fortunate enough to spend a number of winters with my aunt and uncle, first when they lived on West 11th Street near Washington Square and then later when they moved to Gramercy Park and eventually to 74th Street. I lived with them there when I first got out of college, and I spent many a summer on the farm in Redding. I recall particularly when they lived at Gramercy Park, Uncle Charlie used to come home in the afternoons between three and four o'clock and go upstairs to his study to work on his music. Quite often I happened to be in the same room, and he'd talk to me about it while he was composing at the piano. I remember in particular the *Concord Sonata,* which has always impressed me as his greatest work. He illustrated what he was attempting to do by reading passages from Emerson, the Alcotts, Hawthorne, and Thoreau and then playing passages after he had read them to convince me that the music was expressing the words of the author. He also took passages from other authors and showed me how these had been set to music by other composers. He showed me how with quarter-tones the means of expression could be multiplied in almost a geometrical fashion, and the breadth of expression that this gave to music.

When I took an apartment on Third Avenue overlooking the El, Uncle Charlie, on his visits, would always lean out of the window. He loved the sound of the elevated train as it approached and left; it brought back to him memories of old New York. He had a real fondness for New York as it was in earlier years. I remember his office with the rolltop desk in the old Mutual Life Building downtown. Whenever he went out to lunch, he was always careful to pull down the top of his desk as it was an unholy mess. But he could find his papers when he wanted to, and he actually had an orderly mind, even though you'd never know it by looking at his office. He was a great keeper and never threw anything out. Willie Verplanck, who was in his office, sometimes used to go to lunch with us. Uncle Charlie knew and loved all of the old restaurants. Verplanck used to tell me that Uncle Charlie could be spotted a mile away and that there wasn't a single man in Wall Street who didn't know him. They could see him coming because of the crazy hat he'd wear, and they all were fascinated with him, because he was a real old-fashioned Connecticut Yankee with a sense of humor and eccentric ways. They knew him as a talented businessman more than as a composer.

Uncle Charlie helped all of us with our educations. He used to send me money at college regularly, as Father couldn't do it all with six children and a small-town legal practice. Uncle Charlie made up for whatever was needed and more. When I was able eventually to pay him back, he sent me an amusing letter in which he genuinely protested but finally accepted, because he knew I really wanted it that way. He was so intensely generous that it's sometimes hard to believe. He naturally wanted to help anyone who seemed handicapped in any way, and he was never interested in acquiring worldly possessions of his own. I think that he regarded money as something that should be distributed on as thorough a basis as possible, and yet he rebelled at the idea of a welfare state. He felt that it was the individual's duty to be charitable to the point where he would be, in fact, sharing with everyone who came his way. One of my brothers [Moss] was physically handicapped, and he was the one that Uncle Charlie was closest to and insisted on helping all of his life. He made special provision for him and always was genuinely fond of him to the point where he came above all the others in the family.

I always thought of Uncle Charlie as quite an accomplished pianist, and at one point he must have been a really accomplished organist. He worked hard at his music and so did his brother, my father, who used to complain jokingly that when they were boys, he had to stay underneath and pump the organ for Uncle Charlie who sat up and played it and got all of the credit. Father played the flute, but he didn't play it particularly well. Uncle Charlie believed in making all of us work at music. Each one of my brothers studied music, but the only one who really had talent in our family was my sister, Sarane, who became a talented pianist and teacher. Uncle Charlie urged her to go on with her music, and she had the chance to discuss music with him in a more learned way than the rest of us could ever do. Unfortunately, Sarane died in 1956.

Aunt Harmony is a sweet, beautiful person whom everyone adores.* She used to read aloud to us a great deal. I remember so well her voice as she read *Heidi* and other wonderful stories outdoors on the lawn at Redding. She was an avid reader, whether in German, French, or English. She had rare literary talent and wrote beautifully. Being a minister's daughter, Aunt Harmony was always religious, but she too was interested in new ideas. She was interested in the theater and the opera, and she used to take me to both as a boy. Uncle Charlie had never indicated any particular interest in either one, although he liked to talk about Eugene O'Neill, and Bernard Shaw amused him. Aunt Harmony as well as Uncle Charlie always avoided

*Harmony Ives died April 4, 1969.

most newspapers except the London *Times* and the *Christian Science Monitor*. Father loved newspapers and would bring them with him when he visited, much to their horror!

Uncle Charlie and Aunt Harmony adopted Edith when she was an infant. She was with a family of six or seven children and was the youngest—only a baby in arms. The family was living in the guest house near the entrance to the farm at Redding. Edith's mother was having a difficult time with her as she was a sickly child, and Aunt Harmony took her into the house and cared for her. Aunt Harmony had been a nurse and loved the idea of having a child to care for. They both became fascinated with Edith and arranged with Edith's family for an eventual adoption. Edith became the center of their lives for many years after that. She seldom left home as she was not physically well and, in fact, was handicapped with illness all of her life.

Uncle Charlie was an amazing person, one that I don't believe any of us will see again. He was basically an innovator, not only in his music, but in all of his ideas. He had little patience with conventional things; he had little respect for conventional people. He was always interested in the underprivileged and physically handicapped. He had a sincere interest in

Harmony Ives with Edith Osborne Ives, ca. 1916.

anyone who needed help. His thinking was many years in advance of our own. He was as concerned about the Negro problem twenty-five years ago as we have become about it today. In the same way, he was equally concerned about the development of Nazism in Germany in the days of its infancy. He detested Hitler perhaps more so than any other human being and used to hold forth on this at length. This was long before Hitler reached his full power. And he had little patience with the German people for having put up with him.

Father and Uncle Charlie had been brought up in the Congregational Church in Danbury. Both were confirmed Protestants, and Uncle Charlie was a religious person. Yet despite his Protestant connections, he had great respect for Catholicism and all other forms of religion. I remember that when he supported Al Smith, he made it clear that he thought that it was about time we had a Catholic in the White House, and that he felt that Al Smith was sincere in his attempt to help the common man.

The common man to Uncle Charlie was all-important. This was at the root of his political beliefs. He sincerely felt that the basic decisions of great moment in our political lives should be made by the people rather than the politicians. He felt that all politicians were somewhat suspect, and always thought of the people as the proper and final forum that should be given the respect that was their due. He proposed a twentieth amendment to the Constitution to state the principle that Congress would not have the right to declare war without a popular mandate.* I could well imagine what he would have said about the Vietnam affair in which not even Congress had the opportunity to express itself. This would have brought Uncle Charlie out fighting.

---

*The "Twentieth Amendment" (see next page) was at first an article of six and a half pages which Ives sent to the *New York Times* and other leading New York papers. He received a rejection slip from the *Times* on which he scribbled the following: "My article may have but little value, but whatever it has, is, I am reasonably certain a little greater, than that of the society column . . . ." An abridged "A Suggestion for a 20th Amendment" was printed by Ives with the idea of distribution at the Chicago convention of 1920. Ives asked Darby A. Day, manager of the Chicago Agency of Mutual Life, to take charge of the distribution. Correspondence indicates that these handouts did not arrive in Chicago in time for the convention. Ives then sent them to various newspapers and magazines and to such government representatives as: President Wilson, Governor Calvin Coolidge of Massachusetts, Senate members, the Governor of Illinois, the attorney general's office, Herbert Hoover (then secretary of the Navy), the War Department, and William Howard Taft (then Kent Professor of Law at Yale). The replies were unenthusiastic. Taft wrote: "My dear Mr. Ives: I have your letter of May 26th. I am very much opposed to approve such an amendment as that which you suggest. It is impracticable, and would much change the form of our Government. It would be introducing a principle of the referendum, which I think has already been demonstrated to be a failure in securing the real opinion of the people." Ives answered: "You are the only one who came out saying exactly what he thought . . . . "

A SUGGESTION FOR A 20TH AMENDMENT

The following letter was sent to eight leading New York newspapers a few months ago. To date none of them have printed it. Some of the papers returned the copy saying that space prevented their using it. The letter is long, but requires little more space than that which most of the papers give daily to the society columns. It should not be assumed that because these papers did not see fit to publish this letter that they were opposed to it; they may have thought, probably with good reason, that the plan was not well expressed or presented. However, whatever the reason, the fact that it was not printed would indicate that the editors are not especially interested in the idea. Hence this means of presentation by a circular is tried.

If you won't read all of this, read that part in **large print**—**at least read** the **proposed 20th amendment.** If you do not believe in the idea fundamentally—tear this up; or better, sit down and think out your objections and then present them in any open and fair way you can.

If you believe in the plan show it to others, then **sign your name** on the opposite side as indicated **and mail it to** one of **your representatives** in Congress, **or to the President.**

"The following contains an attempt to suggest a '20TH AMENDMENT' to the Federal Constitution—AN ATTEMPT clumsy and far from adequate, we admit, either in form or in substance, but as its general purpose is **TO REDUCE** to a minimum or possibly to eliminate, something which all our great political leaders talk about but never eliminate, to wit: **THE EFFECT OF TOO MUCH POLITICS IN OUR** representative **DEMOCRACY**—we submit this for what it is worth.

As our political parties today, together with a great chorus of candidates, are by their own declarations out for 'the common good' —that is—'for the people,' and as the people believe that politics are to blame for many of their ills and as political parties generate 'politics,' is it not inevitable and logical that all parties will jump at the chance of embodying in their platforms any plan which will eventually eliminate the cause of these troubles—in other words, all political parties?

We hope the Republican party will not become so over-enthusiastic about this proposed amendment that it will claim a prior right to it—even a monopoly!

But seriously—if it is so and it apparently is, that a dispassionate examination of social phenomena in this and other civilizations indicates that **THE INTUITIVE REASONING OF THE MASSES IS MORE SCIENTIFICALLY TRUE AND** so **OF GREATER VALUE TO** the wholesome **PROGRESS** of social evolution **THAN** the **PERSONAL ADMONITIONS** of the intellectual only—that is, in the ever-flowing undercurrent of the man relation, the ethical and religious impulse predominates—the intellect being a stabilizing rather than a primal organic force—if this is so, is it not only natural but essential, that mankind do more towards registering the results of this intuitive reasoning, and its deeper impulses and to formulate more direct means for their expression? And if this mass intuition and deeper consciousness has been valuable, even in the crude way it has had to function, of how much greater value will it be to society if **THE VARIOUS PREMISES WHICH IT NEEDS TO ACT UPON** more accurately can be more clearly and universally presented. If one will admit that God made man's brain as well as his stomach, one must then admit that the brain (the majority brain) if it has the normal amount of wholesome food —truth (in its outward manifestations, specific knowledge, facts, premises, etc.—which **UNIVERSAL EDUCATION IS FAST BRINGING**) will digest—and will function, as normally as the stomach, when it has the right kind of food. If one won't admit that, he comes pretty near admitting that God is incapable. The writer believes that **THE AMERICAN PEOPLE** are willing to make or try to make a greater contribution to social progress; that they have faith in themselves and **ARE WILLING TO TAKE RESPONSIBILITY AND** if occasion requires willing to take **TIME TO THINK ACCURATELY** and **SERIOUSLY—AND** further that they, **WITH THE PREMISES BEFORE THEM WILL BE** more **INSPIRED BY THE SENSE OF JUSTICE**, not only social justice, or any relative justice—but justice in the absolute— than are many self or party-appointed leaders. **THE NEED OF LEADERS** in the old sense **IS FAST GOING—BUT THE NEED OF FREER ACCESS TO GREATER TRUTHS AND FREER**

EXPRESSION IS WITH US, and with this greater and deeper freedom, the sum of all consciousness—the people are finding their one true leader—they are beginning to lead themselves. Utilizing public opinion in any but a general way may seem hopelessly impractical to the hard-headed business man (so termed) and to the practical politician, altogether too practical. To photograph with good results, the universal mind and heart will be a big job—a tremendous job—but one that was successfully started in 1776—and the bigger the job the more reason why the American people will tackle it with courage and equanimity. **TO BE AFRAID TO TRUST THE MIND AND SOUL OF THE PEOPLE IS A COMMON ATTRIBUTE OF THE TIMID.** There is every reason to hold with John Bright that the first 500 men who pass in the Strand would make as good a parliament as that which sits at St. Stephen's. Wendell Phillips, a student of history and a close observer of men, as George Williams Curtis says, 'rejected the fear of the multitude which springs from the timid feeling that the many are ignorant and the few are wise; he believed the saying, too profound for Talleyrand, that **EVERYBODY KNOWS MORE THAN ANYBODY.'** Because a man does not express an opinion, do not assume that he has none. Ask him and find out that mankind is thinking—and thinking seriously and is interested in its thought. And we doubt that the quality of the thinking of the masses will be as inferior as some of the practical voices think. In working out a system of universal expression there will be severe disappointments, disastrous sloughing offs, dark days, trials and discouragements, but no greater problems than we have survived. It is the belief of the writer that **THE MAKERS OF OUR FEDERAL CONSTITUTION HAD** in mind **THE HOPE OF A BROADER DEVELOPMENT OF** direct **POPULAR EXPRESSION.** Obviously, more **DIRECT EXPRESSION** was as **IMPOSSIBLE IN 1780** as it is **POSSIBLE IN 1920.** The process does not change the form of our government. It tends to protect and perfect it. We respectfully submit the following:

SECTION 1.

Article 20. (20th Amendment.) On a day, nine* months previous to the day on which the people shall meet in their respective states to vote by ballot for electors (Article 12) for President and Vice-President, the said people of the United States shall submit to Congress all and whatever plans, opinions and suggestions which each and all desire to offer in relation to future Federal legislation; and in this connection and upon the same ballot there shall be contained not over twenty questions, the subject matter of which shall relate to whatever Congress considers, does most fundamentally and vitally affect the public welfare.. Such questions shall be presented as clearly as is possible so that the answers may readily indicate the opinion of the public. All citizens of the United States, male and female (and over the age of 21, possibly 18), shall be required to return answers or opinions to these specific matters and questions which shall be returned to the Government in addition to the other suggestions, opinions, etc., that the people may wish to submit (as suggested above). The result of these suggestive ballots shall be made known to Congress who shall analyze, classify and orderly arrange these plans, suggestions and answers into subdivisions and make the complete findings public. Whichever ten of the foregoing plans and suggestions as a result of these ballots shall have been the most numerous, shall then be suitably assimilated, condensed and presented to the people in the form of proposed laws (together with an essential digest of each) five months before

---

*This was drafted some years ago but revised recently in the hope that it could be put before Congress so that it might be a definite help in the coming election. This is hardly possible now, but the "plan in principle" should be publicly and seriously discussed. The sooner some such amendment is enacted the sooner will the duties of Congress be made more manifest.

There will be no plank in any party platform more important!

Uncle Charlie always supported the cause of the workingman as against the man of affluence, and I think that he basically felt that we in this society put too much emphasis on dollar earnings and too little emphasis on sincerity of purpose. He always showed his respect for the farm hands at Redding, the neighboring farmers, the mailmen, the grocery clerks. He treasured them as friends just as much as he did other neighbors who were independently wealthy. He was always offended by those who stressed their rank in society or who were at all snobbish.

He was a bashful person basically, and yet at the same time when he had anything on his mind, he was very facile at expressing himself and did so in no uncertain terms. He always had respect for new ideas, whether they were expressed in the business world or in the field of arts. I know that he was interested in Picasso, Matisse, John Marin, and many other artists. And I remember spending many an evening with him discussing modern painters and their approach to painting. He was fascinated with a new approach to painting or a new approach to sculpture. I had a very dear friend who was an architect and who had done a number of original buildings. This delighted Uncle Charlie as much as anything I can recall. He was at pains to express interest in anything that was new, and he made it abundantly clear that he had no respect for those who followed an effortless and conventional way of doing things. He felt that that kind of person was mentally lazy and not worthy of his keep.

During the last ten years of Uncle Charlie's life I was still a bachelor and would stop in regularly each week to spend an evening. After dinner we'd usually get off on a discussion of either politics, economics, or music. I repeatedly asked him about other composers. He always showed great respect for the old masters: Bach, Beethoven, and Brahms in particular. I have a book of his entitled *From Grieg to Brahms,* and in it are many passages of Brahms that he underscored. As far as modern composers were concerned, he had great admiration for his good friend Carl Ruggles and for another innovator, Henry Cowell. I doubt that he actually heard too many examples of other modern composers, as he simply didn't have the physical opportunity to do so. His hearing bothered him for many years. Time and again, I would ask him if I couldn't play some recordings for him, but he would always protest saying that this set up a disturbance in his ears and that it made his head buzz and he couldn't listen. He never wanted either a radio or a phonograph in the house, but on occasion he would listen, usually with the complaint that it bothered his hearing. He actually did attend one or two concerts in later years. At one in Carnegie Hall they called for the composer, and he slouched in his seat and was embarrassed to have himself identified. This shyness grew out of the derision which he had to face in earlier years.

I think that one thing about Uncle Charlie that should be expressed in all fairness is that senility took its toll in his last several years. His doctor toward the end of his life was also my doctor, and when he strongly urged an operation for a double hernia condition, pointing out the risk involved in avoiding an operation, it seemed the only thing to do. As it turned out, Uncle Charlie was not able to survive it.

Aunt Harmony has now outlasted them all. I've never known of two people who were more wrapped up in one another than she and Uncle Charlie. They were so close that the rest of the world didn't get to see as much of them as they otherwise might have.

Harmony and Charles Ives at West Redding, ca. 1948. Photo Halley Erskine.

BIGELOW IVES, nephew of Charles Ives, was interviewed on March 12, 1969, in Danbury. His memories of his uncle go back to about 1914 when the Iveses lived at 27 West 11th Street in New York.

We children always thought it was a very high privilege to be invited into New York to visit with Uncle Charlie and Aunt Harmony. My earliest recollection of them was a visit to New York about 1914. I can recall, at that time, musicians and dancers coming to Uncle Charlie's house. I particularly remember being introduced to and being very much impressed with a ballet dancer, when I was about six or seven.

We saw a great deal of them when they were in Redding in the summertime, and that was always a lot of fun. We would pitch a tent down by the pond and stay there for several weeks at a time. Uncle Charlie would always take time out from his composing in the music room to come out and play ball with us. He'd insist on a game of catch at least once a day. I thought he was a little unfair, because I was still a little fellow and he'd throw the ball really hard at me. I was rather frightened to be faced with playing catch with the real ballplayer I thought he was. He'd put on his old baseball cap when he did this.

I recall with particular amusement the times when Uncle Charlie would attempt, and I use that word advisedly, to drive the old Model T car. He was really one of the world's wildest drivers, and he had this Model T Ford which he kept there in Redding just to drive between the house and the West Redding Station. On one occasion he tried to go up to Bethel with it. That was quite an extensive drive of six miles or more, and farther than he usually went. I remember going through a very narrow, twisting tunnel under the railroad tracks, and it was a fairly dangerous spot. Uncle Charlie said that he'd always wanted to blow the horn real loud here, because it was very dangerous. He said, "I was killed here once, and that was enough for me."

We didn't see a great deal of Uncle Charlie in Danbury because he was reluctant to come back to his boyhood town and kept himself pretty much in the circle between New York and West Redding. I can recall his coming to our house only once. Danbury recalled a past that could not be recalled, and he got quite emotional whenever he came into town. I remember very late in his life, after my own father died, he did come up to the old house where he had spent so much time as a boy. The house had been moved back away from Main Street up onto Chapel Place, and the visit was probably the first one back to the old place in maybe fifteen or twenty years. Uncle Charlie spent the night there and wandered through the old house and spoke very feelingly about the north parlor, and recalled how changed it all was. I went out walking with him late that evening, and we went up as far as the Civil War monument in the City Hall Square. That was only about half a block from the old house. He actually moaned aloud when he got up there and saw how it had all changed from his recollection of it. There were no longer any elms, and there were strange new buildings not very compatible with his vision of the old town. He leaned up against a sandbox which was on the corner by the curb, and he buried his head in his hands and moaned. "I'm going back," he said, "You can't recall the past." And he turned around and went back to the old house and said he was sorry he had gone out at all. From that I had an inkling of how deep his love was for a bygone way of life that he apparently had nurtured ever since having left Danbury as a boy.

I never had any compunction about violating the privacy of Uncle Charlie's music studio. In fact Uncle Charlie never called it a studio. That would have been too fancy a term. It was just a room where the piano was. Whether in New York or Redding, we never thought that we were intruding on him, and he never seemed to resent it. He would draw you in when you came into the room. He would say, "Now what do you think of this?" and he would cease working on a difficult passage that might be beyond our depth and break into one of these ragtime pieces or a march, and he'd do it with such spirit that it was really thrilling. He would occasionally play on the big grand piano out in the living room at Redding, but more often he preferred the little upright in the studio. When he was out in the main living room, playing on the grand, I recall his sticking pretty much to Negro spirituals when I was there. I don't know whether he was trying to lead me easily into an appreciation of music or what.

During the First World War, he was so agitated about the peace movement and wrote the song *He Is There!* It was rather a simple and brief song, but he was still toying with its final form. He tried to get me to sing it, and if I didn't sing with enough spirit or gusto, he would land both fists on the piano. "You've got to put more life into it," he'd say. There was one little passage which called for a real shout, but I shouted very timidly and he nearly hit the roof. "Can't you shout better than that? That's the trouble with this country—people are afraid to shout!"

Uncle Charlie didn't discourage, nor did he encourage, visitors other than the family, and he kept so out of the limelight that his circle of acquaintances in the Redding area was limited to the neighbors. The neighbors came and went, and they were treated just like members of the family. He thoroughly enjoyed that. But he fled from a formal visit from the outside world. Members of Mrs. Ives's family, the Twichells, would occasionally visit, and Mrs. Ives's father, Reverend Joseph Twichell,* used to visit often. He spent a summer down there. And while Reverend Twichell was living, they practiced the old-fashioned New England habit of family prayers. Before breakfast we all assembled in the living room, and old Joe Twichell would lead everyone in prayer.

During his very creative period, which lasted roughly from 1900 up to 1920, he was so filled with trying to put it all down that he couldn't be bothered with the details of cataloging his music. And when that period of creativity passed, he was exhausted, and the scores which he had scribbled out were here, there, and everywhere. They weren't only in the barn; I remember when he decided to use a horse stall for storage space. My brother Richard bought filing cabinets for him here in Danbury, and there was a great to-do about setting up the storage spaces for these scores. But then, what did he do? He just dumped them in there. They came from all over. They came from the rooms on Umpawaug Hill, they came from New York, they came from his office, and probably from under the seats of railroad trains where he did some of his composing.

Uncle Charlie was very much concerned with cataloging all of the reviews which came to his attention and any of the correspondence that seemed of particular interest. It all had to be copied and stored away in his scrapbook. The inordinate amount of time spent in that seemed to me most unusual. I remember how affected he was by one of the earliest performances in Europe of his music by Nicolas Slonimsky.† Nicolas sent him one of the billings that they paste on the walls outside the concert hall, and that went on the door to the music room down in Redding. And how excited Uncle Charlie was over Slonimsky's promotion of his music in Boston! I remember Slonimsky coming to the house at 74th Street, and Uncle Charlie was so delighted to hear him coming. Uncle Charlie's studio was in the attic, but he seemed to know when Slonimsky was in the house. He'd shout down to him and Slonimsky would shout back, and there were four floors between them. What a racket was created by those two! They'd get up there in the music room, and Uncle Charlie would go right at it. "Now what do you think of this?" And then they'd begin experimenting.

*Joseph Hopkins Twichell (1838–1918) was a prominent minister in Hartford and a close friend of Mark Twain.
†Nicolas Slonimsky, pp. 147–55.

All the family knew that music was important to Uncle Charlie, because it was a lifetime avocation. We felt that his music was difficult and strange, and we wondered why he insisted on composing such hard-to-listen-to music. We used to confront him with that, Father particularly. If Uncle Charlie's own brother wanted to criticize him, it was his privilege, but we children were a little more reluctant. Having heard Uncle Charlie's music over a period of years, I've become exposed to it to the point where I begin to appreciate it. It's wonderful, exciting music for me to listen to now. Years ago, it was always through the medium of Uncle Charlie's piano. It's quite a discovery to be presented with a recording done by the New York Philharmonic, playing a full symphony, of these works we heard played by Uncle Charlie in snatches as we were growing up.

CHESTER IVES, the youngest nephew, was interviewed in New Canaan, Connecticut, on May 7, 1969. According to John Kirkpatrick,* Chester Ives talks with inflections very much like his Uncle Charlie's.

The first recollection I have of Uncle Charlie is from when he and Aunt Harmony came to visit us in Danbury. We had an upright piano that he played, and so expressively that any child would respond to it. I remember wondering when he was going to come again to play for us. And we used to visit him in New York when they lived in Gramercy Park. I was very young, but they always had plans to entertain us children. They took us to see the sights in town, and Uncle Charlie took us down to his office on William Street. After 1930, when he had to retire from business, Uncle Charlie was able to give more time to his personal life, and we began to see him even more often.

Everything for us with Uncle Charlie was always built around baseball and other sports. As a child, my impression of him was this enthusiasm to be a sportsman, and he could always share your enthusiasm and give advice if you were a ballplayer. I remember I said I played second base. "Oh, no. You want to get over to shortstop. Anybody goes to sleep on second." Of course he pitched. I can remember going up on top of the hill alongside of the barn at Redding and he'd show us how to pitch. He'd wind up—he really had a classic way of the windup, just as any professional player. My

---

*John Kirkpatrick, pp. 213–26.

Charles Ives with a team-mate, Hopkins Grammar School, 1893.

poor father was always catching for him. Father used to lose his interest in catching the ball for him, and Uncle Charlie would get mad and say, "Come on, Moss. Pay attention when I'm throwing."

One Thanksgiving, Uncle Charlie joined our family at a football game between Pennsylvania and Cornell at Philadelphia. My brother Brewster has a lot of the spirit of Uncle Charlie. Brewster got very enthusiastic during the game, yelling out advice to the coach as to what player to use in the game. Uncle Charlie had the time of his life watching Brewster.

Another time I remember was when Mr. David Twichell, Aunt Harmony's brother, accompanied us with Uncle Charlie on a walk to a swimming hole. I was about twelve years old. There was a rocky cliff, twelve or fifteen feet high, and they were trying to encourage me to try diving. Uncle Charlie said, "Try it, Chester." He was standing on the side, because he wasn't swimming in those days. But Dave Twichell was in the water and he treaded water for about fifteen minutes waiting for me, and Uncle Charlie was on the sand encouraging me. I finally dove off, and it was wonderful to get his enthusiastic praise afterward. I felt like a million dollars going back to the house. I even lost my shoes in the stream and it didn't make any difference. He made me feel so good about my triumph.

My ambition, I told Uncle Charlie one time, was to be on the crew. He said, "Oh, my God. You want to be on the crew? You just go to sleep. You don't use your head. You just sit there and pull an oar, and let somebody shout at you all the time." He would encourage me to be in competitive sports, like football.

I got discouraged at one time, because I had wanted to go to Dartmouth, but the family talked me into going to business school. Other members of the family influenced me to go to a city college, so I went down to Pennsylvania, and after a half a year there I withdrew. It was then that Uncle Charlie encouraged my coming around. He realized that it was disappointing when you have an experience like that, and he began to help me with my reading. He gave me some works by Emerson and Thoreau. And when I was reading *Ivanhoe,* he'd sound me out as to what I thought of certain characters in the story. This was during the Depression, and they were encouraging me to work out my own ways of training myself. He got my sister and me to read his *Essays Before a Sonata*—I don't remember his literally coming out and saying, "Here, read it," but we approached it through his words and his ideas behind it. I remember sitting out in the woods reading it aloud with my sister. I wished he could have done more with Sarane. She died the same year that Edie did [1956]. I remember I was with her in Houston, and one of the last things she played was his *Emerson,* and she did it well. I just wish that Uncle Charlie had listened to her play more. But there was something about music. He'd said, "Oh, don't get into that. Who wants to be a musician?"

Sarane and I talked a great deal about Aunt Harmony and Uncle Charlie as being an almost ideal couple. They helped us so much. Father was busy with a big family. It's unfair to say you look to one person more than another, but it's just that they had more time for us. We often went walking through the woods, and he would try to show me the wonders of nature. There was a path leading out to a bench in the woods, and it was a lookout over the Redding hills. We'd go by an opening in the trees, and he'd say, "Take a look at that up there. Do you see anything?" And I'd say, "Well, sure, sunlight." He'd say, "Do you know that it's just like a cathedral? You get the same effect in a cathedral. You'd better be a little more aware of what you're looking at." They got me reading Washington Irving's writings, and he said, "You come out here. Go out to the bench and just read it and think about it. You don't have to rush through it." They don't do enough of this kind of reflective reading in colleges. And this was the age when I should have been in college.

Soon after that, I went to New York and got a job with a bookstore. I lived at the Ives's apartment. They were away during that winter, and Mr.

Henry Bellamann,* a music critic from the South and a man who was very interested in Uncle Charlie's music, stayed there also. I got marvelous postcards from Uncle Charlie. One of them said, "Middle of the ocean, still on board."

I finally got a job with a publishing company, and the Iveses asked me to live with them on 74th Street. I used to walk from work on 34th and Sixth Avenue all the way home. I'd purposely rush home after work in order to hear him play between five and suppertime at seven. Aunt Harmony gave me some things to read on the lake poets, Wordsworth and Coleridge, and I have always associated all that playing of the piano with that kind of reading. He'd shout and sing along, and I always had fun listening to the way he was doing it. He had an awful lot of vitality in everything he did.

Father would kid Uncle Charlie and say, "So why don't you compose something pretty, Charlie?" And Uncle Charlie would kid him back. Uncle Charlie didn't have any newspapers in the house, and I remember, when Father would visit us, Uncle Charlie saying, "Oh my gosh, here comes a newspaper." Father would bring in the *New York Times,* and Uncle Charlie would say, "What do you have to read that for? That's just the same old stuff. The politicians are running everything."

Edie went to the same school her mother went to at Farmington. When she had graduated from school, I used to take her to Dr. Fosdick's Presbyterian Church downtown. Uncle Charlie didn't go to church then, because it was hard for him to get out, so I used to take Aunt Harmony and Edie. Uncle Charlie encouraged us to get out of religion what we could, but mainly to think for ourselves. It always came back to that.

I finally went back to Danbury, as I had the opportunity to buy out a small bookshop there. To do this I needed some money, and I had to borrow it from Uncle Charlie. This was supposed to be a business loan with interest at four percent. Later on, when I repaid it, he wrote [February 11, 1940]: "Send this interest to your mother during her lifetime; then to the one of her children who, by popular vote, is said to be the nicest." Then he signed it: "Chassy Ives." I remember talking to him about money and his saying that he felt that a hundred thousand was enough for any man to earn. Beyond that he said to give it to some cause that he believed in.

One evening, I talked with him about Beethoven, and I said that I felt what he [Uncle Charlie] was doing was what Beethoven would have done

---

*Henry Bellamann was a poet and writer who later achieved fame as the author of the novel *King's Row* (New York: Simon and Shuster, 1940). Bellamann was one of the earliest proponents of Ives's music, and he wrote several articles and reviews of Ives's works. His wife Katherine Bellamann, a singer, was an early performer of Ives songs.

had he been able to keep on living. And he said that was the way he felt about it—a sort of continuing spirit.

There was one thing he said about his father that always impressed me—that Grandfather always felt that anyone could sing. Never mind if they were on key or not, if they had the right spirit, the right feeling about it. When Grandfather had choruses, he used men to sing who were way off pitch. People made fun of this, but he'd say, "What of it? They have the spirit of it." In fact, sometimes when Uncle Charlie sang, I felt I could sing better than he could!

When I had to leave for the service, Uncle Charlie was very worked up and very emotional about it. He really felt sorry to see a young man have to go into it, and when I came back, there was a wonderful welcome. Aunt Harmony used to say that when Uncle Charlie traveled in Germany, he used to go up to the German fellows and ask them how they really felt about World War I. He would ask them what they would do to prevent another war, and wouldn't they like to have a chance to vote on it, if they had to go to war again. Of course, this was before Hitler came in. There were many conversations my brother and I used to have with Uncle Charlie about the state of world conditions.

Uncle Charlie respected his mother, although he felt that she couldn't really understand what he was doing. But one time he said that when he was at Yale, he wanted to go out for football, and she encouraged him not to do it, because he wanted to play the organ and she said he'd hurt his fingers. Uncle Charlie idolized his father. In fact, he used to speak of his father as if he felt his presence all the time.

He was always teasing me, so I had my chance on April Fools' Day one year to get back at him. They had a cook named Ida, a wonderful girl. So Ida and I arranged to fool Uncle Charlie by saying an interior decorator was going to come from one of the department stores in New York to fix up his music room because it was very plain. He was shocked, and she could hardly keep from laughing. He just straightened up, walked out of the room like a little boy and went down to see Aunt Harmony. He said, "What's all this about an interior decorator coming to fix my room?" Ida giggled and burst out, "April Fool!" Uncle Charlie had a great time laughing about it.

❧

*Ives's eldest nephew, RICHARD IVES, lives in Danbury and was inter-
viewed there on June 2, 1969. The winter of 1915 stands out in his memory.
He recalled that it was when he was thirteen years old and not feeling well,
and the Iveses took him to live with them in New York and showed him the
city. Richard remembered that through the years, his father and uncle discussed many topics which interested both of them, including the American
Constitution and J. Moss Ives's particular fascination with the contribution
of the Jesuits to the founding of this country.**

*In describing his uncle, Richard Ives said, "Once his health failed, he
just put on an old pair of pants and an old soft shirt and he never dressed up
for anything. He always wore the same old brown felt hat which had several
holes in the top and was the darndest-looking thing. I guess he had that hat
for about thirty years." The brown hat, along with Ives's baseball cap of
Yale '98, his father's cornet, pictures of his father and of Lincoln, and the
upright piano, are in the little studio room off the dining room in the house
in West Redding. The room is kept the way Ives had it when he was there,*

---

*In 1936 J. Moss Ives published a book about the Jesuits, *The Ark and the Dove* (Long-
mans, Green).

Ives's studio. Photo Lee Friedlander.

The inside doors of Ives's studio, West Redding, Connecticut. Photo Lee Friedlander.

and on the wooden doors which Ives used as a bulletin board, are the programs, pictures, cartoons, and news items tacked there as they struck his fancy through the years. Brahms and Franck, the Kirkpatricks, old team pictures, and a large yellow and red Ives & Myrick poster form an extraordinary collage of Ives memorabilia.

Sarane Ives was the youngest child of J. Moss Ives and the only one of the six who showed a talent for music. She married a musician, ARTHUR HALL, in 1944. Sarane Ives Hall died in 1956. Professor Hall, a composer and teacher (now retired), was head of the music department at Rice University in Houston, Texas, where he was interviewed on March 22, 1971.

I was introduced to Charles Ives at his former home on East 74th Street in New York by his nephew, Richard Ives. As we entered, Charles Ives just looked at me and sort of nodded his head. He said nothing, but he came and grabbed me by the elbow and led me into the living room over to the mantelpiece and pointed at a little French clock on the sill above the fireplace. Then he made many gestures imitating the stiff movements of the hands of this little clock. Still he said nothing. And of course I was completely flabbergasted. I felt very much like a fool because I couldn't understand his motions. He went back through the same mechanical gestures again, and then said to me, "That's like Toscanini conducting the *Eroica Symphony*." Up until that time he said not a word. I told Sarane about my meeting with her uncle, and she said it was exactly like him. He was testing me out, as he was curious to know what kind of friend his nephew had brought into his house.

Sarane's study with her uncle was completely informal and mutually enjoyable. But it was not, as far as I know, any real systematized work with him. As a matter of fact, I don't think he would have cared to try to influence her with his characteristics at all. He did advise her as to what teachers would be good for her. While at Dana Hall, Sarane had known the piano teacher [Helen Coates] that [Leonard] Bernstein had studied piano with, and Sarane and Bernstein had quite a happy reunion when Bernstein came down to conduct the Houston Symphony one time. When we were married in 1944, Sarane had just finished a tour with E. Robert Schmitz.* She studied with him over a longer period than almost any other teacher she had, and she was very fond of him. She studied with him both in New York and in San Francisco.

Mr. Ives and I didn't discuss music at all. I felt that doing that was like talking shop. I think Sarane always took her Uncle Charles's music seriously. But I think some of the other members of the family took it with

*E. Robert Schmitz, pp. 124–30.

tongue in cheek until he began to get publicity and recognition. They made indirect references to their former ideas of what his music was like, which, of course, are not fit for publication.

The only thing of Charles's that I ever heard Sarane really work at was the *Concord Sonata.* Once when we were on a summer tour in New England, we went over to Concord one day. We went into a church and there was a piano with a tag on it that said, "The Alcott Piano on which Nancy Alcott practiced." And so we got permission from the curator of the museum there, and she actually opened up the piano for us. It wasn't in bad shape at all. Sarane sat down and played the slow movement [*Alcotts*] from the *Concord Sonata,* the one that supposedly refers back to Nancy Alcott practicing and improvising on the theme of Beethoven's *Fifth Symphony.*

My association with the Iveses lasted only from 1944 to 1956—that's the time that Sarane and I were married. The second time I saw Ives was when Sarane and I went to Redding with our children and were there for a whole day. The children went down to the swimming pond. They came back, and Charles got hold of the youngest one's hand and walked around the lot right there, and he looked as if he was having such a wonderful time. The boy, of course, didn't realize what was happening, but he was having a grand time too. Fortunately, I have a photograph of that occasion.

We have Charlie's piano. It was given to Sarane. I have just about made up my mind to give it to my son George, a musician. He's the youngest, the one who walked with Charlie, and I think he got an infusion from Charlie when he walked with him.

The last photograph taken of Charles Ives, ca. 1949, with the son of Sarane Ives Hall.

T. FINDLAY MACKENZIE came from Australia to New York in 1919 to pursue graduate studies in economics. In 1920, he took a position as tutor to the Ives's nephew Moss, and as a result, he and Mr. Ives began a friendship which lasted for many years. "MacKenzie" received a Ph.D. in 1933 from New York University and became a professor of economics at Brooklyn College. Mr. and Mrs. MacKenzie were interviewed at their home in Croton-on-Hudson, New York on October 28, 1971.

When I first came to the States, I went to the Albert Teachers' Agency to find some supplementary work to help me with my expenses, and they advised me to get in touch with Mrs. Ives who was looking for a tutor for Mr. Ives's nephew, Moss. I wrote to Mrs. Ives, and she answered saying that she could not use me at the time. But later, perhaps about the end of January [1920], I got a note from her and I went down to see the Iveses. They lived in Gramercy Park in a lovely house with a beautiful garden in the back.

Mrs. Ives took me on and I did work with the boy, and we got along very well. Moss was fifteen. He had some kind of handicap; I don't know what it was. He wasn't abnormal, or arrested, but he just couldn't come across, and so the Iveses wanted a tutor for him. Moss played the violin and had quite a good ear for music. He lived with the Iveses at this time, and they treated him like a son. They took it for granted that Moss would never make his own living, and this was like a transition period for him. He must have stayed with the Iveses for a year in all. Mr. Ives just said it was too bad he was handicapped, and that we were going to do everything we could to help him.

I met with an accident in June of 1921. I phoned the Iveses, and when I told Mrs. Ives what had happened, she invited me to West Redding. I stayed there for about two weeks to rest. She wouldn't let me out before that. I heard Ives play his music there—he'd play all kinds of things. I got so used to his music that I began to accept it—I could see what he was driving at. I met Mr. Ives's mother in Danbury in 1921, during that time I was recuperating in Redding. Mr. Ives and I drove up to Danbury in the car one day. She was a nice-looking woman, rather petite with dark hair and dark eyes, neat and very bright. She was very pleased to see us.

When Edie was growing up, the Iveses used to have me take Edie and her cousin Sally Ives places. I would go to dinner at their home and take the girls out. I remember going to *William Tell,* and we sat in the orchestra of the Metropolitan Opera House. It was very nice for all of us. One evening I asked Edie and Sally out to Harpur College where I was giving a course, and they came all dressed up. I said to the class, "I'd like to introduce you to some friends of mine. One is Marlene Dietrich, and the other is Greta Garbo." We had a wonderful time.

There were many Thanksgiving dinners, and some Christmas dinners with the Ives family, and then later on I used to go at least once every three weeks for afternoon tea on Sunday to the house on 74th Street. I met Henry Cowell there. He was a great devotee of Ives's music. Ives was a brilliant pianist, a master in command of the keyboard, and once when I was in Redding I said to him that I thought maybe we could go on a tour together. I said, "I'll be your manager, and you'll play and get up and give witty addresses and funny remarks, and we could make a fortune!" And did he laugh at that idea! It would have been a wonderful stunt.

I was always interested in singers,* and Ives said to me one day about Emma Eames, singing Mozart, "Oh, Eames, singing all that sweet stuff. Like fat pussy-cats, these old ladies." And I thought, well, this is a little hard on Mozart. But I think Ives just wanted to go overboard on the modern part.

Ives called me "Mac" or "MacKenzie." He always was pleased to see me because he could be himself, and I'd rib him, I'd tease him, and he liked to go one better if he could! He loved fun and anything that was a good joke, and he would punch me sometimes in a friendly way, and I would just pay no attention.

When I became a citizen, Mr. and Mrs. Ives came to sponsor me. We went to a city court in downtown New York. Everything was going along all right, until some fellow came out to tell people where to go to be tested. And this fellow who was talking was muttering so we couldn't understand a word of it. Ives stood up and said, "Why don't you talk English? We don't understand a word you are saying." And he sat down. About twenty minutes later, another fellow, much worse than the first, came out. And he was terrible. Ives couldn't take it. He stood up in righteous indignation and he said, "What's the matter with you people? You can't talk so anybody can hear you, or understand what you say. It's disgraceful!" So an attendant came over and said, "See here, gentleman, you sit down and keep quiet, or you won't get your papers." A New Englander! You won't get your papers!

---

*Mr. and Mrs. MacKenzie had a long-standing interest in singing and singers which culminated in a book: Barbara MacKenzie and Findlay MacKenzie, *Singers of Australia: From Melba to Sutherland* (Melbourne: Lansdowne Press, 1967).

And his wife was there, embarrassed. "Charlie, Charlie, sit down," she said. Mr. Ives was so chagrined. He said to me, "This won't hurt you, will it, Mac?"

BARBARA MACKENZIE, a psychologist, was brought to meet the Iveses by her husband shortly after they were married in 1944. She was at first put off by Ives's penetrating gaze and manner and his "nonsense" talk with MacKenzie. She noticed that whenever Ives would see Mac, "he would walk quicker and flash his hand out to him in a way that belies the introspective concept of a person." Barbara MacKenzie felt that Ives reacted to only certain individuals consistently, including her husband, and when he did, "it was like a light going on to be with him. If you ask me what one word I would associate with Charles Ives, it would be 'incandescence.'" Barbara MacKenzie admired Mrs. Ives and felt comfortable with her from the start. She said, "People might have thought her prosaic, but she wasn't. She opened doors, and she sewed seams, and she was never in doubt that Charles Ives was a genius, and so he was never in doubt."

Considering Ives's attachment to the towns and hills of New England, it was not at all surprising that he and Harmony looked for a country place soon after they were married, and that they chose a site in West Redding, Connecticut, overlooking the Danbury hills. There on Umpawaug Hill in 1912 the Iveses built the house and barn which became their home and which gave them great pleasure for many years. It was a fortuitous choice, and not the least of its many assets was the proximity of the Ryder family.

WILL RYDER, like his father Frank before him, is a farmer. The elder Ryder helped care for the Ives property until his death in 1927. Will Ryder continued his father's work. The friendship which developed between the families was of such natural warmth and duration that Mr. Ryder's reticence about discussing Mr. Ives with others was surely understandable. It was therefore a surprise and an added pleasure when Will Ryder came in from his fields to join LUEMILY RYDER in this talk about Charles Ives which took place in the Ryder house, next door to the Iveses' in West Redding, on October 9, 1969.

LUEMILY RYDER: Mr. and Mrs. Ives came to Redding in 1911 or 1912 when my husband was fourteen or fifteen.

WILL RYDER: He built the house in 1912. The property was originally my father's. They didn't buy it from us, but from Miss Seymour next door, who had bought it from my father. It was fourteen or fifteen acres. Gene Adams, a carpenter here in town, built the original, and then the addition was put on in '22 by Adams' son-in-law from Ridgefield.

Mr. Ives used to take the month of October off to dig his potatoes and do his gardening until he had a heart attack in 1918. Afteryears, the neighbors planted and took care of it. Mr. Ives and Mr. Hill planted the apple trees up the driveway, and they had a tennis court put in right across the field toward the little house. After '18 he was not as active as he was before. In 1917 he was going to go to Europe for the Red Cross, and this was when he had the heart attack. Then he gave the Red Cross a $1,000 check. He was very upset by the war, and I believe he was right to be.

MRS. RYDER: He was upset with people. He wanted the best for them, and if he was apt to be a little explosive in his thinking, it was always because he was upset.

MR. RYDER: When we knew the man, he was a sick man, let's face it. At first when Mr. Ives was well, I was not involved, because my dad was the neighbor then, so whatever he did in the line of work for the Iveses, I was second string. What I did for them was after my dad died in '27. I don't know what the intention was when they built the little house near the road, but it was used mostly by the people who worked for them and their friends. Edie and her husband George* used it some afterward.

MRS. RYDER: Some of the New York church people made use of it so that the city folks could come up with their children. I think Edie's family must have come to the little house through the church. One family in particular was burned out, and the Iveses let them come into the little house. I'm sure they gave them more than just the little house too.

MR. RYDER: In this neighborhood four families lived close to each other for nearly fifty years and were friends to the end. These friends were at Edie's wedding. I remember one, a Frenchman, wanted me to have some champagne, and I turned it down. Mr. Ives had funny names for all the neighbors. I don't know what he called us. He never did say.

The Iveses had a horse called Rocket. Right now in our attic there are a pair of mittens that were made from Rocket's skin. There were two horse stalls, but only one horse. I built the shelves where Rocket's stall was for Mr. Ives to store his music.

*George Grayson Tyler, pp. 103–05.

Ives with a neighbor (left), Mr. Guilliame, and a friend.

MRS. RYDER: They had a dog too, Jimmie. And they had one fantastic cat. She lived to be twenty-two or twenty-three years old. She had a chair that used to be reserved for her. She sat by the table with her paw on Mrs. Ives's arm, and Mrs. Ives would feed her asparagus or tidbits. Her manners were good!

MR. RYDER: The first car they had when they came to Redding was a Model T. They had one driving lesson from a college fellow, and then Mr. Ives proceeded to come from White Plains to Redding with it on his own. One morning, he picked me up and drove to the station to take the 6:12 instead of the 7:12, because he had an important appointment for ten o'clock in New York with a man who was going to take a million-dollar policy. He drove right up to the railroad crossing which was just below the station and stopped. He jumped out fast and onto the last car of the train. That night he asked me, "Who stopped that car, did you or I?" Many nights during Prohibition, he used to come back from New York with three or four bottles of bitters. I'm sure that there's a case or two of bitters that have been there in the basement forty years, down by the furnace.

Mrs. Ryder: One time Mr. Ives called up here, and this tiny little voice on the telephone wanted to know if Harmony was here. I said "no." He said, "I've been to the dump and I've been up in the attic and I went down to the cellar and I can't find her *anywhere!*" So I said, "Well, perhaps she's down at Mrs. Hill's." And I went down to the Hill's and she was just leaving. I said, "Your husband is looking for you and he's very upset." Well, we went home and when she climbed out of the car, he put his arms around her and said, "Harmony, oh Harmony! I couldn't *find* you!" She kept him alive with her training and her concern. She gave up a great deal for his career, too, because he was not social minded. She told me one time that he would not go out in the evening. At first he did, but he hated it. And so she decided that she could either go alone or stay home, and she decided to stay home. She sort of retired along with him. She was moderately active in our little church here, and I guess she participated a little in the New York church.

Mr. Ives's music was very difficult to play, and as an organist* I never felt that I could do it justice. I know he felt that people just didn't want to tackle it, and that would provoke him. I have played a few little things that were within my scope, but not anything that would please him, I'm sure.

He came here to our place after the *Second Symphony* premiere with Mrs. Ives to listen to it rebroadcast on the radio [March 4, 1951]. It was Bernstein conducting. Mr. Ives sat in the front room and listened as quietly as could be, and I sat way behind him, because I didn't want him to think I was looking at him. After it was over, I'm sure he was very much moved. He stood up, walked over to the fireplace, and spat! And then he walked out into the kitchen. Not a word. And he never said anything about it. I think he was pleased, but he was silent. I was thrilled to think that he came here to hear it. It was my privilege. He was pleased to have the Pulitzer Prize [1947] and to be elected to the National Institute of Arts and Letters [1946], and yet he didn't brag about it. Speaking of it, you had to drag it out of him.

Most any time you were at their house, he'd go into the music room and give a little demonstration on the piano. And he would tell little anecdotes along with it. Usually it was something that we knew, only played in his own fashion. They were hymns or popular tunes that he used. He had such an abounding energy to get out what he wanted to get out, and I guess he had

---

*Luemily Ryder played William Monk's hymn *Abide with Me* on the upright piano at the Ives house in West Redding for Charles Ives's funeral, and then on the organ for Harmony Ives's funeral service at the Long Ridge Methodist Church, West Redding, Connecticut.

to do it in the few years he had the strength to do it. He was a family man, and such a loving person. You could feel it with his wife and Edie. But he was just as nice with his neighbors. He would say sometimes when I was over there, "You're going back? Say hello to the best man in the world!"

Mrs. Ives was the one who did most of the traveling back and forth, coming here. And once in about 1950 or 1951, he came here for dinner. I don't think he had been to anyone else's house for dinner in a good many years. But he liked roast pork, and I had mentioned that we were having it. She said, "Charlie likes roast pork so much." I said, "He wouldn't come for dinner, would he?" Well, she called me back and said yes, they would come! Our daughter called up that night from the hospital where she was training, and he talked to her on the telephone, which was unusual. He hated the telephone. The day he couldn't find Mrs. Ives, she said that "it proved that he could use it if he needed to, and that was quite an accomplishment."

One time when Mrs. Ives was having gallstone trouble, the maid couldn't stay, so I went over and cooked his dinner. My husband's fifty-third birthday happened to be at that time, and he said to me, "I want you to write a check out for Will." And I said, "Oh no, I'm not going to do that." So he sat down and wrote one out himself, for $53.53. He was like that. He was like a family to us, our own family. That's the way we felt toward them both. A wonderful part of our lives.

Life for the Ives family settled into a pattern of long summers at West Redding and winters in the New York house. Social life at Redding consisted of visits from neighbors and family. Harmony Ives kept close ties with her family. She was one of the nine children of the Reverend and Mrs. Joseph Twichell. It was a large family, and although reunions were not their custom, members of the Twichell family often visited the Iveses through the years. DEBBY HALL MEEKER, interviewed in Washington, Connecticut, on September 24, 1969, was Mrs. Ives's niece, the daughter of Louise Twichell Hall. She was a close friend of Edith Ives. Her mother owned the Mayflower Gift and Tearoom for a number of years in Washington, which was not far from Redding. Debby Meeker's favorite aunt was her Aunt Harmony. She remembers that her mother's older brother, Edward Carrington Twichell, was "one of Uncle Charlie's great friends. He used to call him E. C. America, but the rest of us called him Uncle Deac."

Harmony (right) with older sister, Susan, ca. 1896.

MRS. BURTON TWICHELL, interviewed in New Haven, on September 18, 1970, was a sister-in-law of Harmony Ives and recalls that her four children thoroughly enjoyed visits to the Iveses in Redding. When her youngest son was about seven, he was learning to play hockey and kept losing his puck and his baseball. Mrs. Twichell said, "He had to save his pennies for a long time to replace them. One Christmas Uncle Charlie sent him six pucks and four baseballs, and the excitement was intense." Another son used to go into the woods with Uncle Charlie to dig garnets out of the rocks with a hammer, and they would look for grasshoppers together to feed to the trout in the pond. Mrs. Twichell claims that "the greatest fun that we all remember was the clog dancing. Charlie and Deac clogged with the children, clapping hands and keeping a tune going. It was real old-fashioned clogging and Charlie always made a lot of noise. The children loved it."

Young friends of Edith's were in and out of the house. GERTRUDE SANFORD, interviewed in Redding, Connecticut, on July 29, 1969, and her sister (now Mrs. Janice Jones) lived above their family store in West Redding. Miss Sanford recalls that Mrs. Ives came by almost every day for groceries and to pick up her sister who was very close to Edie, and they were all carted to Compo Beach in Westport quite often on good summer days. Edie wrote short stories, and Miss Sanford says that she remembers "hearing some of them—little imaginative stories about woodland creatures —very much like Mr. Ives's fantasies to us children about things that were happening down in the woods."

When Miss Sanford and her sister visited with the Iveses in New York, she recalls that "Mrs. Ives always dressed for dinner. I can remember her particularly in a long blue dress, and she was very beautiful." In later years, Mrs. Ryder and Miss Sanford visited the Iveses in New York every year for two or three days at a time, and Mrs. Ives had tickets for the women to go to an opera or a concert. There were several times when Miss Sanford and Mrs. Ryder traveled into New York for concerts in which Ives's music was performed. One evening Miss Sanford particularly remembers is when they were having dinner "and Mrs. Ives asked Mr. Ives to ask the blessing, which he did very nicely. And then, immediately afterward, all of a sudden he banged his fist on the table and he said, 'Goddamn that Hitler!' It shocked everybody. Even Mrs. Ives said, 'Oh, Charlie!' Then he became so overcome that he couldn't speak. This usually happened when he talked about the war."

In 1924, when the Iveses traveled to Europe for the first time,* Edith was ten years old. When they left on their second trip in May 1932, she was a young woman of nineteen. Ives had retired, Edith was out of school, and there was no reason not to be leisurely. After two months in England, they spent about a month each in France, Switzerland, and Germany, and then traveled to Taormina, Sicily where they stayed for the winter. By April of 1933 the Iveses were in Florence. Here they met a young man, JAMES THOMAS FLEXNER, who was to become a well-known author and outstanding scholar in American art and history. Mr. Flexner was interviewed in New York City, on December 11, 1970.

---

*There were four trips to Europe: 1924, 1932–33, 1934, 1938.

I got to know Charles Ives's daughter Edie Ives, and my contact with the Ives family was altogether through the daughter. I originally met the Iveses in the Pensione Annalena in Florence in April 1933. It was an amusing situation, because I had lived in a walk-up flat across the backyard from the Ives's house on 74th Street and had noticed a pretty girl across the backyard. And she had, as a matter of fact, noticed me. And then we ran into each other at the Pensione Annalena. Edie was nineteen years old and I was twenty-five.

The pensione was on the far side of the Arno, facing the Boboli Gardens. It was up several flights of stairs in an old palazzo, and it was run primarily for young students and artists. The Prix de Rome people stopped there on their way up from Rome, and art students stopped there. It was well known as an agreeable place where you would meet people with artistic and intellectual interests. Groups would sometimes go out together. I remember upon one occasion Edie was supposed to be the partner of a very sour individual who was very much annoyed because he insisted that he was Edie's escort, and Edie went off with me. The pensione was a simple place where everyone ate at one table, and you ate what was put before you unless you happened to be on a diet.

The Iveses were, however much money he may have made in the insurance business, traveling simply. From the point of view of their daughter this was infinitely better, because she landed up with other young people, which she wouldn't have done if they had lived at the Grand Hotel. I got to know Edie then and subsequently I saw a certain amount of her. For the record, I'd better say that there was nothing very great between us, but nonetheless we became good friends, and as a result of that I was on occasion entertained both at the Ives's house on 74th Street and at the house in West Redding.

As everyone knows, Mr. Ives for some reason felt very strongly against publicity. One time I was having lunch with them in New York, and some mail arrived, and Mr. Ives got a letter from some disciple of his in California. Enclosed was a clipping which this man was sending to Mr. Ives thinking that he would be pleased. It was of something he had told the papers about Mr. Ives. Mr. Ives was so upset that he got his beard in the soup. I think he must have done this before, because it didn't upset him the least.

I got the impression that he was a very different man in New York from in the country. In New York he seemed to me very nervous and jumpy. In the country he was very much more relaxed. For some reason, I remember a particularly elegant wine-colored smoking jacket he wore. I have a vision of him taking me out over quite a considerable estate to show me cows or pigs or something of that nature. And I got the impression that he very much enjoyed being a country squire.

Upon one or two occasions I served as the male escort who accompanied the two ladies, Mrs. Ives and Edie, to a concert in which Charles Ives's music was played. I was told, probably by Edie, that her father was unhappy about going to such concerts now that people no longer booed or walked out when his music was played. He felt he was becoming a bourgeois because people sat with a polite air of appreciation and then applauded.

Edie told me many things, and I don't really know how much of what she recounted was accurate. She was not a very happy young lady, and I think she was lonely. After I had known her for some time, she confided that she was an adopted child. I got the impression that Edie was unfamiliar with her natural family, and that she had been told very little if anything about them. She was rather inimical about her father's music. She told me once that he was writing a piece of music that had so many instruments in it that the audience would have to sit on the stage and that the orchestra would fill the hall. However, one has to remember that young people like to show themselves independent by deriding their parents to one another.

Edie was a charming girl—gentle and intelligent. I think that Mrs. Ives probably was very conservative in an old-fashioned way, and Mr. Ives seemed to be withdrawn. However, he was always extremely courteous to me. Edie said that he had previously made her miserable by his anxiety when she went out on dates. But my experience showed none of this. I don't remember that any restrictions were made as to where I could take her or when she had to be home.

GEORGE GRAYSON TYLER met the Ives family after they returned from Europe. He met Edith first in 1934, and he frequently saw Mrs. Ives in connection with functions at the First Presbyterian Church in New York, of which they were all members. Edith Ives and George Tyler were married on July 29, 1939, at the house in West Redding. Mr. Tyler, an attorney, became Ives's attorney and the executor of the Ives estate. He was interviewed in New York City, on March 18, 1969.

I met Mr. Ives in January or February of 1935. He didn't have a great deal to say to me, nor I to him. But as time went on, I got to know both Mr. and Mrs. Ives quite well. It was much easier to know Mr. Ives in the country atmosphere of Redding than in New York. He seemed more at home there.

Mr. Ives certainly had a formidable exterior, but as I got to know him, I could say truthfully that he was one of the kindest persons I have ever met. He was extremely generous, and he made a great many gifts that he said nothing about. Indeed, I would have known nothing about them at all except that some time later Mrs. Ives might mention the fact. In addition to his generosity to particular individuals and to charitable organizations, Mr. Ives for many years refused to take any deductions on his income tax returns for charitable contributions. He said that he gave to charity because he wanted to and not because he could get deductions. After I became a member of the family, I was able to prevail on Mr. Ives to take deductions for two reasons. First, the rate of tax had gone up considerably; and second, he was made to believe that if he deducted them on his income tax returns, he would have more money to give to charity.

I remember Edith saying to me very shortly after I met her that her father would be remembered as the greatest American composer. I didn't know Mr. Ives at all well at that time, and I hadn't heard anything about his music. I naturally discounted this statement as something that a daughter might say about her father. At that time, the only recognition of Mr. Ives's music had been in Europe. Edith played the piano, but she never had any inclination to play professionally. She was very much interested in listening to music, and she was very fond of her father's music.

Mr. Ives used to talk to me about the musicians who liked what he would call "soft notes for soft ears" or the "lily pads." He would sound off about it—not to them, but to members of the family. Another thing that used to arouse his ire and make him rush around waving his cane in the air was when an airplane would come over his farm in Redding. He would call out a good many uncomplimentary remarks to the pilot, who, of course, couldn't possibly hear him.

Mr. Ives's expressions were original. I can just hear him saying, "A poor joke is better than a good one." And he had a lot of peculiar names that he'd call people, like "Little Willie Pickleface" and "Ratneck." Mrs. Ives tells an amusing story about one of their stays at an English hotel where there was a little kitten that Mr. Ives was playing with, and the kitten was running down the corridor. Mr. Ives came after it on his hands and knees, yelling "Little Willie Pickleface." He didn't realize that the kitten was leading him into one of the hotel drawing rooms where a number of other people were present. I think even Mr. Ives was a little embarrassed on that occasion. Our son, Charles Ives Tyler, remembers his grandfather calling him "Ratneck" as well as "Little Willie Pickleface." One thing that his grandfather was always amused at was little Charlie's description of his hair. Mr. Ives had a fringe of hair. He was bald on top and little Charlie used to refer to grandfather's "half hair."

I often heard Mr. Myrick say that he really didn't think that Mr. Ives would live for more than a year after his retirement in 1930. Of course, he lived to be seventy-nine, and this was in large part due to the wonderful care that he received from Mrs. Ives who had been a registered nurse at a time when comparatively few women went into any profession at all. Mrs. Ives watched him like a hawk. In addition to his heart condition he had developed diabetes and he was one of the people who was actually saved by the discovery of insulin. As time went on, he completely overcame his diabetes, and his heart seemed to be in good condition in later years. For many years his hand shook from a palsy. He used to be very much ashamed of his signature because it was so wavy. He used to say that it had "a lot of scallops" on it. He hated to write and he wrote much better with pencil than he did with pen. But his handwriting was very difficult to read.

At the time I knew him, he didn't read the papers, and he really didn't have too much contact with what was going on in the country, except as he would hear about it in conversation. One time in the thirties, he said to me, "George, whatever happened to Charlie Hughes? I knew him when he was governor of New York and used to see him in connection with his investigation of insurance companies." And I said, "Now he's the chief justice of the United States." And he said, "Oh, is he? I hadn't realized that." He was quite out of touch with the current scene by the time I knew him.

Mrs. Ives was a most extraordinary woman. She used to read to Mr. Ives every night after dinner. She would read all the novels of Dickens one after the other right through, and then to Thackeray and maybe Jane Austen, and then when she finished their favorite novels, why she'd start right over again. I often think of them sitting beside the fire in Redding in the evening. We would all sit back and Mrs. Ives would read to us, sometimes for as long as two hours after dinner.

Ives with grandson, Charles Ives Tyler, 1946.

CHARLES IVES TYLER, grandson of Charles Ives, is chairman of the English department at the Berkshire School in Sheffield, Massachusetts. He was interviewed there on February 26, 1970. Charles Tyler was eight years old when his grandfather died.

I was not really old enough to understand Grandfather Ives, and that's something I've always been very sad about. I'd love to talk to him, being aware of the things that I am aware of today. He was an enigma to me, and I was frightened of him at times. I especially remember that he used to glare at me and call me "Ratneck," which was a personal joke of his, but that always used to frighten me. Grandfather could look very devilish when he was playing a joke on somebody, and as a matter of fact, I almost always think of him telling a joke.

Grandfather had a song that he sang on various occasions called *The Royal Star Bazoonya* which was a nonsense song. He usually sang it whenever he got frustrated with anything. He would burst into it with vitality and it was something about "fishcakes in the sky." I wish I could remember more of it. The music sounded like one of those Yankee tunes that he often put into his symphonies. When grandfather would get in a low mood, he'd walk into his study and pound out *Onward, Christian Soldiers* a few times, and he'd feel better.

Grandfather had to drink milk every day, and since he hated to do this, he would take his milk outside, throw it in the bushes, come back with the least little bit left in the bottom of the glass, and walk into the house draining the glass to the general applause of whoever was there. One day I followed him out, and he was trying to get rid of me. He said, "Look at the little bird up in the tree." I looked at the bird and quickly turned around to catch him emptying the contents of his glass into the bushes. I followed him back into the house, and I said, "Grandfather didn't drink his milk." Everybody knew, I'm sure, that this was what he did. But it had never been spoken out before. It was the cause for a great altercation in the family. He hated the milk, but one of his favorite drinks was mulled ale. He used to get ale, and put it in a beer mug, and pop it down by the fireplace until it got nice and warm. He would sometimes drink whether people liked it or not. He wasn't allowed to take sweets either, but he did.

My mother told me that one time he was suffering from a cough and decided that he was going to take some cough tablets. So my grandmother said, "Oh, they're right over there in the drawer." He reached into the drawer, and pretty soon this tremendous coughing was heard and muffled curses. They found that he had taken moth balls instead—just reached in and grabbed them!

I can remember vividly on Washington's Birthday one year when his *Washington's Birthday* was being played on the radio, my parents spent forty-five minutes convincing him to come down and listen to his music. That was at 57th Street at our place in New York. He was over for the day. He refused adamantly, but finally he was cajoled into coming down. He lasted for about five minutes before he burst into a rage against poor conducting.

I can never remember hearing any disparaging comment or criticism from anybody in the family about grandfather's music. My grandmother Tyler, who died two years ago never was able to understand it—it was a total mystery to her. She had a great respect for him, but she said, "I never can understand his music." I can remember listening with her to a television show they had on the NET, I think, two or three years ago on the *Fourth Symphony*. She was completely baffled.

We often spent summers in the little house at the entrance in West Redding. It's lovely out there, and I would like to see it all stay just that way forever. I have loads of memories, and my father does too, tied up there, and we'd hate to see it change. I'm hoping that there will be some way that I can preserve everything as it always was when Grandmother and Grandfather Ives lived there.

Ives's friends in Redding were chosen from among the townspeople. If he needed his hair trimmed and he liked the barber, the barber and his wife were invited to dinner. If work had to be done in the house and Ives discovered some appealing trait in a workman, or that he enjoyed talking to the architect, the architect and the workman became his personal friends. In the same way that the housekeeper was treated as one of the family, a secretary was made to feel a close friend.

One of the local residents who became friendly with Ives soon after the Iveses moved to West Redding was DR. CHARLES KAUFFMAN, an osteopathic physician in Brookfield, the town next to Redding. Dr. Kauffman was interviewed there on June 25, 1969. He is the kind of free-thinking, independent personality Ives enjoyed. Both men had unconventional philosophical and political ideas, and they took pleasure in sharing them with each other.

I was born in Pennsylvania, of Pennsylvania Dutch ancestry, and perhaps that was one reason why I got along well with Ives, because I carried some of the old stuff along, and we learned to think for ourselves.

I met Ives through his brother, Judge Ives, and his brother-in-law, Reverend Joseph Twichell. That was in the early 1920s. Ives had a little trouble with his hearing and sinus, and so I took care of that and then we got to be friends. I was so stimulated by him—not by what he said, but by what he was. He seemed more like my own folks back in Pennsylvania, although he was a New Englander, and perhaps there was a common bond there. I was so impressed with Ives's house because there was not a status symbol in the whole place. His bookcase—no knickknacks in his bookcase —books. That's what's supposed to be in there. And his den was a delight.

It reminded me of my aunt: just a plain couch, an upright piano. When I was in that room, I noticed he had an old washboiler alongside of his desk with music stuck in it, and I asked him where he got that, and he said, "Off our dump. The music fits that, and it fits the music."

He had a cat called Christofina that lived to a remarkable old age, almost thirty years. It was a gray cat with a stubbed tail that had been cut off. One day, the cat was up on the piano, meowing, and he went over and took the cat gently, put it on the floor, and said, "This cat can get up on the piano, but there's something wrong with her leg, and she can't get down." So I manipulated it and the joint was a little bit askew. I gave it a treatment and the cat looked at me gratefully. I wish you could get patients like that. Then the cat jumped up on the piano and jumped down. She did it three times, as much as to say—look what I can do! Cats have a characteristic which Ives had. I call it detachment. Now detachment doesn't mean not caring. It means you can detach yourself when you have to, if you're going to survive. Ives was particularly sensitive, and during the war I just happened to mention something about it, and he almost went crazy, walking up and down the floor cussing. His wife heard and she said, "What's the matter?" And I said, "I'm awfully sorry, but I just let something slip about the war." And she said, "Well, he just doesn't want to talk about that." People mistook Ives's detachment for aloofness. In fact, it was his caring too much that made the detachment necessary.

I wrote a pamphlet called *Universal Law and Democracy*. Well, there was no response to that, because Ives and I were the only ones who believed that each man has a spark of genius in him. Ives was very enthusiastic about my pamphlet. He sent a copy to Yale, and they never even acknowledged the letter, and wasn't he mad!

Ives never mentioned Christ or the Bible. He was not a stereotype, brainwashed church member. I don't think he went to church often. Of course, his brother-in-law was a fine minister and a man who was different from other ministers too. Ives was not a Fundamentalist, although some people thought he was, because he chided his daughter for reading one of these esoteric, popular books. I think it was because it was popular and written for money. I think he objected more to the writer than the subject. He was very strict on morals. I don't know what he'd say today about these new books and plays.

One day I went to Ives's house with my five-year-old daughter who was studying piano. Ives brought her in and sat her down at the piano and said, "Play me something." So she played one of those first tunes that they have, and he looked at her nice and all he said was, "Cute." Now my daughter is

Chas. E Ives
Room 435

or Some true temp conceptions to what matter

The accompanying four pieces grouped together
and called-(for want of a more exact name)-a sonata though
in form or substance neither justifies or deserves it,
is an attempt to present (one persons) impression of the
spirit of transcendentalism that is associated in the
minds of many with Concord, mass, over a half century
ago. This is undertaken in impressionistic pictures
of Emerson and Thoreau, a sketch of the Alcotts, and
a Scherzo supposed to reflect a lighter quality which
is often found in the fantastic side of Hawthorne.
The first and last movements do not aim to give
any program of the life or any particular work
of either Emerson or Thoreau but rather
composite pictures or impressions, so general
in outline that, from some view points, may be
as far from a too impression as the valuation, which
they purport to be of the influence of the life, works
thought and character of Emerson & Thoreau
is inadequate.

How far is anyone justified, be he an authority
or layman, in expressing or trying to express in
terms of music (in sounds, if you like) the value
of anything, material, moral, intellectual
or spiritual, that is usually expressed in terms
other than music? How far afield can music
go and keep honest as well as reasonable, i.e. artistic? Is it

The first page of Ives's ink manuscript, Essays Before a Sonata.

Reproduced from Charles Ives, *Essays Before a Sonata, The Majority, and Other Writings,* by permission of the publisher, W. W. Norton & Company, Inc.

married to a professor at Duke, and she always talks about the time she played for Ives. She said that she wouldn't have done it except that I ordered her to.

Ives predicted that some day we would communicate with music—with sound instead of spoken language, and, of course, I agree with him. I believe that you can get more from a tone of voice than you can from the words. This is in Ives's book, *Essays Before a Sonata*. He says more in that book than Yale can give you in four years. That's my private opinion. Ives once said to me, "You're the only one who seems to understand that book." I only talked to him about it a little. Mostly I'd go home and write a poem and send it to him or give it to him.

People thought Ives was a hermit and didn't go anywhere, but he used to call on Philip Sunderland, and he'd often come to my place first thing off the train when he came to Danbury, and I'd often see the piano tuner, Brownlow* at the Ives's house. The one thing about Ives is that he always had time when he was with you to say something. He never was in a hurry. His eyes would light up when he'd see people, and there was no put-down in him.

When Ives was at our cottage here in Brookfield, he sat and looked over at the hills, and then he bought the ten acres next to me. He thought he might build there, but he built only a little shed which opened up to the hills, and he had a chair there. He would come up now and again to sit and contemplate the distant hills. He was a follower of Thoreau and loved nature. He gave me a set of Thoreau. That was March 3, 1931. I've got them up on the top shelf there. Want to read the letter? "I hope you won't mind my depositing a few books of Thoreau in your library, just to remember me by—and Thoreau. Please remember us kindly to Mrs. Kauffman and the children. Hoping to see you before long. Sincerely, Chas. E. Ives / Please excuse this very bad writing."

On August 22, 1967, I saw Mrs. Charles Ives, who was as much a part of Ives as one person could possibly be. She was living less than a mile from their old home in a quiet and comfortable nursing home run by Mrs. Emma Goldhorn, wife of a former prominent physician. Edith Ives died two years after Mr. Ives, and Mrs. Ives had to bear that grief alone. She said to me, "Isn't it nice that my husband was recognized." I said, "But he was very patient about recognition." "Yes," she answered. "He always said if people finally liked his music, that was all that mattered." And later she said, "I haven't been out to the old place; it is so sad." Then I reminded her that

*Harry Brownlow died on the very day he was to have been interviewed.

Ives firmly believed in life after death, and she said, "Yes, he'd always say he would see and talk with his father."

Once when Ives played for me, I told him it reminded me of mountains. He looked quite pleased but said nothing. I've never heard that music played since. Therefore, I believe it may have been from his *Universe Symphony*. He was always working on this, but the theme was so gigantic that it was not intended to be finished.

ANTHONY J. ("BABE") LAPINE of Bethel, Connecticut, was Charles Ives's barber and friend. The interview took place in Babe's barber shop in Bethel on June 30, 1969. An article in Sunday's New York Times *(June 8, 1969) about the interview, "What Will Babe the Barber Say?", caused a stir in the town and made Babe a local celebrity.*

I met Charlie over thirty years ago. I had my other shop in the center of the town then. Mrs. Ives would drive him down to English's drugstore, and he'd cross over to the shop.

Charlie (I called him Charlie) never dressed up in street clothes as long as I knew him. He used to wear overalls with the bib and straps, a big brown hat, and farmer shoes. He walked very fast, but he stooped. And I never took him for a musician.

One time I was trimming his beard, and he was looking in the mirror and says, "You know, Babe, your work reminds me of mine." I says, "Gee whiz, Charlie. How does my work remind you of yours?" He says, "The way you're trimming my beard; you're shading it. That goes into my work." When he said shading, I took him for a painter. But I didn't go into it at all with him. I never would take him for a musician—Gee whiz, old overalls, old shoes. My God, he looked like a gentleman farmer. But one day I'll never forget. I had the apron over him, and the radio was playing in the shop. I pay no attention to the radio—I'm cutting his hair. And all of a sudden, like a shot out of a gun, he lifts up the apron and he says, "Will you shut that damn thing off?" I'll never forget that. Well, has that got anything to do with him being a musician?

Later, when he was failing, I used to go over to his house. I went to that house at least a half-dozen times. We'd go into the garage in the back there, and he'd show me all his things—a football, the knee pants, baseballs, spiked shoes, and a lot of stuff like that. I'd trim his hair and beard on the patio outside, and then he always liked to take me in that goldarn garage. His wife didn't go for it much. "Now, what are you showing him? He's seen that a hundred times already." But I think he liked to talk to me because he hadn't too many people to talk to.

When I got married, he and his wife came over to my house. I was about thirty years old then. We had bought a new house, and he brought me over a little blue creamer and sugar for a wedding present. I should have saved that creamer and sugar. If I thought that Charlie Ives was going to pass away and be noted, I would have kept it. The day he came over he invited us over to his home on Umpawaug for dinner. It was a fish dinner. Mrs. Blackwell cooked and served. We were there twice, in fact. Both times fish.

One time he said, "This is the last haircut you're going to give me for quite a while." And I says, "No kidding. What's going on?" He says, "I'm going to London." I said, "Well, gee Charlie, how about sending me a card?" So, by golly, he goes to England, and I didn't get that card for over a month or more. After a long while he came back. I said, "For God's sake, I got that card all right, but it took you long enough." "Well," he says, "it took me long enough to get over there. It took me thirty-one days." He sent me two cards, actually. I should have saved those cards. After he passed away, I found out that he was a musician. Not until after he passed away.

WILLIAM A. GREY is an architectural engineer and a resident of Redding, Connecticut, where he was interviewed November 11, 1970.

In 1939 Mrs. Ives asked me to undertake a project at their residence on Umpawaug Road in Redding. The work in the house was completed in about four or five months. It was mostly small changes, except that there was an entirely new heating system put in. This was quite a job to do in that house without disturbing them. The work was started in the spring of 1939, went through the summer and spilled over to fall.

In the course of this work naturally I had many conversations with both Mr. and Mrs. Ives and became friendly with them both. Most of the detailed conversations of what was required were with Mrs. Ives, but periodically we reviewed the matter with Mr. Ives. In some cases he was assisted downstairs and we sat in the living room, but that was seldom. I had met Mrs. Ives earlier, but I had never met Charles Ives before. Almost nobody around here knew the Iveses. They seemed to keep very much to themselves. I think that Mr. Ives had little contact with the outer world other than Mr. Ryder, his neighbor. What impressed me so much was Mr. Ives's calmness and self-control in the face of the constant torture that he suffered, and in all my dealings with him I never remember a single complaint.

Music was never mentioned in our conversations. Actually I was interested in his music, but from all appearances he had banished music from his life, and you think carefully before you bring up a subject like that. The piano looked like it had not been opened for years. From appearances, nobody would have guessed that a distinguished composer lived there.

CARRIE BLACKWELL worked for the Ives family for seventeen years and eight months, beginning in 1942. On September 10, 1973, Mrs. Blackwell said with great feeling that the Iveses were the most wonderful people she ever knew and that they made her feel like one of the family.

When my husband died in 1942, I went to work for the Iveses in West Redding and winters in New York. I didn't expect to be there but a short time, but each week went by and I liked it better all the time. Sometimes we'd stay in the country until almost Thanksgiving.

Mr. Ives was not bedridden. He was always able to go out on the lawn and he was lively. He was always joking with me. He'd help me with the dishes once in a while. Mrs. Ives asked me to let him. I never in the seventeen years and eight months I was with the Iveses heard Mrs. Ives cross. She never said a word to me about the house. I remember one day I came down and I commented on some dust I'd left somewhere, and Mrs. Ives said, "Carrie, you keep my house immaculate." And cooking for them was nothing. Neither of them ate much, and Mr. Ives was not allowed any sweets, so I didn't do much baking—the only real cooking was when Edie and her husband, Mr. Tyler, came on weekends.

The Iveses gave me a radio and it was the only radio in the house. Sometimes when Mr. Ives's music was being played, I'd bring it down into the living room and we'd all listen. Every Sunday Mrs. Ives would call me into the living room, and she would read to me and Mr. Ives from the Bible.

One day Mrs. Ives brought me a little kitten. She'd found it in a restaurant and she brought it to me with a little red ribbon round its neck. "Carrie, I got a present for you." I was so crazy about that kitten. Mrs.

Ives named her Daffodil and she followed me around everywhere. One morning, Daffodil went with me to the mailbox. I got the mail and left the cat there on the lawn. When I went back later, I saw a car coming fast up the road, and when I looked, there Daffodil lay in the middle of the road. I picked her up in my arms and went screaming for help. "Mrs. Ives, can't you do something for her?" Mrs. Ives said, "Carrie, she's gone."

Mr. Ives was always at the piano and he could make that piano talk. It always sounded sweet to me—he played a lot of hymns. I'd always hear him when I was setting the table and he'd be in his little room next to the dining room. Sometimes he'd get so excited and he'd knock down on those keys like thunder.

Christine Loring was a mystery for a long time. She was known to have done secretarial work for Mr. Ives at the house in West Redding, but she could not be traced, and no one seemed to know what had become of her. Long after a seemingly fruitless search, it came to light that a MRS. ROD-MAN S. VALENTINE of Refugio, Texas, had known Charles Ives. Here was the elusive Christine Loring. Mrs. Valentine was interviewed in Refugio on March 23, 1971.

When I worked with Mr. Ives, I was Mrs. Christine Loring. We lived about two miles from the Iveses—they were up on the hilltop and we lived in the valley. When we came to Redding in '38, I went to a church in the Center, and about two years later we began to go to the Long Ridge Church, Methodist by denomination but with many denominations in it. There I met Mrs. Ives. She was a very active, beloved, and generous member.

I had done secretarial work long before I came to Redding, and then for several years I did none. In Redding, my typewriter was unboxed for the first time in years, and when Mrs. Ives asked if I would do some work for Mr. Ives, I was delighted. This was about 1943. Whenever Mr. Ives wanted me to take dictation, I brought my typewriter over there. I worked in the little room that was off the dining room, or in the dining room itself. Mr. Ives had masses of material, correspondence, and articles that were just in boxes. I copied and copied, and once in a while he would dictate a letter. At that time he did very little writing. Once I asked him for an autograph for my son and he said, "The only time you get my autograph is on a check."

I thought Mr. Ives was very handsome, and others did, too. He had grown a beard, and he must have been over six feet tall. He used to tell me over and over how he used to love to pitch hay and do some of his own work outside. He had the greatest respect for farming and nature in every form, from a pebble to a star. He felt that everything in the universe had a right to live its own life. I think one reason he liked me a little bit was because I understood this. Even when he was hardly able to do it, he loved to walk. When Mrs. Ives used to call for me to take me home, Mr. Ives would walk out with me to the car when he was able. If there was a stone, he'd whang it with his cane and say some little thing to it. He'd look up all around and try to see, but he couldn't see much.

Mrs. Ives told me about earlier times when Mr. Ives would come home from a strenuous day in the insurance business, have his meal, and then go to the piano and forget all about time until the wee small hours. He would be completely absorbed in his music. And she told me about how their little girl had learned to adjust. He couldn't take any interruptions because he was listening to what was inside him. He'd play, and the little girl was allowed to sit there underneath the piano and play with her dolls, but she must not make a sound. Mrs. Ives must have led a lonely social life in a way, but she was active and very interested in many worthwhile things. She wrote beautiful poems, and Mr. Ives set some of them to music. She taught me to see the beauty in November—the tans and browns in the landscape, and the beauty of the bare trees.

I came to the house until about three years before Mr. Ives died. I was in the house a lot more than probably almost anyone except the Ryders. Mr. Ives called Bill Ryder "the boy," because when they came up there he was a young lad in his twenties. He was probably married then, but Mr. Ives always called him "the boy." That amused both Lu and Mr. Ryder. In the last years when Mr. and Mrs. Ives really had to have someone looking after them, the Ryders were right there looking after everything and dropping in often.

Some people thought that Mr. Ives was a little bit tetched because sometimes he would sing nonsense things. He sang one thing about the codfish hanging in the sky. Oh, and he could roar. But he only did that once in a while, and then he'd always laugh. Mr. Ives resented his physical infirmities. He wasn't reconciled to them. He'd forget, even after he had been disabled for so many years. He used to bang with that stick of his. He'd pound the thing on the floor and he'd say, "I don't need you." And he'd call the cane his "governor." And then he'd laugh and not be able to catch his breath.

The piano drew Mr. Ives like a magnet. He couldn't sit still for long, and it seemed like he couldn't keep away from that studio. He'd go in, he'd come out, and I'd be typing. Everything would be so still except the type-writer. Then I'd hear these crashing chords out of the deathly silence. Once in a while he'd play gently, and sometimes he'd come out and talk about the music. He asked me once if I had ever gone to a barn dance. When I said yes, he went in and picked out different parts sounding like barn dance music for about fifteen minutes. He had the best time. But then he disap-peared, and I knew he'd gone to lie down. He told me once that he didn't like canned music because, he said, "There's so much of the music that doesn't get recorded." Another time he said something about the fact that no two performers see the same thing alike or feel the same thing alike. Mr. Ives mentioned his *Universe Symphony* to me more than once. It was to be played by at least two huge orchestras across from each other on mountaintops overlooking a valley. It was to be religious (a paean of praise, I believe he said), and it was a real and continuing interest for years. Once after he stood looking out the picture window toward the mountains, he restlessly paced about, not conversing but as if he were thinking aloud with gestures, and humming and singing bits of music. He said. "If only I could have done it. It's all there—the mountains and the fields." When I asked him what he wanted to do, he answered, "the *Universe Symphony.* If only I could have done it."

Moment of Light, a book of photographs by CLARA SIPPRELL, was published in 1966 by the John Day Company. In it is a very fine portrait of Charles Ives taken in 1948. An inquiry to Miss Sipprell in Manchester, Vermont (where she was subsequently interviewed on December 31, 1971), brought forth several pictures of Mr. and Mrs. Ives which had not been seen before, and the following story about how they were taken.

I began making pictures in about 1902 when I was sixteen or so. I used natural light then, and I've never used artificial light in all these years. I have been very lucky and very fortunate through my life. I have the gift of portraiture. People came to me because of it and were willing to give of themselves.

I had an exhibition at the Town Hall Club in New York in April, 1946. Mrs. Ives saw the exhibition. She had been trying to convince her husband for about twenty years to have his picture taken. She looked at those pic-

Charles Ives, 1948. Photo Clara Sipprell.

tures of mine and she took my name and address and wrote it somewhere in her checkbook. Two years later she finally got Charles Ives to agree to have me make his portait. He loved her so and he hated it so, but he said yes.

She sent me material so that I'd know about him and she did everything she could so that I'd understand him. Then she made an appointment for them to come to my studio. I opened the door and there she was, this lovely, tender woman in a red dress. He stood with his blazing eyes, and his hat on one side. He looked at me as if to say, "I dare you." That's the spirit that he came in with. And he put on the most amazing show for me. He wanted to please her, but he couldn't make the grade. When I began to make the pictures, he blew out his cheeks and sat on his hands. He acted like a contrary child. Mrs. Ives would look at him and say, "Oh, but I want a picture of you." He looked at her tenderly, but he fought it tooth and nail. And so I made a picture of her instead. I did the best I could with him and I made the proofs and mailed them. Several days later, the Iveses invited me for tea. Mr. Ives opened the door. He bowed low. "I apologize," he said.

We sat near the fireplace, surrounded with the proofs, and Mrs. Ives was so eager. It meant so much to her to have the pictures. I don't think he was crazy about them because he wasn't crazy about himself, you see. But she was.

MUSIC

The first page from the manuscript of Autumn, *the first movement of the* Second Violin and Piano Sonata.

Charles Ives composed steadily and furiously up to the time of his serious heart attack of 1918. He had had reason to wonder about his health since 1906, and that knowledge, combined with the fact of his father's death before his fiftieth year, may have determined Ives to write his life's work in half a lifetime. His connections with the world of professional music making were almost nonexistent. There are no programs at all in Yale's Ives Collection for the years between 1902 and 1921—the amazing fact is that no performances of Ives's music were given, other than those instigated by himself, from the time he quit his post as church organist at Central Presbyterian Church in 1902 until copies of the Concord Sonata, *printed and distributed at Ives's own expense, reached Clifton Joseph Furness, a music teacher at Northwestern University who promptly began to play the* Alcotts, *and Henry Bellamann, who was lecturing in the South, began to illustrate his talks with sections of the sonata played by a young pianist, Lenore Purcell. None of the composers who later were closely involved with Ives and his music were so much as acquainted with him during the time of his greatest creativity. In the* Memos *Ives indicated that he was concerned with the performance aspect of his music in these years; he described readings of various chamber works by musicians whom he invited to his house in New York for this purpose. And when Ives met someone he thought might be interested in modern music, he extended an invitation to attend a rehearsal.*

MRS. ARTUR NIKOLORIC was invited to one of these sessions. She was an American pianist who studied abroad and returned to this country with her husband before World War I. Mrs. Nikoloric had an active teaching career after a few years as a concert pianist. She was interviewed in Bethesda, Maryland, on January 29, 1971.

Mr. Keyes Winter* had a law office in New York City, and when my husband came over to this country from Vienna, he was able to get a clerkship at Mr. Winter's office. This was during the First World War. Mrs. Winter was a charming person and was very anxious to have me have a

---

*Keyes Winter (1878–1960) graduated from Yale in 1900, entered New York University Law School, and joined the group of Yale men at Poverty Flat, 317 West 58th Street, where Ives had been living since 1898. Winter became United States district attorney in New York and a Republican congressman.

pleasant time in New York, and so they invited us to dinner one night. They said that they thought maybe we'd have a good time, because I was a pianist and they were having a couple that were interested in music.

We went to dinner and met Mr. and Mrs. Ives. I had never heard of Charles Ives then. He was a businessman and was very successful. After dinner Mrs. Winter said, "Will you play the piano for him?" And I thought, my, what shall I play? You don't know what to play for strangers, and you take an awful chance anyway. I thought, well, what do most people like? The rank and file of people mostly like Chopin. So I played a little Chopin Nocturne and was greeted with politeness but nothing else. Then afterward Mr. Ives asked if I liked modern music. And I said I did—very much so. Mrs. Ives asked if I would like to come sometime to a rehearsal of Mr. Ives's works. He had written quartets and various other kinds of chamber music and had rehearsals at their house. It happened that he was going to have a rehearsal the following week, and they asked me to come.

I went and was very much impressed. It was a rehearsal of either a quartet or quintet. After hearing some of his things, I didn't wonder that my playing of a little Chopin Nocturne left them cold!

I kept in touch with Mr. Ives's music, not personally but through a friend of mine, Henry Cowell. I played the premiere performance of *The Tides of Manaunaun,* a piano piece by Henry, in Town Hall. He took me to hear Charles Ives's music many times. My husband wasn't very interested, but we both enjoyed Henry. He would call and announce that Charles Ives's or Carl Ruggles's music was to be played, and didn't we want to come? So I heard a great deal of Ives's music, and I was sorry not to have followed up the personal introduction I had.

E. Robert Schmitz (1889–1949), French pianist, had studied at the Paris Conservatory, knew Debussy, and conducted his own orchestra in Paris before World War I. He was dedicated to the cause of little-known and contemporary music, and Pro Musica (at first called the Franco-American Society), which Schmitz founded in 1920 and directed, did a great deal to further this cause during its eighteen years of existence. Due to his extraordinary abilities as an entrepreneur and to the magnetism of his personality, Pro Musica had over forty chapters by 1930, some in remote areas of this country and in other parts of the world, whose function was to acquaint the public with new music and with the composers themselves.

Ravel, Bartók, Honegger, Milhaud, and many others were brought to this country for the first time under the auspices of Pro Musica.

Schmitz first visited Ives at his office in 1923 in search of an insurance policy, and to Schmitz's great surprise, he found a composer behind the desk. Ives was invited to become a member of Pro Musica. The friendship between Schmitz and Ives deepened and gave pleasure to both men, and it was important to the cause of Ives's music. Considering his almost total isolation from the music world, one can imagine Ives's appreciation of the seriousness with which Schmitz listened to his ideas and to his music. Here was the first professional musician to pay close attention to him. In 1925 Schmitz arranged to include two of Ives's Three Quarter-Tone Pieces *in a concert sponsored by Pro Musica (then still the Franco-American Society) in Town Hall, and in 1927 Eugene Goossens (1893–1962) conducted Ives's* Prelude *and second movement from the* Fourth Symphony *at the Pro Musica International Referendum Concert.*

When Robert Schmitz arrived in New York from France with his wife and infant daughter in 1918, his health had been severely damaged and his career interrupted by four years of war. His ideas and the vitality to project them, however, seemed indestructible. Germaine Schmitz assisted her husband with the activities of Pro Musica and with the business and paper work of the organization. (In fact, under the name of Ely Jade, Germaine Schmitz edited Pro Musica Quarterly.) *The Schmitz's daughter Monique grew up during these interesting, tumultuous years in which her father successfully combined a rigorous concert and teaching career with his directorship of Pro Musica. Musicians, particularly composers, were close friends of the family for many years. In an interview in Montreal on May 18, 1971, MONIQUE SCHMITZ LEDUC recalled sessions where Sergei, Béla, or Darius discussed with her father what kind of modern music would be tolerated in Dubuque, Kansas City, or Seattle. She finds it a little startling now to realize that these men were Prokofiev, Bartók, and Milhaud.*

Ives came to the financial rescue of Pro Musica any number of times. I remember Father saying that he could not say anything about this in the newspapers—that Ives would not bear with it. I questioned Father about this, and he said, "Ives is not interested in that type of thing at all. He doesn't want people to be grateful, and he doesn't want to have his name printed in this, that, and the other thing. Not at all." As a child I found this difficult to understand. It was only much later that I could perceive the type of person that this behavior would indicate. It was rather extraordin-

PRO-MUSICA, Inc.

130 West 42nd Street, New York City

Founded in 1920

OFFICERS

E. ROBERT SCHMITZ,
President

MRS. HENRY P. LOOMIS,
First Vice-Pres.

MARCUS L. BELL,
Second Vice-Pres.

WILLIAM S. VERPLANCK,
Treasurer

SIGMUND KLEIN,
Secretary

TOWN HALL

January 29, 1927, Saturday afternoon, at 3 o'clock

INTERNATIONAL REFERENDUM CONCERT

ORCHESTRA CONCERT

With 50 men from the Philharmonic Orchestra, New York

Under the leadership of EUGENE GOOSSENS and DARIUS MILHAUD

PROGRAM

CHARLES E. IVES—Prelude and Second Movement, from a symphony for orchestra and pianos—(World Première).
Pianists: E. Robert Schmitz, Marion Cassell, Elmer Schoettle.

CLAUDE DEBUSSY—Musique pour le "Roi Lear"—(American Première).

DARIUS MILHAUD—Les Malheurs d'Orphée, opera in three acts—(American Première)

Soloists: Minna Hager, Greta Torpadie, Rosalie Miller, Radiana Pazmor, Eric Morgan, John Parish, Irving Jackson and Dudley Marwick.

The next concert will take place in February, 1927, at the Residence of Mrs. Reginald deKoven, 1025 Park Ave., New York. Sonatas by Tansman, A. Steinert and Chamber Music
(reserved for members)

MEMBERSHIP

Upon presentation of their Membership Card for the current year, Members can be admitted to all concerts given by Pro-Musica, in New York and its Chapters in Kansas City, Denver, St. Paul, Minneapolis, Montreal, Los Angeles, San Francisco, Portland, Chicago, and Paris, and to receive the PRO-MUSICA QUARTERLY, whose contributors are among the most pre-eminent musicographs of America and Europe and which includes articles on modern music, musical science, biographies, etc.

Founders—$500 or more	Entitled to 1 box for each concert
Life Members—$100 once	Entitled to 2 seats for each concert
Associate Members—$5 yearly	Entitled to 1 seat for each concert

---

AEOLIAN HALL

Saturday evening, February 14, 1925, at 8:15 o'clock

Franco-American Musical Society, Inc.

Founded 1920

INTERNATIONAL REFERENDUM CONCERTS

Season 1924-1925

Second Concert

(Programs are suggested by the International Advisory Board)

RAYMONDE DELAUNOIS	HANS BARTH
ROBERT IMANDT	SIGMUND KLEIN
GERMAINE TAILLEFERRE	E. ROBERT SCHMITZ
WOOD-WIND QUARTET	

(*This will be Germaine Tailleferre's first appearance in America*)

Program

I. 1st Sonata (for piano and violin) - - - - - G. Tailleferre

GERMAINE TAILLEFERRE and ROBERT IMANDT

II.
Adieu a la Vie - - - - - - A. Casella
Air Tzigane } (First performance) - M. D. Milhovitch
Le Pigeon
Myosotis d'amour fleurette } - - - I. Strawinsky

RAYMONDE DELAUNOIS

III.
Etude
Nocturne (No. 2) } - - - - A. Tansman
Improvisation (Nos 1, 3, 5) - - - B. Bartok
Cortège Nocturne - - - - - Petyrck

E. ROBERT SCHMITZ

IV.
Largo } World premiere
Allegro } - - - - - - Chas. E. Ives
Chorale } World premiere
Sonata (3rd Movement) } - - - - Hans Barth
For quarter tone Chickering Pianos

HANS BARTH and SIGMUND KLEIN

V.
de Fleurs (from the "Proses Lyriques") - C. Debussy
Brodeuses (from the "Crépuscules d'automne") - L. Aubert
Sheherazade - - - - - - M. Ravel

RAYMONDE DELAUNOIS

VI. Deux Mouvements (First performance) - - Jacques Ibert

WOOD-WIND QUARTET

Mr. E. Robert Schmitz uses the Mason & Hamlin Piano   Tickets at Box Office, 50c. to $2.00
Messrs. Barth & Klein use the Chickering Piano   Boxes (seating six) $15.00, tax exempt

BOGUE-LABERGE CONCERT MANAGEMENT

Franco-American Society concert program, 1925, lists the Three Quarter-Tone Pieces. Actually only the Largo and Allegro

Pro Musica International Referendum Concert, 1927.

The first page of Ives's manuscript for **Largo**, *the first of the* **Three Quarter-Tone Pieces.**

Darius Milhaud, Aaron Copland, and E. Robert Schmitz, ca. 1928.

ary, particularly in the 1920s when the whole American scene was crazy and wide open, especially in New York, and then you find a perfect gentleman who is assuredly the most important thing in music for America who doesn't want anything to do with any of this. It's quite a contrast. I think perhaps this explains a sense of security Father had in terms of his friendship toward Ives. Father was himself a rather shy person.

When we got together at the house on 74th Street [1926–ca. 1931], Father and Mr. Ives did a great deal of work together—always playing and talking around the piano. They alternated at the piano. One would push the other one off—not literally, of course, but I remember they would change places at the piano or else bring another chair to the piano, and the two of them would go at it with four hands. I presume that they were working on orchestral scores. They were sight-reading from large formats that were not published. Father was a very good sight reader. This came from the Paris Conservatory, where he studied as a boy, and where they were very strong on sight-reading, sightsinging, and score reading. Also, Father had directed an orchestra [Association des Concerts Schmitz] and had conducted enough modern works, so that the technique and the attitude was not foreign to him. By that time, Father had tackled some music which had prepared him for Ives, and I think this was why he was so valuable to Ives.

When Father had occasional objections, he made them straight to Ives. There were some parts that he felt could be done another way at the piano —the same exact notes but distributed in the hand differently so that it might be a little easier to play. The scores were extremely difficult. Ives would answer with "Never mind" and with something about how his mind was carrying on, and the fingers would have to follow. I don't think either the complexity of the harmonic textures or anything like that bothered Father. It was his concern to perceive how the music was organized.

I considered it strange that Ives was so vigorous at the piano. It surprised me that he was capable of so much Latin effervescence, and that he could be so proper, but then suddenly so free. Perhaps this was because of his passionate interest in music.

As a result of Father's and Mr. Ives's friendship the women and children became acquainted. Mother felt slightly awed by Mrs. Ives. Mother was always awed by New Englanders, and Mrs. Ives definitely had a New England way about her. I wouldn't have been too surprised if she had said that cleanliness was next to holiness. She gave that feeling of steadiness, a certain mellowed sternness, and at the same time a good deal of warmth, but the kind of warmth you associate with very nice people from New England, not the kind of warmth you associate with Latin climes. I felt instinctively that she wouldn't particularly appreciate frivolity in a person, or bright colors. Mr. Ives struck me at first as mildly scary, and it was only little by little that I discovered that perhaps Harmony was more scary than he was. I came to the conclusion that with Mr. Ives we could do all kinds of nonsensical things. He'd say something very serious, tongue in cheek, but then his eyes would be sparkling. A child will react to that immediately because it means there's a complicity—a sort of a secret between them. Also, I think children respond to someone who is shy, because they are shy themselves. I felt he was shy, and much more than that, retiring. But there was a part of him that he would give to others only after a great deal of time.

Edie and I weren't too involved in what the adults were doing, but we'd sometimes hear crashing pianos, or long discussions, or we would be summoned for tea. Edie at that time had long blonde hair. She was tall and thin, and I was plump and small and darker, so I felt that we made quite a contrast together. I conceived of her as somebody gentle and in some respects poetic, a little bit mysterious, and in a way not terribly full of childishness. She was much more reasonable than me by a long shot, and much less impulsive. She was a few years older, but I don't think that was what was causing it. We used to play that she was a sleeping princess who

Edith Ives, ca. 1925.

would be awakened one of these days. I was her lady-in-waiting and I'd trot around, but she would always automatically be the princess. There was no question about that. On 74th Street Edie had a room of her own, and since I was sharing a room with my aunt, I felt green with envy.

The Iveses had told Edie way back that she was adopted. I remember a discussion between Mrs. Ives and Mother about their telling Edie, and the pros and cons. I remember thinking that Mrs. Ives had the right point of view that the confidence of the child in her parents would be so much greater knowing than not knowing. And I remember Mother was a little bit startled by it, but she eventually came around. I was happily surprised when I saw Edie as a young adult, because she was much less far from reality than I expected her to be. And I don't mean that unkindly, but all of a sudden I found a young woman who was shopping for a trousseau, who had her two feet on the ground, actually getting married.

After we moved to the West Coast [early 1930s], there were letters and talk about a visit to us by the Iveses. But this never happened. The Schmitz family were happy to have the friendship of the Iveses. Father was particularly grateful to have Ives's friendship, because he felt that he was one of the greatest musicians alive. And yet you didn't have to come with your engraved card and deposit it and wait in consternation in the parlor. There was no barrier. Father always admired people also who were able to do more than one thing—musicians who were at the same time either politicians or businessmen or something like that. He felt it meant that there was a tremendous intelligence at work. Father would have been surprised to think that there were not many people who took Ives seriously as a composer. It never occurred to him that this was the case.

When a copy of the Concord Sonata *found its way to Clifton Joseph Furness (1898–1946), at Northwestern University, Furness, who was interested in the contemporary arts, was enthusiastic. He began a correspondence with Ives, who subsequently helped Furness secure a teaching position at the Horace Mann School in New York. There, Furness introduced composer ELLIOTT CARTER to the music of Ives. This was in 1924, and, "It triggered an interest in Ives that has never stopped." Mr. Carter was interviewed near South Salem, New York, on June 20, 1969.*

Elliott Carter saw Ives several times during his high school years, and when he applied to Harvard in 1926, Ives sent a letter of recommendation to the dean:

> *Carter strikes me as rather an exceptional boy. He has an instinctive interest in literature and especially music that is somewhat unusual. He writes well—an essay in his school paper, "Symbolism in Art," shows an interesting mind. I don't know him intimately, but his teacher in Horace Mann School, Mr. Clifton J. Furness, and a friend of mine always speaks well of him—that he's a boy of good character and does well in his studies. I am sure his reliability, industry and sense of honor are what they should be—also his sense of humor which you do not ask me about.*

In 1924, when I was a student at Horace Mann School in New York City, my music teacher, Clifton Furness, who knew Ives, showed me some of his music. Furness was interested in contemporary arts of all kinds—it wasn't merely Ives's music, but also various performers of new music like Katherine Ruth Heyman, artists like the Russian refugees, David Burliuk and Nicholas Roerich. Also, through Eugene O'Neill, Jr., a fellow high school student, we followed the lively productions of the Provincetown Playhouse on MacDougal Street. It was an exciting time for contemporary arts: *The Dial* was in full swing; *Ulysses,* which we all read, was banned; and O'Neill wrote one remarkable play after another stirring up a great deal of controversy.

Miss Heyman, a very progressive pianist for those days, had been a friend of Ezra Pound in London before the First World War, had befriended the much neglected Charles Griffes here, and was regarded by her circle as a spokesman for the avant-garde "great" from the immediately previous period, both as a musician and a conversationalist. It was at her

C-22 George Smith Hall
Cambridge, Mass.
Feb 19, 1927

Dear Mr. Ives,

I am very sorry that I was unable to come to see you that Sunday afternoon nor later to hear your symphony. As I am interested very much in your music I would like to hear it once instead of having to work over it to make it sound at all.

I wonder if it would be possible to have a few more records made of your violin sonata. — Or is the stamp lost? Recently I have been greatly interested in recordings. I have eight records of "Pelleas and Melisande" "Pacific 231", Stravinsky's "Petrouchka," "Fire-Bird" "Ragtime", as well as Scriabin's "Poem of Ecstasy" — only to mention the moderns. I find the victrola a great help in studying Beethoven and Brahms. Unfortunately very little good Bach has been done.

I am sending you a very interesting magazine dealing with recordings entirely. In it, this month, has appeared an account of private recordings. I wonder if Pro-Musica could not have a department for recording its more popular modern works. "Pierrot Lunaire" and other things are waiting to be done as well as some Scriabin.

The subscription record idea seems a very good one (at least to me) and would help in the understanding of modern music.

I wish that it were possible to start a modern music group up here in Boston — it has never been done though we hear a great deal from Koussewitzky.

I am coming to Miss Heyman's concert Sunday evening Feb 27 & I hope I shall see you there.

Sincerely yours

Elliott C. Carter Jr.

The first letter from Elliott Carter to Charles Ives.

weekend afternoons, in a loft-apartment on 15th Street and Third Avenue, in a little triangular building (now razed) that I first heard parts of the *Concord Sonata* around '24 or '25. She played much other new music for her friends then, particularly Griffes, Emerson Whithorne, Dane Rudhyar, Ravel, Debussy, Schoenberg's opus 11, no. 2, and especially Scriabin. The group that came to these dimly lit gatherings admired the latter very much. I myself, enthusiastic, soon acquired all the late works at considerable effort and practiced the polyrhythms in works like *Vers la flamme* and the *Eighth Etude* of opus 42. Ives used to appear occasionally at these private recitals, but whether I met him there for the first time or where, I really couldn't say.

Both Furness and Miss Heyman, along with a few habitués that came to these séances, were involved with what might be called extra-musical ideas. She was committed to mysticism, having been a member of the Annie Besant theosophical circle in her London days, while Furness was drawn to Rudolf Steiner's anthroposophy. I myself read quite a number of Steiner's works with great interest in those days. Therefore, the mystical, transcendental aspect of Ives's music had a particular appeal to the group. There was, however, a strong feeling among this group against Schoenberg's music, which was considered a kind of dangerous black art (the "Satanic" side of Liszt and Scriabin, on the other hand seemed perfectly OK). From this point of view, Ives was considered a kind of white god and much reverenced. The mystical bias in all of this appealed to an adolescent, though it was not long before I began to feel these judgments unreliable when it came to artistic matters. In retrospect I would have thought that Ives would not have liked this kind of thing.

My impression, then, however, was that Ives had a rather restricted world of musical contacts, limited to the few that really admired his music, and it was understandable that he would be drawn to interested musicians, no matter what their other views, in a desire for human talk about contemporary music.

Ives was certainly involved and interested in music of his time and didn't remain aloof from it: as much as he could be, he was part of it. He was very generous to *New Music*, which published modern scores quarterly for years, of which Henry Cowell was editor. Later, when I succeeded Cowell, for a while we continued to receive an annual contribution from Ives of a thousand dollars, which, in those days, went far to printing modern scores. Besides this help to other composers, Ives subsidized the printing of many of his own music scores and his *Essays Before a Sonata* and sent these around to libraries all over the country, including, to my surprise, the library of the American Academy in Rome, where I found copies a few years ago. He was not a recluse in the sense that he didn't want his music to be unknown to the music profession, which he looked on with some suspicion; on the contrary, I think he was making a distinct effort to take his place among the composers of his time.

When Ives expressed opinions about the music profession as it existed in his time in America, there was much anger at its timidity and its secondhand cultural attitudes. He expressed himself in the *Essays*, verbally, but also in the many marginal comments in his music manuscripts. Some of the music itself is a direct reflection of his scorn and anger—poking fun at the music profession and sometimes, I think, punishing it by intentionally peculiar cacophony or vulgarity. Every American composer cannot help but understand this attitude. During Ives's lifetime, Dvořák was brought over here to explain and demonstrate what American music should be, and now we subsidize Stockhausen and others as if they could show us the way.

Like many composers of his time, he was sensitive about the criticism that the modern composer really didn't know how to write "music." Once in talking about this he told me that in order to prove that he could write in a conventional style, he had written his *Third Violin Sonata*. He then played this with comments for me on a privately made recording by a violinist who had played all four sonatas the previous year, I think, at Aeolian Hall. It was at this same meeting, I believe, that he showed me the score of his *First Symphony,* written as a student of Horatio Parker, and pointed out details Parker had objected to, particularly modulations that did not follow the then accepted sonata-form formulas. How scornful he was of the latter—saying, as has often been said more recently (and also at that time by Debussy), that the great sonata writers had never followed the rules.

One of the most vivid memories I have of Ives is of an afternoon when he lived on East 22nd Street, near Gramercy Park. It may have been our first meeting, where we were invited after a concert on a Sunday afternoon which I described in an article in *Modern Music** when my memory was fresher. It was perhaps in the years '24–'25 when I was occasionally invited to sit in the Ives box (which he subscribed to for the Saturday afternoon Boston Symphony series at Carnegie Hall), and I remember returning with him to excited discussions of the new music at his house. I was then very surprised about his attitudes and so remember quite distinctly what he

*Elliott Carter, "The Case of Mr. Ives," *Modern Music* 16, no. 3 (April 1939): 172–76.

thought. He invariably felt that each of the new pieces like, I think, Ravel's *Daphnis et Chloé* or Stravinsky's *Rite of Spring,* although I am not sure it was the latter, revealed extremely simple-minded ways of dealing with new harmonies and rhythms. I remember vividly his "take-off" at the piano of the Ravel chord and of the repetitiousness of Stravinsky. Ives was very literate and sharp about this—he seemed to remember quite clearly bits of what he had heard and could parody them surprisingly well. His point was that most all contemporary composers of the time had chosen the easy way out. Perhaps out of deference for our interests at that time, I don't remember his taking off on Scriabin, although both *Le Poème de l'extase* and *Prométhée* were heard occasionally then. Scriabin's music might well have been criticized for the same reasons as the others—excessive repetition, mechanical formalism, and the isolation of some small formula in an unwillingness to deal with a large body of musical material. Ives's *Essays,* too, which contain rather pointed asides about Stravinsky and especially Debussy, express some disagreement with his musical contemporaries. But, in spite of what he said, I think Ives had a genuine interest in new music. I remember seeing, to my surprise, the score of Prokofiev's *Love of Three Oranges* lying on a desk in his house in Redding. I couldn't believe he could be interested in Prokofiev at that time, although it was right after the opera, commissioned by the Chicago Opera, had been performed. One of the myths that has grown up about Ives is that he never knew about and never heard contemporary music. This may have been true in his early years, but by the time I met him it was not. By then surely he had heard some of the piano pieces of Schoenberg* and Scriabin, and works of Stravinsky and others, and had read about all of these and others in the pages of the *Pro Musica Quarterly,* copies of which he must have received as one of its sponsors, and also the scores of *New Music* which printed many new works besides his own.

I seem to remember—it's hard for me to believe now—that it used to be said among us that after a few social evenings early in their married life, at which Ives's excited, enthusiastic outbursts had overpowered the gathering, Mrs. Ives had considered it more prudent not to accept such invitations any more, as her husband could not be counted on to take a social situation into account. He was, as is well known, secretive with his business asso-

---

*Mr. Carter later supplied the following footnote: "After having made this statement, I read in *Charles E. Ives Memos,* edited by John Kirkpatrick, that Ives wrote E. Robert Schmitz in 1931 that he had never heard a note of Schoenberg's music, and I realized that he must have been absent on each of the infrequent occasions when Miss Heyman played the Schoenberg piece (opus 11, no. 2)."

ciates about his music. He would tell how he had gone up in the elevator to his office with someone who said, "Ives, you know, yesterday I heard *Parsifal* at the opera. It's a fine thing. You should go to the opera sometimes." He seemed ruefully proud that he kept all of this from the people in the office, but the other side of the story, apparently, was that they all knew of his music but played the game.

He was a complicated, quick, intelligent man with, obviously, an enormous love and wide knowledge of music, and with a determination to follow his own direction, believing in it deeply. Yet he seemed to have been almost unwilling to witness the imperfections of the performances he had and reluctant to face and solve them. It may have been too disturbing for his excitable nature to discover his works did not come out as he wanted, either because they were not carefully or practically enough marked with dynamic indications—the score of the second movement of the *Fourth Symphony*, printed after the 1927 performance, shows an elaboration of dynamic markings seldom found in others—or else because musicians had not rehearsed sufficiently. So he seems to have avoided concerts where his own music was played, although attending the rehearsals, as he did with the performance of the *Fourth Symphony* movement. The suspense and excitement of public performance and the ensuing reaction was said to be too much for him to bear. I remember a dismaying demonstration of this over-excitability which occurred when he was playing parts of *Emerson* for me at Redding. A vein on the side of his neck began to bulge as if it were going to burst with the tremendous energy and excitement he was putting into the performance. Apparently accustomed to this, he stopped playing, pinched the vein as if to stop the flow of blood and went to lie down on a sofa to recover, his wife bringing him a glass of milk. Perhaps he had been warned by a doctor that he must avoid excitement, and it's possible that for this reason he did not go to concerts.

In any case it seems in retrospect he had already begun to withdraw from active life by the time I met him, although this tendency, perhaps, had always existed. But it seemed clear even at that time that there had been a great disillusionment with America as it emerged from the First World War, a crass, materialistic society that no longer lived up to the ideals he so worshiped. I suppose his reputed refusal to read the New York newspapers, subscribing instead to the London *Times* was a symptom of this. For in talk about contemporary politics, he seemed profoundly disturbed by the bungling and compromising that had gone on, with the peace settlement and the postwar negotiations which had destroyed the illusion that the war had been fought for a noble cause.

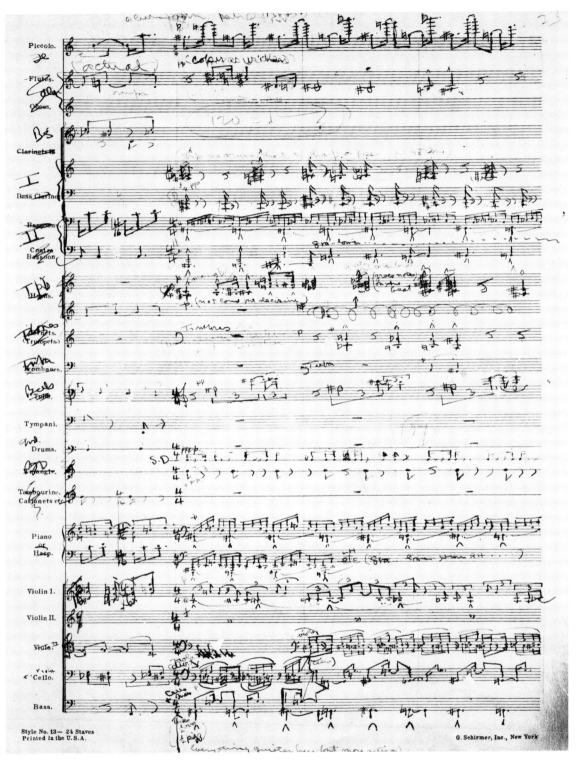

A page from the autograph score of Ives's Fourth Symphony, *second movement.*

© 1965 by Associated Music Publishers
Used by permission

Yet being the idealistic man he was, such things were not in the fore-
ground of his thought. It was part of his attractiveness that he was so lively,
so full of enthusiasm and, except in the instances mentioned above, not
given (at least at any time I saw him) to bitterness and pessimism. In fact,
he was so uncritically enthusiastic about the things he cared for that there
seemed to be little counterbalancing cool judgment or cynicism, which
might have helped him to be more realistic about the notation of his more
intricate scores.

A matter which puzzles me still is the question of Ives's revision of his
own scores. I can remember vividly a visit on a late afternoon to his house
on East 74th Street, when I was directed to a little top-floor room where
Ives sat at a little upright piano with score pages strewn around on the
floor and on tables—this must have been around 1929. He was working on,
I think, *Three Places in New England,* getting the score ready for performance. A new score was being derived from the older one to which he
was adding and changing, turning octaves into sevenths and ninths, and
adding dissonant notes.* Since then, I have often wondered at exactly
what date a lot of the music written early in his life received its last shot
of dissonance and polyrhythm. In this case he showed me quite simply
how he was improving the score. I got the impression that he might have
frequently jacked up the level of dissonance of many works as his tastes
changed. While the question no longer seems important, one could wonder
whether he was as early a precursor of "modern" music as is sometimes
made out. A study of the manuscripts would probably make this clear.
It's obvious to me both from his music and his prose that Ives was really
familiar with Debussy, for there are many piano figurations and conceptions of music that seem derived from the French composer although, of
course, he transformed them in a most original and personal way. Ives,
although he was not aware of it, probably, belonged to the 1890–1920
period with a strong retrospective view of the transcendental–Civil War
period. This was brought home to me very intensely at our last meeting.

When my father and mother were living in Westport, Connecticut, I
remember driving their car over to Redding with some music, showing it to
Ives and spending a whole day with him talking and walking around in the
woods behind his house. My family was so upset about my becoming a
musician that I thought I ought to get the advice of respected people before

---

*Three Places was being prepared by Ives and Nicolas Slonimsky for the premiere performance of the work (1931) by Slonimsky's Boston Chamber Orchestra. The work was
originally scored for full orchestra, and so it was necessary for Ives to rescore it to accom-
modate Slonimsky's small orchestra.

I really broke away and became the rebel I had to be. This was in '28 or '29, during my college years. Ives was certainly not enthusiastic about the neoclassic music I was then writing. My memory is that he had seen other music of mine before I went to college which he thought more promising and had on the basis of that encouraged me to go on. (Just before Henry Cowell died, he returned one of my boyish compositions submitted to *New Music* in the '20s that had gotten lost in his files. It wasn't much good, I must say. It's a wonder Ives or anyone else could have seen anything in it.) That day was the last I saw Ives, except for occasional times when I used to take the morning train from Westport to New York during the summer, which stopped at South Norwalk and picked up passengers from the Danbury spur, among whom occasionally was Ives on his way to his office. When I saw him get on, I usually would wait until the last stop before New York before going to talk to him.

Ives's influence on my music has varied greatly from '24 to now. It was very important before I actually decided to become a musician. But when I began to study music formally at college in '26, its value diminished a great deal, because I was anxious to learn how to write music step by step, not only by traditional methods but from the new music that was within my grasp to imagine auditively and to formulate clear ideas about. From that time there was a mounting sense of frustration when I returned to Ives's music, which I have done frequently, because much of it then seemed so disordered and even disorganized that, given the point of view I held then, it was nearly impossible to understand how or why much of it was put together as it was. This experience coupled with a growing antiromantic outlook, characteristic of most young composers of the '30s and '40s, led me to try to cultivate clarity and sharp definition of musical material, qualities antithetical to Ives's work.

Out of this attitude, a distressing dilemma arose, for when John Kirkpatrick finally gave the first performance of the complete *Concord Sonata* at Town Hall in 1939, I was disappointed in the piece that had previously meant so much to me. Unfortunately, being the critic for the magazine *Modern Music* and being quite knowledgeable about the sonata and about Ives, I felt I had to write a long review of the work expressing my views.* The critic's obligation to speak his thoughts frankly, painful as it was to me as one who wanted to admire Ives, made me very sad. After what I wrote then, I never had the heart to see Ives again.

Later in the mid-40s, I began to think I had been wrong about the

*Carter, "The Case of Mr. Ives."

Carter

I am writing for ———

He greatly appreciates your interest in his music and your kindness in writing that article in the Modern Music Review. You put things in a most interesting way — and it is well written. There are some matters not quite accurately referred about — though that is hardly your fault — data should have been sent you.

For instance — the 2nd Symphony was, for the most part composed before Mr. Ives' father died, 50 years ago — (though it was fully scored a few years later) — Mr. Ives then had not heard or seen any of Dvorak's music which you assume influenced this Symphony. The themes in this, were a kind of reflection of — or at least the hope to express in some way the spirit of Stephen Foster — even if some of the old barn dance tunes were occasionally strewn over it — also themes from the old camp meeting Hymn tunes; and in the last movement the stirring excitement the boys

The first page of a letter from Ives to Elliott Carter in response to Carter's 1944 article in Modern Music. *The remainder of the letter continues in print.*

felt when the Danbury Cornet band of the '80s was marching down Main St. playing "The Red, White and Blue."

The 3rd Symphony, particularly the 1st and 3rd movements, he played as organ pieces and so not as fully as in the score in church services over 40 years ago and before he had heard or known any of Caesar [sic] Franck's music which it is inferred influenced it.

The last movement of the Holiday Symphony "Forefather's Day" Mr. Ives feels strongly is not dithyrambic—at least he hopes it reflects in no way the sallies of a crowd of revellers of Bacchus—no more than does that great solemn old hymn which a chorus sings towards the end of this Movement "O God, beneath thy guiding hand Our exiled Fathers crossed the Sea."

In his chamber music there may be, he says, a poor joke or two but no parody of modern music was intended.

We hope that the inference in the last paragraph that no real consideration has ever been given to his music will not be misunderstood, that is, taken too literally, nor seem unfair to those who have played, sung, conducted some of his music, written about it and "stood up for it" even when, as he says, some of them felt that in so doing they would probably get in wrong with some of "the powers that be"— and be not for that matter.

However, most of the above matters are secondary and rather unimportant. He feels that your thoughts as to the fundamentals of music are "thoughtfully and beautifully expressed and that they seem to suggest something that may be seen in a cosmic landscape of an Art-Philosophy"—

He is deeply grateful for what you have done in behalf of his music and sends you his sincere thanks.

We were so glad to see that your Symphonies are being played and hope they were well performed and fully appreciated.

Mr. Ives hopes when he is better to have the pleasure of seeing you again.

With kindest remembrances from both of us I am

> *Sincerely yours*
> *Harmony T. Ives*

Concord Sonata, that I should go back and reconsider all of Ives's works more closely.* I plowed patiently through the eleven-volume photostat collection of his unpublished works that Ives had deposited at the American Music Center. As I did, frequently surprised and delighted, I began to list pages out of order, hardly legible, or apparently missing. It became clear to me that a great deal of work needed to be done to get some of the manuscripts in shape for performance, and it would help if Ives could be consulted, even in his sickness before he died. I got in touch with Mrs. Ives to propose such a project, asking if Ives would cooperate. They agreed, so I began to work on one piece after another, raising questions, planning for copying. Unfortunately I found very quickly I was temperamentally unsuited to unscramble the confusion of many of the manuscript sketches. Not only would they take inordinate amounts of time (with no certainty that an actual piece would emerge), but I could not make the rough decisions necessary, for only too frequently there was a palimpsest of three or four alternatives. The mounting sense of confusion his music has at times overwhelmed me with, was at this juncture too much for me to take, and I stopped, but not before finding others, in particular Lou Harrison and Henry Cowell, who were devoted to the project and more able to face its problems. At about the same time, I planned a book on Ives with [critic] Paul Rosenfeld, but the latter's death put an end to this.

As I scanned the Ives manuscripts, the *Fourth Symphony* looked the largest and the most important. However, unlike the other three movements, the last was scribbled in pencil with many perplexing alternatives sketched in the margins. I remember a few measures for six trombones, a number never called for again. I began to wonder whether this movement could ever be gotten into playable shape. The second movement was printed after a concert performance in 1927 (Ives had invited the New York Philharmonic percussionists to his house and beaten out the complicated rhythms on the dining room table until they learned them). Its markings, as I have said, are much more elaborate and carefully done than in any other Ives scores—which usually content themselves with very vague indications that force the performer, often, to invent his own. Perhaps if Ives had had more and better performances during his life, the other scores would have been similarly marked.

The first and third movements of the *Fourth Symphony* have been printed very much as they appeared in the photostated volumes. The third,

*Carter wrote a second article in 1944 discussing various works by Ives. Elliott Carter, "Ives Today: His Vision and Challenge," *Modern Music* 21, no. 4 (May-June 1944): 199–202.

which is about seventy-five percent the same as the first movement of the *First String Quartet,* has a few irregular bar lengths, polyrhythms, and dissonances added especially at the expanded climax near the end. Comparison between these two show, in small, how Ives revised his works to suit the changes brought about by his musical development, as do, in a much more problematic way, the incorporation of parts of the *Hawthorne* movement of the *Concord Sonata* into the piano part of the second movement of the *Fourth Symphony.*

It is most mysterious that it took musicians and public so long to catch on to the fact of Ives's music, once the contemporary movement began to take hold in the United States during the '20s. Quite late, perhaps during the Second World War, I think, I can remember talking Ives over with Goddard Lieberson,* who in turn arranged a lunch with Stokowski to try to convince him that there were a lot of remarkable pieces that ought to be played. The latter was very cautious, saying that the works were complicated, hard to rehearse, and would take much more time to prepare than could be arranged for.

With this, and similar scenes in mind, I attended the ISCM [International Society for Contemporary Music] festival in Baden-Baden in 1955, the year after Ives died, being one of the members of the Central Committee and having my Cello Sonata played there. I was immediately impressed by what was, to me, extraordinary, for I witnessed what was said to be the fiftieth (or so) rehearsal of Boulez's *Marteau sans maître,* at which the conductor, Hans Rosbaud, was still picking apart little details, patiently getting an instrument to play the part exactly as written with the right dynamics, and so on. I immediately talked to the director of the Südwestfunk [SWF], Dr. Heinrich Strobel, saying, "You know, there's a very wonderful work of Ives, the *Fourth Symphony,* that the SWF Orchestra should play. It is probably the only orchestra that could afford the rehearsals of such a complicated piece, and with its conductor who is so interested in new music and so painstaking with it, you would be helping the cause of new music by presenting this important work in a fine, well-rehearsed performance." Strobel got in touch with the various people in the United States who had custody of the score, as I suggested. This led to those in the United States being disturbed by the possibility that the German radio might get the first performance of the work, and so they busied themselves with getting the score, especially the last movement, in shape, copying the parts and finally convincing Stokowski to do it. It took a request by the

*Goddard Lieberson, pp. 206–09.

German radio to get the ball rolling, which ended in the typically American "big-time publicity" given to Ives's music.*

Many another remarkable work like the *Browning Overture* had to wait until the publicity had sifted down and done its work, while prior to this, efforts to get the orchestral works played in America by the major orchestras met with the kind of rebuff I described (except during the '30s when Nicolas Slonimsky conducted a few, as did Bernard Herrmann).

In spite of the efforts of some of us to get Ives's scores in shape, the declining health of Ives and his consequent inability to check on the orchestra parts of some of his available works meant that some of these were very badly, at times unprofessionally, copied. I know this, because when I was on another jury in Italy, I happened to have with me the old printed score of *The Fourth of July,* which I'd owned for a long time. When I presented this score to the music director of the Italian radio (who had never seen it), he burst with enthusiasm and said, "We've got to play this—it's one of the most interesting pieces I've ever seen." (Quite different from the reactions one used to get from musicians in important positions in the United States.) So the radio sent for the parts, which turned out to be so mixed up and confusing that the radio librarian had to have them copied all over again. The director of the radio station was quite angry and almost canceled the performance because of the mess in the original parts, which, I believe, Ives had had extracted for *New Music.* Now the work is published by another publisher, and there are probably better parts.

Each work has its difficulties because of Ives's inability in his later years to cope with musical situations. I remember that after I had looked through the volumes of photostated manuscripts, two of the works which intrigued me a great deal were *The Unanswered Question* and *Central Park in the Dark.* As I was then teaching at Columbia University and there was an annual Ditson Festival, I persuaded the festival committee to include premieres of these two works on the program [May 11, 1946]. I wrote to Mrs. Ives to ask if these were in fact first performances and for other program information. She wrote back a very charming letter quoting her ill husband, that they would not want to say those works were having their

---

*During the preparation of the score and parts of the *Fourth Symphony* for its first complete performance by the American Symphony Orchestra under Leopold Stokowski (April 26, 1965), it was discovered that a few pages from the fourth movement were missing from the American Music Center's collection of photostats of Ives's music. A search was made and these pages were found. It was claimed that the fourth movement had been lost and was recovered as a result of the first performance preparations. Actually, all of the manuscript pages were complete and safe in West Redding, and it was only a few pages of negative photostats which had been temporarily mislaid.

premieres—Mr. Ives wanted to be fair to those "old fellers" who had played them in between the acts of a theatrical performance around 1907 or 1908.

I don't think Ives had much influence on other composers until the *Fourth Symphony* publicity after his death; for Ives's music is, for the most part, very programmatic, and during the period of his life most composers of concert music were interested in writing "abstract" music, that is, music that depends on its design for its expression. Movie scores are different, and certainly those of Bernard Herrmann, who performed a lot of Ives's music with the CBS Symphony in the late '30s and '40s, were much influenced, particularly the one for *The Red Badge of Courage,* which sounds very much like Ives, I think.

As for myself, I have always been fascinated by the polyrhythmic aspect of Ives's music, as well as its multiple layering, but perplexed at times by the disturbing lack of musical and stylistic continuity, caused largely by the constant use of musical quotations in many works. To me a composer develops his own personal language, suitable to express his field of experience and thought. When he borrows music from another style and thought from his own, he is admitting that he did not really experience what he is presenting but has to borrow from someone else who did. In the case of early music, like masses on *L'homme armé,* or cantatas on Lutheran chorales, the original melody has a deep religious meaning so that, understandably, a very devout composer feels he needs to borrow.it as a basis, since its expression transcends his own religious experience. These old tunes both united the composer to his listener and were very close in style to the music for which they formed a basis. At the other extreme of borrowing are the endless variations on popular or famous tunes in the nineteenth century, a very few of which produced great music, not really because of the tunes. Then there were the entertaining potpourris or medleys of patriotic airs, sometimes arranged humorously for band concerts; these have no artistic pretentions and reveal little fundamental musical imagination. Some of Ives's works belong close to this latter category, except for his daring "take-off" technique that often makes these pieces resemble "realistic" sound pictures of festive scenes. It is, to me, disappointing that Ives too frequently was unable or unwilling to invent musical material that expressed his own vision authentically, instead of relying on the material of others. But what is striking and remarkable in his work, like much of the *First* and *Second Piano Sonatas,* is an extraordinary musical achievement.

Henry Cowell with Charles Ives.

The year 1927 was an important one for Ives's music. Aside from the Pro Musica Referendum Concert in which Goossens conducted some of the Fourth Symphony, *the year marks the beginning of the important relationship between Henry Cowell (1897–1965) and Ives. CHARLES SEEGER* in an interview (March 16, 1970, in Los Angeles) said, "I had just received Ives's* 114 Songs *when Henry came to see me. I showed them to Henry, and he took to them immediately, although they didn't particularly move me." From 1927 on when they met, Cowell was responsible for most of Ives's contacts with other musicians. Not the least of these was Cowell's introduction of Nicolas Slonimsky to Ives.*

*Charles Seeger is an ethnomusicologist, musicologist, and author. At the time of his introduction of the Ives songs to Cowell (ca. 1922), Seeger and Cowell were both in New York. Cowell had been one of Seeger's students in California.

NICOLAS SLONIMSKY was born in St. Petersburg, Russia in 1894. After a few years as an opera coach at the Eastman School of Music, Slonimsky worked with Serge Koussevitzky in Boston and founded the Boston Chamber Orchestra, which he conducted from 1927–34 and which gave the world premiere of Ives's Three Places in New England *in 1931. Slonimsky conducted many concerts including those for the Pan-American Association here and abroad. His programs reflected a predilection for contemporary music, and he was responsible for many first performances of works by Henry Cowell, Wallingford Riegger, Carl Ruggles, and Edgard Varèse. In recent years, Slonimsky has become well known as the author of* The Lexicon of Musical Invective, Music Since 1900, *and other musicological reference works. Nicolas Slonimsky was interviewed in New York City on January 29, 1969.*

I was twenty-eight years old when I came to the United States, and I had numerous jobs: as a pianist, as an opera coach, as secretary to Serge Koussevitzky. Then I began to compose and got in touch with Henry Cowell who was instrumental in having my first work published in his collection, *New Music,* which was largely financed by Charles Ives. This first composition of mine was called *Studies in Black and White,* and it was a typical modern composition of the time with a trick. The right hand played on the white keys and the left hand played on the black keys of the piano, and there were all kinds of contrapuntal combinations which seemed very modern at the time. I wrote some more pieces along the same lines, and then gradually I drifted into conducting. I realized that new music demanded new approaches, and I developed all kinds of new methods of conducting. I devoted myself to the problem of interpretation of what were then called ultramodern music works, particularly by American composers, and first of all by Charles Ives.

I met Charles Ives in New York, and we somehow hit it off together at once. He was very much amused to learn that as a boy I had read Mark Twain in Russian, and that Mark Twain was one of my favorite writers, as he was the favorite writer of so many Russian boys of my generation, and for that matter of the present Soviet generation. It was particularly interesting to me that the Ives family through the family of his wife, Harmony Twichell, was connected with Mark Twain, so there was a certain meeting of the minds between Ives and me despite the total difference of cultures. I don't know how, but I understood almost intuitively that here was a great man and that that great man was composing great music. That was at the time when there were mighty few people who could find anything in Ives except eccentricity and experimentation which had no purpose except to amuse a few similarly eccentrically minded people.

And then Ives suggested to Henry Cowell, who introduced me to Ives, to rig up a concert—I remember his expression "rig up a concert"—that of course meant that Charles Ives would be financing this concert. So it happened that first I gave some concerts of American music on my own in Boston with the Boston Chamber Orchestra, and there I gave the world premiere of *Three Places in New England* by Charles Ives, of which of course I'm very proud.

For *Three Places in New England* I developed a method of conducting two different beats simultaneously, one with the right hand and one with the left hand; I felt that the music of Ives required it because of its polyrhythmic combination. In the second movement there is a scene which represents the meeting of two marching bands in the village, and they play the same marching rhythm but at different tempi because they are coming from different directions. Although Ives wrote it out so that it could be conducted with a single beat in 4/4, I, being adventurous, decided that it would be more to the point to actually conduct one group with my right hand and the other with my left hand. So four bars of my left hand equaled three bars of my right hand. And amazingly enough the orchestra could follow me. There was no difficulty. I merely told one-half of the orchestra to follow my left hand and the other half to follow my right hand. Some critic said my conducting was evangelical, because my right hand knew not what my left hand was doing. I believe that this was the first time when a really stereophonic or rather bilateral type of music was played and conducted.

A few years after my performance, Ives decided to have the work published. It was his first published orchestral score and naturally he asked me to supervise the publication. I got in touch with Birchard in Boston [C. C. Birchard & Co.] because I was situated in Boston at the time. The publication was financed entirely by Ives who also very generously gave me a fee for my work. I went over the entire score, and I arranged this business of two simultaneous different bars in the second movement. This was not in the Ives original, but it was done with his permission. Needless to say, I didn't change a note. I merely suggested that it could be arranged in unequal bars. I had a lengthy correspondence with Ives and numerous meetings about various minor details in that score.

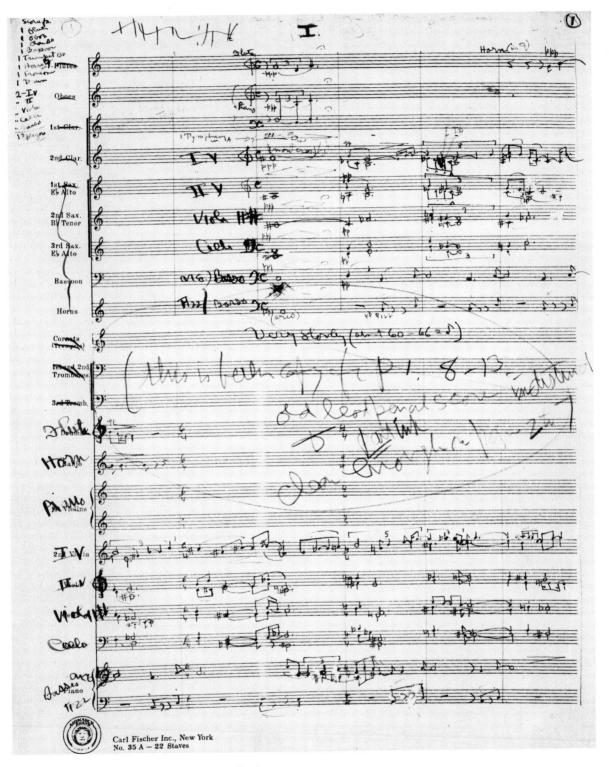

Manuscript page from Three Places in New England.

At that time people were still saying that Ives was an amateur who really didn't know what he was writing. Nothing could be more wrong. Ives was a professional musician, with an academic education. His *First Symphony* is entirely orthodox except for a few flights of fancy and sparks of genius. But in this particular work, *Three Places in New England,* whenever I raised the question about some changes, he would always point out to me why he did it otherwise. For instance, I remember a very strange situation in the viola part: an A sharp that was immediately changed to B flat, and I could not find any justification for the use of that A sharp, and I wanted to change it to B flat so as not to confuse the player in his part. But Ives said no. He said that A sharp was important because it was proceeding from A as a sort of an unfinished chromatic, that it would have gone to B but it just didn't, you know, and so therefore B flat would be wrong. What was amazing was that he would not compromise on any of those details. And while he had an idea that the performance should be free, there was an insistence on the letter of his writing. Now I believe that this is one of the most important features in the working mind of Ives during the creative process, because it did include every detail of composition including notation.

It's no secret that Ives financed not only *New Music,* but also my concerts in Paris, Berlin, and Budapest, which included American programs, programs of some of his music but also other music. He was extremely generous when I went on my trip. He insisted on adding an extra thousand dollars, and so he gave me a letter of credit of four thousand dollars, which was an amazing sum of money in 1931. And he always tried to send me a hundred dollars. At that time I really needed money. He didn't want to offend me by just giving me money, but whenever there was any suggestion that a fee could be justified, he would always send me those checks.

Ives came to my concert in Town Hall in New York on January 10, 1931. He told me he would come, but in a characteristically Ivesian manner, remarked something like, "Don't pay any attention to me, just go ahead and conduct your Boston Symphony men [at this concert I had my Chamber Orchestra of Boston which consisted of Boston Symphony men], and I will just sit back and listen to you." I recall that my concertmaster Theodorowitz (who was second concertmaster of the Boston Symphony) kept saying after each piece on the program, "So far, so good." Actually the performance was excellent. After the last residual chord of *The Housatonic at Stockbridge* I made an attempt to espy Ives in the hall, and I remember clearly that I put the palm of my right hand against my forehead and looked around like an Indian scout in a movie. Of course, Ives never acknowledged his presence, and nobody in the audience knew that he was there except from the evidence of my trying to find him. One of the minor radio stations in New York promised to broadcast the concert, and changes in the order of the program and the time of intermission had to be made to take advantage of this possibility. I had to make some announcements to that effect from the stage. Ives told me that he liked the informal manner of the whole concert. He said that it was like "a town meeting" and that everyone seemed to enjoy it. He seemed happy, in his reticent way, about the whole affair, and told me so when I had dinner with him the next day.

Well, it would take me hours and hours to tell the story of Ives. I stayed with him in his house in West Redding, Connecticut, near Danbury where he was born. Ives had only a few friends whom he accepted, and I was one of those fortunate people. Outside of myself, of course, there was Henry Cowell and then John Becker, Carl Ruggles, and Henry Bellamann, a writer—not even Varèse or other American composers who were admirers of Ives. Of course there was John Kirkpatrick later on. I tried to induce Aaron Copland to pay a visit to Ives, and of course Aaron Copland was only too willing. I mentioned this to Ives. He asked me one question—"Is he a good man?" So I assured him that Copland was a good man. But then Ives became too ill, so the meeting never took place.

He never owned a radio, and he never read newspapers, and he never played phonograph records. Of course at that time there were no phonograph records of his works. Again I must say with pride that I was the first to record an Ives composition. That was the *Barn Dance* from *Washington's Birthday,* a New Music recording made in 1934 [vol. 1, no. 5].

Ives asked me to orchestrate some of his songs, which I did under his supervision, and I still own a volume of his *114 Songs* with indications of instrumentation. This was not too successful even though I did it under his supervision. When I performed those songs in 1934, there was something wrong about it. I'm still dubious about orchestrations or reorchestrations of any of his works. I think they ought to be played the way he planned them. Of course, he was extremely liberal in letting people arrange his works, but I always believed that only his original idea was right.

I recall his peculiar sense of humor. It was in a way very old-fashioned and quite different from the genius he revealed in his music. I think that it went together with the simple tunes that he used in practically every one of his works. For instance, I remember the last time I saw him, shortly before he died here in New York, I asked him how he was. He said, "Oh how am I? Look, I can't even spit into the fireplace." Then he suddenly asked me, with a twinkle in his eye, whether I knew why a fishmonger named Jones was not successful in his business. I was completely amazed, so I said, "Why?" You know why—"because he was ine*fish*ent." This was his idea of a joke. He liked puns, and if I were a writer of literary essays I would bring together the love of puns and genius through Shakespeare and James Joyce. They all liked puns, the lowest kind of humor.

There are so many other things to remember about Ives. Of course his complete separation from the world was most amazing. I remember very well that I told him about the second election of Roosevelt to the presidency. He simply didn't know about it. And then I told him what was going on in Germany in 1933. He stood up erect with great emphasis and tremendous thunder in his voice and said, "Then why doesn't someone do something about it?" The brutality of it was simply unacceptable to him. You might think that it was Thoreau or Emerson who was speaking. "Why doesn't someone do something about it?"

Ives was to me an experience, as he was to anyone who came into close contact with him. I believe that it was due to his illness that he found it difficult to meet with people. He suffered from diabetes, and it was difficult for him to write letters or even to speak. He had to have his injections of insulin three times a day, and that made it difficult for him to perform any social functions, if indeed any of his life could be connected with society. But in his mind he was always on fire. I have quite a collection of his letters, copies of which have been deposited in the Yale University Collection of Ivesiana, and it's amazing to see his hesitant writing, sort of like seismographic, oscillographic design. Yet he attended to many details with the few people with whom he did correspond, and I was one of those who was fortunate to be in the Ives circle.

I asked him once whether he ever heard any of the music of Debussy, Stravinsky and so forth, because in one of my articles I stated that he had never heard that music. I believe it was Harmony Ives who corrected me and said that he did hear Stravinsky's *Firebird* way back, maybe in 1912, and perhaps Debussy's *La Mer*. When critics said that he was influenced by Stravinsky or by anybody, it was perfectly ridiculous. He never heard a note of Schoenberg, and he never, never examined any score by Schoenberg. So he was an individual completely separated from the mainstream of music. His world was still old music and romantic music. Of course, he knew his Beethoven, and he knew his Brahms, and in many compositions he has the *Fifth Symphony* of Beethoven. The last movement of *Three Places in New England* is also based on the Beethoven theme, although it is disguised because of the addition of an extra note. Nevertheless, it's still that *Fifth Symphony,* and in the *Alcotts* movement in the *Concord Sonata* there is that Beethoven *Fifth Symphony* again. He felt free to interpolate any kind of musical material that he felt related to the subject. Since the *Fifth Symphony* of Beethoven was a favorite composition in nineteenth-century America, in describing nineteenth-century America—and of course his music really was the portrait of that America, not new America at all—he felt free to use occasional quotations from Brahms and other sources and any number of tunes which were popular late in the nineteenth century.

When I see signs of recognition of Ives, I can't help smiling almost wistfully, remembering what terrible things critics said about him forty years ago. You know, one rather friendly individual asked Ives why he wouldn't compose something people would like to hear. He said, "I can't. I hear something different." Now the world has grown up to what he heard, and the extent of his fame is extraordinary. When I went to Russia five years ago as an American citizen and as an emissary of the State Department on the cultural exchange program, the Russians even in remote districts asked me about Ives, and they knew specifically what they wanted. Needless to say, Ives did absolutely nothing to precipitate his fame, which is largely posthumous anyway. There is a great satisfaction for all of us who believed in Ives when nobody believed in him forty years ago.

I don't believe that he would have enjoyed any kind of honors or even performances of his works. When he received the Pulitzer Award, he said, "Awards and prizes are for school children, and I'm no longer a school boy." He was always satisfied when his music was recognized, or when there were people who believed that he was on the right track. But beyond that I doubt whether it would have made any difference to him. I doubt whether he would have been particularly happy about this tremendous growth of appreciation. He probably would have said, "Well, I wrote my music the way I heard it." Basically it made very little difference to him whether he was or was not played or recognized. He felt that he was doing the right thing, and nobody could change that conviction.

Ives's position was very biased in relation to his friends. People whom he liked, he would stand by—no matter what they did, it was right. Apparently I was one of those people who were, in his mind, doing the right thing. Cowell said in his book on Ives that I perhaps was the first martyr of the cause and that I could have gotten a big orchestra to conduct. Possibly I could have, perhaps the Los Angeles Philharmonic, which was quite serious about this, but I fed them a big dose of Ives and Varèse. It's ironic that forty years ago [December 29, 1932] I conducted *Three Places in New England* in Hollywood, and that was to them anathema, completely unacceptable. Now this very work is programmed this spring by the Los

Programs of Nicolas Slonimsky conducting Three Places in New England in 1931: New York, Budapest, Paris.

Angeles Philharmonic in the Hollywood Bowl as a great attraction because the name of Ives draws. I feel a certain satisfaction because I was the one who conducted it for the first time.

I think that on the whole Ives had a happy life. He was happy with his family, and he was not a tortured human being. Another composer, being a genius, and knowing that he is a genius, might be terribly unhappy about the failure of the world to recognize him. But he didn't seem to be unhappy about it. I don't remember who said it, that in order to achieve universal greatness you must first achieve national greatness, and in achieving national greatness you will become universal if you express your national soul with utmost sincerity and with utmost conviction. This is what Ives did. In his works he seemed to be very provincial, quoting all those tunes from nineteenth-century America, and yet he projected his music universally so that it is understandable to almost anyone anywhere.

Unknown to Ives, a "fan club" was forming in New York in the midtwenties. Composers Jerome Moross and Bernard Herrmann were teenagers from the DeWitt Clinton High School when they discovered Ives. They tried to get everybody they knew interested in Ives—and they succeeded with Arthur Berger when they were all at New York University, and Lehman Engel, whom they met at the Juilliard School. BERNARD HERRMANN became a composer and conductor, particularly active in radio and films. He was the musical director at Columbia Broadcasting Company, conducting the CBS Symphony Orchestra for many years. Herrmann became a successful film and television composer. His films include: Citizen Kane *(1941),* The Snows of Kilimanjaro *(1952), and* Psycho *(1960). Bernard Herrmann now lives and works in London. He was interviewed during a visit to New York on November 12, 1969.*

I must have been only about sixteen or seventeen when I got into Ives [1927 or 1928]. I went to the library (I think it was on 23rd Street off Second Avenue), and they had a small branch that was devoted to music. There I found Ives's *114 Songs.* I was very taken with it. It had his address on it, so I wrote him a note saying how much I liked it. And then I met him shortly afterward. That is how I first knew about him. I just knew the songs. A lot of them I understood and some I didn't.

The people that I mixed with weren't particularly interested in Ives, except Jerome Moross. In the beginning Copland didn't care for Ives's music. Later on, when he really investigated the music, he picked out a selection of the songs for Cos Cob Press, and he became an Ivesian. I studied with Albert Stoessel at the Juilliard Graduate School, and I remember I brought the music to him and he thought it was a big joke, although I lived to actually see him conduct some Ives later on. I guess I put my foot in it all the time with these people, because they didn't know what it was all about.

I conducted some Ives when I was at the Juilliard School with the student orchestra. We did a fugue [from the *Fourth Symphony*] and the piece *In the Night*.* We had a young conductor there named Charlie Lichter† who did some Ives too. And Jerry Moross used to play Ives pieces a good deal. The other piece of Ives's that was played about 1930 was called *Children's Day at the Camp Meeting* [*Fourth Violin Sonata*]. Most people just thought it was all funny, kind of eccentric music. They weren't taken with it at all. Once, I went to see Walter Damrosch, because I was trying to find Ives's *Second Symphony*. Ives thought that he had sent the last copy of the score to Damrosch. Sure enough, Damrosch had it, and we got it back.‡ It was in the same cupboard that he had put it in forty years before. He had never played it.

In 1932, I wrote an article about Ives for a magazine called *Trend*.§ Before I became affiliated with CBS, I played pieces by Ives at various concerts. I went to Camp Tamiment‖ in the Poconos with [critic] Irving Kolodin, who was doing programs there. We did some Ives. I plowed through the movements of the *Concord Sonata*.

I played a lot of Ives's music through the years, and although I always thought there was a certain amount of interest, I never felt that we could

---

*From the *Theater or Chamber Orchestra Set (In the Cage; In the Inn; In the Night)*.

†Charles Lichter has supplied the following information: "My only public conducting of Ives was in the '30s in the days of the WPA orchestras, with one of which—probably the Greenwich Sinfonietta—I programmed four songs with Judith Litante as soloist. I did perform the *Barn Dance* from *Washington's Birthday* at several informal concerts for one or another worthy cause."

‡It is not clear whether this was a score in Ives's own hand or one by a copyist. Indeed, there is now no knowledge of the whereabouts of the "Damrosch" score. Ives was under the impression that Damrosch had lost it. A full score, perhaps by Price or by copyist 9 is listed as "lost" in the Kirkpatrick *Catalogue*. It was necessary for Cowell and Lou Harrison to prepare the published edition of the *Second Symphony* from pencil sketches without the use of a full ink copy of the score.

§"Charles Ives," *Trend: A Quarterly of the Seven Arts* 1, no. 3 (September-November 1932): 99–101.

‖Camp Tamiment was owned by the People's Educational Camp Society, Inc., from 1929 to 1964 or 1965. This was a socialist group which sponsored lectures and concerts by liberal organizations.

THE NEW CHAMBER ORCHESTRA

NEW SCHOOL AUDITORIUM
66 West 12th Street, New York

Wednesday, May 10, 1933
At Eight-Thirty

BERNARD HERRMANN, Conductor

Assisting Artists: Vladimir Dukelsky, composer-pianist; Percy Grainger, composer-pianist; Jerome Moross, composer-pianist; George Rasley, tenor.

Program of British and American Music

Overture to "The Gordian Knot Untied"	PURCELL
Interludes from "Falstaff"	ELGAR
1. "He was page to the Duke of Norfolk."	
2. Gloucestershire. Shallow's Orchard	
†Elegy	McCLEARY
Green Bushes, Passacaglia	GRAINGER
Percy Grainger, soloist	
*Scherzo from Kammersymphonie	JAMES
*Three Songs	HEILNER
1. Canthara	
2. Love Song	
3. K. McB.	
George Rasley, soloist	
*Reel	COWELL

INTERMISSION

Ballade for Piano and Orchestra	DUKELSKY
Vladimir Dukelsky, soloist	
*Fugue from Fourth Symphony	IVES
*Prelude to "Anathema"	HERRMANN
*Ballet	MOROSS
Charleston Rhapsody	BENNETT

†First performance in New York.   *First performance anywhere.

**The British section of this program is under the auspices of the
PERMANENT COMMISSION FOR INTERNATIONAL EXCHANGE
CONCERTS.**

Concert program. Bernard Herrmann conducting the Fugue *from the* Fourth Symphony.
The date is incorrect—the concert took place on May 17, 1933.

get the real kind of interest of a big public. And I don't think that has been achieved even now. I think certain works have a good chance. They have become sort of acceptable, but most people don't have the touchstone for listening to Ives, and much of the music is still alien to the listening public.

In the thirties I tried to get the Budapest Quartet to play the *First Quartet* and they wouldn't consider it, because they said it was just a lot of cheap American religious music themes. That got me irritated, and I said, "Well, it is no different from Haydn." They said, "What do you mean? Haydn is a great composer." And I said, "Yeah, but there were cheap beer garden tunes in his quartets." They said, "Oh, that's different." And I said, "No, it isn't different. You don't mind them, but you mind these. That's all." And they never played Ives, because they never really had a feeling for him.

I worked with Ives on the *First String Quartet*. We worked on the score together, adding a bass part and all that. I still don't know where Kirkpatrick got that fugue which he tacked on, but that's his business. I don't think it belongs there. It belongs to the *Fourth Symphony*. I don't think it fits the *First Quartet* at all.*

I conducted the first performance in England of the *Second Symphony* with the BBC.† And I remember when I first conducted part of Ives's *Fourth Symphony* in about 1937 for the BBC, that they didn't have as much trouble with it as the Americans did, because the English didn't expect anything to happen to the basic material the way Americans do. Americans hear *Bringing in the Sheaves,* and they think it ought to go one way, but the English don't sing *Bringing in the Sheaves,* so they don't mind what you do. They hear it with different ears. Of course, at that time, there was another conductor who was very taken with Ives, the English conductor, Eugene Goossens. What I really resent today, even in England, is that they seem to think that they have just discovered Ives right now. But I don't really feel that from 1930 he was a totally neglected composer. He never got mainstream performances in the sense that Copland did, but he didn't write accessible music, and he wasn't fashionable. Now he is fashionable. But earlier some of the leading composers did a lot of his songs and chamber ensemble pieces at the New School and on the radio. I remember I did an orchestration of the song, *Charlie Rutlage* for CBS.

---

*The *First String Quartet* in its early sources had four movements: *Chorale, Prelude, Offertory, Postlude.* The *Chorale,* a fugue, was transferred to the *Fourth Symphony* after it was revised for orchestra in 1909. The numbering of the remaining last three movements was then changed from 2, 3, 4 to 1, 2, 3. It is the original *Chorale* (fugue) which John Kirkpatrick has reinstated to the *First String Quartet.*

†The performance with the London Symphony Orchestra was May 25, 1956. It was recorded May 9, 1956.

Not all Ives's music is very complicated. If I did something that was simple, I remember everybody, including the critics, would say, "It really isn't typical Ives because it isn't complex." Yet I think his best music is his simple music. It is more original. He really wrote everything for that New Haven theater,* and he always liked the theater-sized orchestra. I never found that he cared really for the full symphony orchestra in the sense that other people do. The most involved or difficult music became the thing that the new crowd seized on as being Ives, but I don't feel that that is the best part of Ives. The best part of Ives is always the very simple parts, the very simple statements he makes. The *Second Quartet* is so much more difficult than the *First,* and I never yet met a quartet that really enjoyed it. They never seem to be able to lick it. But Ives told me he didn't like music that was easy to play and easy to perform. He wanted to give the performers a workout. Well, not everybody wants a workout. I know he told me that he thought Toscanini was just a lot of lady-finger music. He said old ladies listen to that kind of music. I didn't mind any of that. The only thing I objected to really about Ives was the sheer mechanics of getting people to play the music.

Ives was ambivalent about his music. He really financed *New Music,* but he didn't want them to print anything of his. There was a big row about that. Also, he had an instinct that in order to do his works, the people who were really interested in him, all composers themselves, would have to give up so much of their own time, and he didn't want that sacrifice. He would say, "You have your own music to write, why bother with this? But don't forget, put it in ink, put it in ink." I remember his once telling me about how Nicolas Slonimsky went and ruined a marvelous career trying to shove Ives's music down people. He said, "Imagine, they not only invite him to the Hollywood Bowl, but the idiot wants to go and play something of mine. Of course, they will throw him out." I dedicated my cantata *Moby Dick* to Ives. He told me not to, because, he said, "if they see my name on it, they will throw bricks at you." But I paid no attention to him.

He had a negative attitude about his music. After he finished it, he wasn't interested in it. Oh, he was pleased if someone else took an interest, but he always found reasons why you shouldn't bother with it. It wouldn't do your career any good. It was too difficult. It wasn't right. It wasn't worth

---

*Herrmann refers here to the Hyperion Theater where, during Ives's college years in New Haven, a few of his works were tried out by the small orchestra. Ives actually composed some works for this group. It was led by Frank Fichtl. The second and fourth movements of the *Second Symphony* were originally written as overtures for the Hyperion Theater Orchestra.

spending all the time. I think he was more interested in just writing his own pieces and that was it. That is why they all exist in such terrible states. He wasn't interested enough to take off time to do the proofreading.

Ives was completely dependent on what his copyists did, and he never proofread. The first copyist was very good, but later on he got some others who made mistakes. Because of the parts, it was terrible in the early days to try to achieve an Ives performance. All Ives did was get the copyist to photograph the score and then cut it up. They would put each part of the score on a piece of paper so that you would have two bars, and then the poor musician would have to count out fourteen bars silence, and then he would find a few little notes. He would be reading actually from a full score. The parts were not copied and collated and corrected. So it was always very difficult. Anything that I ever did of Ives, I have always found that I had to go from the very beginning and make a duplicate copy of the score and make sure of everything, including all the dynamics, and then have it recopied, which is always a great undertaking. Every time I asked him about a wrong note or anything, he would say, "You know better than I, so correct it." Or he'd say, "If it doesn't seem right to you, you know what to do about it." And many times he couldn't see well enough to know what was the problem. Sometimes you would talk to him for a whole hour and then he would say, "Of course, you can leave off the trumpet if you don't like it or put it back in again." I asked him about one spot, and he said, "*tacet* the trumpet," and I said, "You can't mean that, leaving out that marvelous bit on the trumpet?" And he said, "Well, put it in if you like." I think everybody is all wrong about Ives's attitude on this. I don't think that it had anything to do with giving performers options or varying from performance to performance. I think his music is a kind of abstraction that exists on paper and he just went by and said that would be nice if we added something else and just added to it. But it had nothing to do with the result of the performance or even revision. I never thought of the different versions of the *Concord Sonata* as being any improvement over the original one that was printed. I just feel—well, that's some chips off it or some extra pieces tacked onto it. It is not a matter of which one is the better. Ives, after all, was a very impractical man when it came to performances of music. By not being a professional musician in the sense that he did not have to make a living out of music, he entered into an abstraction of music. Because it was an abstraction, it didn't deal with any of the realistic problems.

I don't think Ives ever listened to other people's music. Of Debussy he most likely knew *The Afternoon of a Faun,* and that is all. It is part of his originality that his music developed without any reference to other music.

I know he told me that they had a manservant working there in the house, and he said, "Oh, this fellow's a great Sibelius man. I myself never heard anything of Sibelius other than *Valse Triste*."

Ives was not much interested in the social aspect. He wasn't like Vaughan Williams in his old age. Vaughan Williams would love to come to every performance even though he was quite deaf, and he would put up this hearing thing and go, "Oh, ha ha. Yes. Doing pretty well, isn't it?" Ives didn't have any of that. He had no interest in it at all.

Ives was the last of the transcendental school. They had a different attitude about things. Ives's writing was part of his function of being alive, much to the bewilderment of his friends, relatives, and most likely of his wife. All the Walt Whitman crowd had their own way of protesting. Their way was either to use commonplaces or to become very metaphysical. Ives, when he got this thing against war, wrote all these pieces of music and articles against war. And when war was declared, what did he do but go off and give the government two completely equipped ambulances.

People looking around at Ives to find his musical technique or form are all wasting their time, because he didn't have any. I think he made up each technique for each piece. It wasn't even a technique; it was some kind of a miasma that hit him and then he went to work on it. Ives's music doesn't go on in time and space. His music is a photographic replica in sound of a happening. His *The Fourth of July* is a replica not of all Fourth of Julys, but of one. *Washington's Birthday* is the same. I once asked him about *Washington's Birthday,* "Do you want the bells at the end or not?" And he said, "Oh well, there are times when they make a lovely sound— you know, like sleigh bells." When I do it, I always try to get sleigh bells. Everything in him is something that he heard happen which he transferred and caught at a moment in time like a photograph.

Nature was very important to Ives in all his music. He resented that there were no longer barns. I used to say, "Why do you stay so long out in Redding?" "Oh," he said, "I love to stay that late; the corn gets so golden and the pumpkins are there. What is nicer than to just sit and watch?"

Ives had some original expressions. For instance, he would have a kind of simple melody and then a little complicated secondary thing that would run across it like maybe a flute doing something very fast. And he said, "That's what I call shadow counterpoint. It's a shadow that the main thing throws off." I was very taken with the expression "shadow counterpoint," and I mentioned it to Schoenberg, and he was quite taken with it too. But I have never seen it referred to by anybody else, although I thought it was a marvelous way of describing that kind of musical happening.

Ives was working at music in a very difficult time in American music. After all, even as distinguished a composer as Edward MacDowell went down the booby hatch. Ives really didn't get on with the establishment in his time, because the establishment were all Germans. They went to Luchows and they heard the same old music all the time. Ives was on 74th Street, and across the street was the David Mannes School. Ives would watch young ladies getting fiddle lessons, and he used to say, "Look at that old guy across there teaching that lovely girl how to murder music. That is where they go every day. They walk into that building and they walk out more ignorant than before." I remember that I met Leopold Mannes at a concert. He never knew that Ives lived across the street from him. And Ives had no real feeling for the real light American music like Victor Herbert had. I remember I asked him about something he used from the theater. I said, "Where did you get that tune, Charlie?" because I knew it wasn't his. "Can you remember the name?" He said, "No, I can't remember."

And then the way he stopped writing music I thought was very odd. One day he just announced to his wife that he was all finished. Now I think I can explain to you what I think happened to him. Not having any kind of audience at all, I think that he became absolutely fatigued and said, "I have had it. Good-bye." The vacuum broke. It just broke for him. The impetus was gone. And then I think that by the time young people came around and began to take an interest in his music, it was too late for him. I always felt that if he had been in the mainstream of practical music making, it might have been a different story. I don't say for the better. Maybe he wouldn't appeal to us now. Any artist who can make up his mind to spend three-quarters of his life being an insurance man and another quarter being an artist is a pretty unique compromise. It is not often done. It is a very difficult thing to maintain the equilibrium, and I think that he fell off it. He couldn't maintain it after a while. Ives was a very great man, and I don't think that he ever really enjoyed the fruits of his music. By the time it came, it was too late for him. Really, too late.

෫

JEROME MOROSS discovered the music of Ives when he was about fifteen. He became a composer of orchestral and ballet music and has written extensively for radio and theater. Mr. Moross was interviewed in New York City, on September 19, 1969.

Whenever I hear the music of Charles Ives, it takes me right back to about 1928 when Benny Herrmann and I found a copy of the *Second Piano Sonata [Concord]* in the Half-Price Music Shop, which has since become Patelson's. At that time it was on 57th Street between Eighth and Ninth Avenues. I was going to school at the old DeWitt Clinton High School which was at 59th Street and Tenth Avenue. Coming home every afternoon we always walked by 57th Street and dropped into the old Half-Price Music Shop. And there we found Ives. I was studying piano then and writing. I saved a dollar out of my weekly allowance and went without lunches to buy the sonata. At first it was impossible for me to play it. But then bit by bit I got to the point where I could play some of it.

We found other things. Benny found a copy of the *114 Songs*. We were always trying to play some of the songs. I remember that a big thing was to play *Shall We Gather at the River,* Benny on the violin and I at the piano. Benny and I were at Juilliard, but I had known Benny from high school. We got Arthur Berger interested in Ives, too. I met him because he lived around the corner from me in Brooklyn. And Lehman Engel we met at Juilliard. The Ives fan club was just the four of us, as far as we knew. We avidly collected anything of his we could find—the few things he had published himself and the things that Henry Cowell had published. Among other things, I had learned the movement *In the Inn* from the *First Piano Sonata.* Benny, Lehman, and I gave a concert at the Juilliard in which we played avant-garde music. The Juilliard was not very receptive at that time to anything new. Among the things we played was a piece of mine called *Paeans* which Henry Cowell heard that night. He got very excited and came backstage and introduced himself to me. I was eighteen at the time, and Cowell was an extraordinarily important figure to a young musician.

We had a meeting after that and we talked and got to know each other, and among other things, I played him the *In the Inn* movement from the *First Piano Sonata.* He asked me to play it at one of his symposiums at the New School. Henry Cowell took Benny and me to meet Ives in his house in New York. Henry and Ives were extremely friendly and from all I could

First Festival

of

Contemporary American Music

Yaddo

Saratoga Springs
New York

April thirtieth and May first
nineteen hundred thirty-two

ASSISTING ARTISTS

ADA MAC LEISH, Soprano   HUBERT LINSCOTT, Baritone
JESUS MARIA SANROMA, Pianist   JOHN KIRKPATRICK, Pianist
GEORGES LAURENT, Flutist

HANS LANGE QUARTET

H. LANGE, First Violin   Z. KURTHY, Viola
A. SCHULLER, Second Violin   P. SUCH, Cello

LEAGUE OF COMPOSERS QUARTET

N. BEREZOWSKY, First Violin   M. STILLMAN, Viola
M. MUSCANTO, Second Violin   D. FREED, Cello

COMPOSER-PIANISTS

GEORGE ANTHEIL   AARON COPLAND
VIVIAN FINE   OSCAR LEVANT

THIRD CONCERT

SUNDAY AFTERNOON   MAY FIRST

At two-fifteen

SONATA FOR FLUTE AND PIANO   Walter Piston
1. Allegro moderato e grazioso   2. Adagio
3. Allegro vivace
MR. LAURENT and MR. SANROMA

* SEVEN SONGS   Charles Ives
1. The Indians (Charles Sprague)
2. Walking (Ives)
3. Serenity (Whittier)
4. Maple Leaves (Thomas B. Aldrich)
5. The See'r (Ives)
6. Evening (Milton)
7. Charlie Rutlage (Cowboy Ballads)
MR. LINSCOTT and MR. COPLAND

* SUITE FOR FLUTE AND PIANO   Henry Brant
1. Madrigal   2. Minuet   3. Saraband   4. Toccata
MR. LAURENT and MR. SANROMA

INTERMISSION

PIANO VARIATIONS (1930)   Aaron Copland
THE COMPOSER

SUITE FOR FLUTE SOLO   Wallingford Riegger
1. Moderato   2. Vivace   3. Molto con sentimento
4. Allegro ironico
MR. LAURENT

✝ SECOND STRING QUARTET   Silvestre Revueltas
Allegro giocoso—Lento—Molto vivace— Allegro molto sostenuto
HANS LANGE QUARTET

Program from the Yaddo concert in which Copland presented seven songs by Ives.

gather, it had gone on for quite a while, because Henry had discovered Ives way back. But nobody had listened.

I remember Ives at that first meeting. He was resting on a chaise longue and looked very tired and very old to me. Of course, he was about forty years older than I was. This was somewhere around February or March of 1932. I played *In the Inn* for him. He was very excited that young men were beginning to get interested. He loaded Benny Herrmann and myself with scores, which he either published or had photostated and bound. We took all our copies and we became great Ives evangelists. I kept seeing Ives. In 1932, Aaron Copland had started a group called the Young Composers Group. One of our main points was to get Aaron interested in Ives. That spring Aaron was doing the first of the Yaddo Festivals, and we insisted that he must play Ives. I brought my copy of the songs; we played some of them for Aaron, and I left them with him. Aaron got fascinated with them and did do a set of Ives songs at the festival.

Earlier the first and second movements of the *Fourth Symphony* had been played by Goossens. I was too young to hear that, but Cowell had published the second movement and it was kind of our bible. Everybody in the group had a copy of this and we pored over it. Benny got some money somewhere to give a series of concerts, and he got me into it, and the two of us were busy working on these concerts. We played a number of pieces by Ives, but the most interesting thing was that Ives gave us the first and third movements of the *Fourth Symphony,* which he said would fit our orchestra, because these movements were for a much smaller orchestra than the other two. He gave us this incredible photostat of a manuscript, and we were just appalled at the start. It took us weeks of calling and going back and checking on notes with him. Benny and I worked on it, and we made a clean copy. He'd work on it some; I'd work on it some. We took it up to Ives twice to check notes and phrasing and things like that. We couldn't decipher the terrible manuscript, and Ives had to make the final decision of what he had meant. Then there was one movement [the fourth] that he couldn't find at the time. The manuscripts were just a mad mess in a closet he had. But we did get the third movement [Fugue] in shape, and we played it at the New School, Benny conducting. This was May 17, 1933. And so by that time, three movements of the *Fourth Symphony* had been presented already. It was startling to everybody, because they thought that the *Fourth Symphony* was this impossible mess of sound. The concert was supported by money contributed mostly by Broadway people. Benny and I got a lot of people like composers Hans Spialek and Robert Russell Bennett and others to contribute money.

I would go over to see Ives every four or five months. That went on for about three or four years. But in the fall of 1936 I went to Chicago and then to Los Angeles. I was not in New York much for a long time, and I never saw Ives again. All the time I knew him, Ives seemed to me terribly old and terribly sickly, and yet he was probably only in his fifties. I never knew what his illness was, but the fact that Charles was sick was a very kind of awesome thing to all of us, and something had to be done about this man before it was too late. I called him Mr. Ives at the start and then once he asked me to call him Charles. That was just before the last time I saw him. I found it very difficult to call him Charles and I would kind of alternate between saying Charles and saying Mr. Ives. He didn't care—he just let it go. Suddenly I have a memory of his once coming down to a concert where something of his was being played. I can't remember exactly what it was, but I have a remembrance of Mr. Ives and Mrs. Ives in a concert hall. He had a shawl around his shoulders, very Victorian and old-fashioned—literally with a shawl around his shoulders! I remember all of us flocking to greet him.

I don't think he ever heard any of my music. Henry sent him copies of everything that *New Music* published, and so consequently he had a couple of my things, but his own music involved him terribly at the time. This is just speculation on my part, but I imagine he was afraid that it might die with him, and he was very delighted to have us doing what we could.

In those days if we had a performance of an American composer once a month in the music listings in the *New York Times,* we thought it was marvelous. It was strictly the European tradition then. Every now and then they would play somebody like Daniel Gregory Mason or Reuben Goldmark. We always used to wait for Koussevitzky concerts, because once or twice a year he'd play a piece by Aaron Copland. Then later on, he played one or two things of Roy Harris. But if you wanted to hear people like Ives or Ruggles or Varèse, you had to go to concerts conducted by Nicolas Slonimsky or by Benny Herrmann.

ARTHUR BERGER joined Benny Herrmann and Jerome Moross in their enthusiasm for Ives's music. In an interview in Boston, on October 19, 1970, Berger said,

We were the three holy terrors down at N.Y.U. . . . I did not go to see Ives—I had just seen my mother through a lengthy illness, and I felt particularly sensitive to Ives's ill health. I was given to understand that provocative discussions about politics or music were to be avoided, since Ives could become unduly excited if he disagreed, and such excitement could lead to harmful physical consequences. I was in the midst of the various controversies of the time, and polemic was a normal aspect of my conversational style.

Berger wrote several excellent articles about Ives, and he delivered a radio talk in the early thirties which included some of his music. Remembering early performances, Berger in his interview said,

Nobody heard really good performances in those days. Perhaps it was because of the movement to have simplified music in the thirties. . . . At one time, my historical sense was disturbed about the mixture of styles in Ives, but it doesn't bother me at all now. Attitudes change—what seemed like crudity then, takes a completely different aspect now. It's the whole gestalt—his life, the typical artist in the American scene, the isolation, the fact that we don't have the tradition here, even now. . . . Would Ives have written differently if he could have felt more comfortable with the background tradition? Would he have fixed up the things which I found defective, or is it really all part of what he wanted to do? . . . I admit that I am unobjective about Ives. I can take the moods of the Concord Sonata *and* Three Places in New England *and love them for the evocations of mood itself. Some of my latest colleagues, the serialists, don't get the Ives thing at all—it's too informal for them— but I admit that I like some things sometimes and others not at all, and I think that Ives would probably be the first to say that some moments are worth going back to and others are not. . . . One time, in the forties, when I was in a very neoclassic period, I went to a performance of the* Second String Quartet *up at Columbia, and I just didn't like it. I saw Paul Rosenfeld, and he said, "Wasn't that ending heavenly?" and I said, "Anything would sound heavenly after all that dissonance." Well, Paul got red in the face and he really let loose at me—"You and your neo-*

classicist friends!" I felt sorry about it because I think it was the last time I saw Paul Rosenfeld. But I have had other times with Ives's music that were gems—like Easley Blackwood playing the Concord Sonata. . . . *I think the real thing that Ives was prophetic about was the whole idea of catching action—that sense of improvisation—and yet it's achieved with the performers playing the notes that are written. . . . There is something that's very real about Ives's music, and it reaches one, doesn't it?*

LUCILLE FLETCHER WALLOP is an author, particularly known for the screenplay Sorry, Wrong Number *and, more recently, for the play* Nightwatch. *In the Ives Collection are fragments of a typescript, "A Connecticut Yankee in Music," written in 1939 by Lucille Fletcher and intended to be a* New Yorker *profile of Ives. Lucille Fletcher Wallop was one of the people influenced by the enthusiasm of Bernard Herrmann (they were married in 1939) and Jerome Moross and what she calls "the stream of excitement and ferment" in the arts during the late twenties and thirties. She talked about this and about Ives in an interview in New York on August 18, 1972.*

I went to Vassar and was the music critic there for two years. Vassar was an ardent school—it was women's lib, way back. I was very active musically and hoped to be a music critic, but the best I could do when I left Vassar was to get a typing job at CBS for fifteen dollars a week, including Saturdays and overtime. And that's where I met Benny. Almost immediately he began to tell me about Ives. Benny played me a lot of Ives's music; we used to go to the Liberty Music Store, get records of all kinds of music, and go to their listening room to play them—and then never buy the records. Benny took me to concerts of contemporary music at Town Hall, and I met some of the composers. They cared about causes, they cared about the underdog, and the social system. They were terribly ardent. I was in the thick of that, and Benny was one of those who really drew me in. I did fan mail for some of the composers—I answered all of Carlos Chavez's mail; he gave me a job because I could speak Spanish. Moross I knew very well too, and Arthur Berger. Benny was so enthusiastic about Ives and on fire about the injustices of American composers not being recognized. It's interesting to think that these boys, who were of a totally different culture, most of them born on the East Side of New York—their parents from Russia—should have been so enamored with this truly American, old-fashioned, New England atmosphere and found it and loved it so. They weren't hammering for themselves—it was a feeling of what the country was. They were also interested in South American music—composers like Villa-Lobos, and they were publishing him very early. And Chavez, too. There was more of a meshing then, too, of the Broadway people and the young composers from the streets and from the colleges than there seems to be now. There wasn't so much snobbism about writing pop. It seemed that there was great hope then for all kinds of music.

Benny suggested that I write a novel about Ives. We used to ride back and forth on the subway, and we used to talk about this novel. And then I started writing it. It was a novel called *Idle Thunder*; and I did that in addition to all the commercial things. But that novel was going to be my introduction to the literary world. I worked on that novel, and I finished it after Benny and I were married. But I submitted that novel to twenty-eight publishers, and nobody wanted it. So it's still there; someday I'm going to fish it out and read it again to see if it's any good. My composer in the book was supposed to have written a cantata on Moby Dick. Well, one day in the subway Benny was hearing about this and he said, "By golly, I'm going to write it myself." And he did, and he got his cantata, *Moby Dick,* performed at the Philharmonic by Barbirolli and the Westminster Choir with Robert Weede, who was then an unknown baritone, singing the part of Ahab—before my novel was even finished. During this time [mid-thirties], I did some pieces for the *New Yorker* and two or three profiles about radio things. They were for the column *Onward and Upward with the Arts.* They would pick an idiot subject. I did one on the history of the musical saw, and that was some research job! And then I wrote one on animal imitators in radio and movies, and I did one on sound effects. So the *New Yorker* got to know me. One day, once the Ives fever began after the *Concord Sonata* concert by Kirkpatrick in Town Hall, they asked me if I would do a profile on Ives. By that time I think I had met him once, or maybe I met him afterward, I don't remember, but as I recall, I only saw Ives twice in all. I went with Benny. Ives met us at the head of the stairs, and he seemed very flushed, very tense and friendly and excited—shaking with excitement. We went into the front parlor, which was all sunlight and old-fashioned furniture, and there was a cat curled up in the chair. Ives talked very feverishly. He would get himself terribly worked up to an extent that he would suddenly gasp for breath and then have to lie down. And nobody ever stopped him from carrying on. He seemed to approve having me write the profile, so I set to work to do the research. Later that fall, Benny and I were married. And that whole year I spent traveling about interviewing people. I went to see Mr. Slonimsky, I went out to Redding to the Ives home, and I went to see Ives's brother a week before he died in Danbury in the old Ives home. He talked to me at great length.

I wrote the article, and called it "A Connecticut Yankee in Music." The *New Yorker's* policy was not to submit a profile for anybody to approve, but I submitted mine to Mr. Ives, and it caused a furor—he wanted practically everything taken out. He wanted to put in a great section on an amendment that he had, and he wanted most of the piece at the end devoted to his ideas on peace. It meant a tremendous amount to him. I don't think he ever read the *New Yorker* or knew the kind of thing they wanted. Well, as time went on, we just couldn't come to any terms at all; the thing was totally emasculated. I decided that he was too old, he was too fine a person, and he was too sick to push it. I couldn't please him, and what I would have left would be nothing. So I said to the *New Yorker,* "I won't submit it— it's not good enough." I withdrew it. It had taken about six months and a lot of legwork, but I told Mr. Ives that he could forget about it. Well, he was very pleased, and he insisted on sending me a hundred dollars. And then when Benny and I were married, he gave us a hundred dollars; and then when my first child was born, he sent her a beautiful little silver drinking cup. He was very sweet; and he was happy that the matter was over. He really did not want any publicity. I don't think that he was a person who had been burned by publicity, but I think in his case it was a true sense of privacy. His music spoke for him, and I think that's what he wanted. Soon after this, Benny and I went to Hollywood, and I didn't see Mr. Ives again.

The Pro Musica concert of January 29, 1927, in which Goossens con-ducted some of the Fourth Symphony, *included also the American premiere of Darius Milhaud's opera* Les Malheurs d'Orphée. *It was during this time that Robert Schmitz introduced Milhaud to Ives.*

DARIUS MILHAUD was interviewed in Aix-en-Provence, France, on July 25, 1970. He recalls with pleasure attending a lunch for himself and his wife Madeleine at the Ives house in New York. "I had a wonderful time with Ives because he was such an interesting man. And I always admired his music from the first I knew of it. There are four composers who had been neglected for a long time, and now are being heard finally: Erik Satie, Edgard Varèse, Charles Koechlin, and Charles Ives."

Another composer who met Ives in the twenties was DANE RUDHYAR. Rudhyar, born in France as Daniel de Chennevière, is a composer of experimental piano music and a poet, painter, and writer. His primary interest in recent years has been in the field of astrological philosophy. He is the author of several books on this subject. A visit was made to Rudhyar in San Jacinto, California, on March 18, 1970.

I met Ives in New York. I am not sure now of the year. But I think I corresponded with him first, and then I went to his house twice. This must have been around '25 or '26. I was in New York those two summers. I had written a piece called *Five Stanzas* for strings which was about to be published, and he offered to have the parts copied for me. He didn't comment at all on my music. He saw the score and he said, "Well, that thing should be copied." He said, "Have you done the parts?" I said, "No, I have no time." And he said, "All right, I'll have it done for you." And then later on he sent me some money to buy a little lot in New Mexico, in Santa Fe, where I was going to build. He was very nice to me. And he was very generous to the New Music Society started by Cowell which I helped to organize.

Once I had lunch in New York with Ives, his wife, and his daughter. When I saw him at first, he had no beard and looked quite young. And another time we climbed to the top of his house and he played something for me. And, of course, I had the experience that everybody had—you expected the poor man to die every second, because he was supposed to have terrible heart trouble and then he would climb to the fourth floor of that brownstone house. When he played on the piano—it was a little upright—he danced, jumped on the seat, shouted, and sang. If Cowell had not told me that he had heart trouble, I would never have known it. He was very exuberant.

The composers who visited Ives, who admired him and tried to get performances going of his works, were not colleagues. They were, for the most part, of a younger generation, and they looked up to Ives as to an elder pioneer in the lonely battle for modern music. They were somewhat in awe

of him, and his long years of illness removed him even further from them.
There were only a few who could really be considered colleagues, and even
these few, but for Carl Ruggles, were between about ten and twenty-five
years younger than Ives. This "group" consisted of John Becker (1886–
1961), Henry Cowell (1897–1965), Wallingford Riegger (1885–1961),
Carl Ruggles (1876–1971), and Adolph Weiss (1891–1971). None of
these composers met Ives until past his fiftieth year, and one strong com-
mon factor drew them together—the cause of modern music. They never
met as a group, or functioned as one, and they did not influence each
other's music. Ives had finished composing long since, and, with a few
exceptions, he neither saw nor heard other composers' works. These com-
posers were not interested in finding similarities of musical styles (although
they all disliked neoclassicism), but they were passionately dedicated to
independent thinking and to breaking with the traditions of the past.

CARL RUGGLES and Charles Ives liked to talk about who was the
greatest modern composer. Ruggles's son, Micah, says, "Dad said Mr. Ives
was. Mr. Ives said Dad was. I never did find out who was. But of all the
composers that my father knew, he considered Mr. Ives the most dedicated
and respected him more than all the rest." Ives and Ruggles are often
bracketed together. They were, after all, the closest in age, and they were
very fond of each other. This closeness extended to Charlotte Ruggles and
to Micah, who became a professional athlete, and this, of course, interested
Ives very much. Ives obviously took great pleasure in Ruggles's salty humor
and his New England rugged individualism, and he chose to ignore
Ruggles's prejudices and extreme political conservatism. Once Ives ac-
cepted a friend, moreover, an all-encompassing loyalty went to work.

Carl Ruggles was ninety-three when he was interviewed on February 28,
1969, in a rest home in Arlington, Vermont, not far from the converted
schoolhouse which had been his home for many years.

Ives saw my *Men and Mountains* in *New Music* [vol. 1, no. 1, 1927],
and he was crazy about it. We met soon after that. Then *Sun-Treader* was
played in Paris [February 25, 1932], and the conductor [Slonimsky] said
he would need more money—it wasn't going well. Varèse was over there,
and he sent word to Ives, and Ives immediately sent him a thousand dollars
for more rehearsals. Slonimsky also conducted Ives's *Three Places in New
England* in Paris. Later, Stokowski conducted my music, and Ives and I
were going to have a concert together, each one choosing from his own

works, Stokie conducting. That would have been something, wouldn't it? But it didn't happen.

There's one man who had a great deal to do with Ives's music. That's Mr. Henry Cowell. You're talking about somebody when you talk about him. Cowell had a great deal to do with Ives's *Fourth Symphony*. Henry had genius, and Ives knew it, and Ives liked him tremendously. Cowell published *New Music*, and I made the cover for one of Ives's works.*

Charlotte and I used to go out to West Redding. Ives had a little adopted daughter, and she had a friend who was crazy about my son, Micah. And Ives thought my son was grand. One Christmastime at West Redding Ives came out from the dining room with a check and said, "Here's something for Christmas, you and Charlotte, and I don't want to hear a God damn word out of you about it." That's a little specimen of him.

He had a different kind of humor, altogether different kind. He used to like to kid my wife and Harmony [by] whispering jokes to me.

I heard him play at West Redding. He was a grand pianist. I wish I was as good a violinist as he was a pianist. I never heard a better pianist in my life than he was. I was there when Ives threw the *Browning* [*Overture*] piece. He didn't like it. He was so sick then. You know, he never ate anything. "To hell with the goddamn thing," he said. He'd swear something terrible. He could even beat me swearing. He said, "The goddamn thing is no good." And he took it and threw it clear across the dining room floor. I got up, went over to get that score back. I said, "I don't think I would say that, when I hear such phrases as here and here and here. Such magnificent music as that. I wouldn't talk like that." He said, "You think that?" I said, "I certainly do." That was the episode.

When Varèse had the chorus in New York, he wrote to Ives. He wanted to make changes here and there, and wouldn't Ives be good enough to let him do it, and Ives told him to go ahead. Nobody knows this.†

I like the beautiful symphonic work called *The Housatonic at Stock-*

Lincoln, The Great Commoner, New Music, vol. 26, no. 2 (1953).

†Varèse was director of the Greater New York Chorus in the forties. Correspondence with Ives reveals that Varèse wrote, expressing his desire to perform the *Harvest Home Chorales*. He was concerned about the rhythmic difficulty of the *Second Chorale,* and wrote Ives (February 29, 1944), "I don't know of any chorus, certainly not mine, capable of keeping up with this computative subdivision." Varèse asked Ives if he should perform only the *First* and *Third Chorales.* Mrs. Ives answered, "Anything you think best to do will be quite all right with him." By July, Varèse wrote: "Beating in 3 (3/2 instead of 2/2) will solve the problem, resulting in a precise subdivision. . . . With your approval it is how I plan to have the work studied." Varèse included a few measures of a musical example. Again Mrs. Ives answered for Mr. Ives, "He says whatever you think best to do in performing the *Chorales* will be quite all right with him. . . . On account of his eye condition . . . he can't see the measures in your letter." After all, reason unknown, Varèse did not perform this work.

Arlington Vermont
May 21, 47

Dear Charles:

Congratulations!
Belated my dear,
But from the Heart,
You certainly deserved
the Honor. It has
taken them a long time
to see the Light, but
that seems to be the
History of all Creators.

I do hope we can
see you this Summer.
Last year we had planned
for it, but unforseen circum-
stances prevented. Our
Love to you and Harmony,

Always, Carl
And Charlotte

"We are living in an age which is fast hardening into a wretched scientific precision. All of Paul Gauguin's creed which is applicable today.

A letter from Carl Ruggles to Ives congratulating Ives on receiving the Pulitzer Prize.

Dear Carl.

Just a few snake tracks from an "ole fellers" shaky paw", to tell you, that you are the best composer in Europe, Asia, Africa, any America — but if you should get a Pulitza Prize sunshine, y'" then that would mean that "you aint" —

we were very glad to hear from you that you + Charlotte are back in old New England whare the Rocky Hills an Plumy Elms sing out "one to River".

we do hope that we will see you both coming up Umpawaug Hill some time this summer, to stay here for a while.

with our love to you both

Ives's response to Ruggles's letter regarding the Pulitzer Prize.

bridge. That's a very fine orchestral work. And if Ives never wrote but one song, he would have been a great composer. That's *General William Booth Enters Into Heaven*. Now, I don't think anybody's said that before, have they? When I was teaching in Florida, I made them hear it. No one there had a voice that could sing it. It's a very great song. It's a song of genius, that's all.

Carl Ruggles, ca. 1960. Photo Clara Sipprell.

Dr. John J. Becker was the only composer of the advanced guard in the Midwest. Becker suffered from incredible neglect of his own works, but he was indefatigable in his attempts to bring the works of his contemporaries to a conservative public. A gauge of Becker's taste and progressive thinking can be made from the ending of an article about Ives which he wrote for the Northwest Music Herald *in 1933: "When the history of American music is finally written one of the most brilliant names in its pages will be that of Charles E. Ives. It will stand forth not only as a sign of a great composer, but as a living symbol of a great man." Becker and Ives became close friends in the thirties. EVELYN (MRS. JOHN J.) BECKER described that friendship in an interview on October 8, 1973, in Evanston, Illinois.*

John had written an article that was published in November of 1930 entitled "Fine Arts and the Soul of America." The article was published in the *Religious Journal,* and Henry Cowell took the article over to Ives to read. Ives was very impressed with it and wrote John about it. I think that the reason that they became friends so quickly was that Mr. Ives was able to take John's measure as a man from that article. John had written,

> People talk about a cultural revival in the United States, and if one considers bad radio programs, moving pictures, material profits, they might be right. But if one refers to a deep spiritual development brought about by deep spiritual contact with cultural things, those things that have to do with soul-processes and those things which after religion inspire one, such as an intellectual contemplation of music, art, and literature, it is not true. America has a soul, but as far as aesthetics are concerned, it is nearly lost and is floundering around and is saved only by the starving creative artist. . . . Where are the small opera companies, orchestras, singers, theatres?

John then outlined a four-year program to include courses in art and music right along with the regular college curriculum, and he wrote: "By aesthetic education I mean a familiarity with the arts that enables one to see the relationship of the arts to God and with this knowledge help men to bring about the development of their own souls." And one can understand why this would especially appeal to Charles Ives. John's educational plan was somewhat carried out when he was at St. Thomas as chairman of fine arts. In response to this article Ives wrote that he had not heard of any other colleges taking such a stand and that, "One usually hears of the burial of Latin and Greek together with the fine arts and over the spot a stone palace with a thousand bathtubs with a pretty sheepskin for the head plumber." Ives asked for extra copies of the article to send to his friends, for those he thought would be interested and "for those who ought to be, if they weren't."

A short time before John met Charlie Ives, he had started to give concerts of modern music in St. Paul, Minnesota, at St. Thomas College. The concerts were without any fee or admission, and neither was any hat passed for a donation. In these concerts John played Ruggles, Ives, Cowell, and Riegger. And these were the first performances that took place of this music between New York and California. At that time, no one in St. Paul had ever heard of Charles Ives or any of these men, so that John had to really bear the brunt of the criticism which was much greater than the approbation, because people couldn't understand what this music was all about. They really thought that John was just not quite all there and that he was trying to revolutionize everything. John had raised the money himself from the community and had engaged men from the Minneapolis Symphony for a small chamber orchestra. These men became very interested in the idea. They gave a good deal of free time for extra rehearsals, so that when the concerts were given, the works were played excellently, and the composers did not have to suffer from poor performances, which was not often the case. In 1933, John played *In the Night* by Charles Ives, *Lilacs* from *Men and Mountains* by Ruggles, *Polyphonica* of Henry Cowell, Wallingford Riegger's *Scherzo,* and John's own *Concerto Arabesque.* There were two concerts in that series before John became ill and was unable to go on. At one concert of John's songs a woman critic wrote that his first songs were quite palatable and she could take those, but that frankly she had to leave, because the others gave her a stomachache! Usually the performers would get excellent reviews. The attitude was that it was marvelous that they could stay on pitch and that they could do these difficult, impossible things expected by the composer. One concert was given at the national meeting of the Federation of Music Clubs. There was quite a battle to get that concert on the program. They didn't want it, but it had been offered to them for free, and they felt they had to take it, so they decided that they would do it during the lunch hour, and in that way it wouldn't be taking up anybody's valuable time. Mr. Ives became very interested in these concerts and thought that it would be wonderful if John could be located in the Chicago area and be giving modern concerts there while Slonimsky was giving his concerts in the Boston area. However, this never worked out.

Program

1. Symphony No. 5—B major..............*Schubert*
   Scored for 1 flute, 2 oboes, 2 horns, 1 bassoon and strings.

2. Siegfried Idyll (*original version*)..............*Wagner*
   Scored for 1 flute, 1 oboe, 2 clarinets, 1 bassoon, 1 horn, 1 trumpet and strings.

INTERMISSION

3. Concertino for Octette..............*Eugene Goossens*
   1st time in Northwest
   Scored for 4 violins, 2 violas, 2 celli and contrabass.

4. Fairy Bells..............**Henry Cowell*
   1st time in Northwest
   Scored for 1 flute, 1 oboe, 1 clarinet, 1 bassoon, 1 horn, 1 trumpet, bells and strings.

5. At Night (from Theatre Set)..............**Charles E. Ives*
   1st time in Northwest
   Scored for 1 horn, 2 pianos and strings.*

6. Concerto Arabesque..............**John J. Becker*
   First performance
   Scored for 1 flute, 1 oboe, 1 clarinet, 1 bassoon, 1 horn, 1 trumpet, strings and piano.

*Contemporary English

**Contemporary American

The contemporary American works are from the library of the Pan American Association of Composers.

The
CONTEMPORARY ARTS SOCIETY
of the
COLLEGE OF ST. THOMAS

presents

The Saint Paul
Chamber Music Society

JOHN J. BECKER
Conductor

ELSIE WOLF CAMPBELL
Pianist

St. Thomas College Auditorium

Monday, December 7, 1931

8:30 P. M.

The first concert at which music by Ives was presented in the Midwest.

Henry Cowell had been very anxious for John to meet Charlie Ives, but he was a little hesitant about it because he felt the men were both of somewhat the same temperament and that John was apt to say something to Charlie that would upset him and get him on one of his rampages that we'd all heard about. However, things didn't work out that way. John didn't say anything, and wouldn't have intentionally, to upset Mr. Ives. They met early in 1932. I have a letter from Mr. Ives dated in May of 1931 in which he wrote that he was very happy that John was going to come to New York the next season, and that he had studied John's *Symphony Brevis* and had found it "strong music and music that carried one high." Then in October of 1931, there is another letter in which Ives wrote that, knowing that John was coming to New York, he hoped that he would be able to stay under their own roof, and that he would also like to have me stay there, if I could come, and that he hoped that John could arrange this and would be disappointed if he didn't. As early as May of 1931, Mr. Ives had sent John bound photostat copies of almost all his music, telling him that he wasn't thinking of John's using the music for concerts, but he would be very happy for these works to be in John's library, and that he hoped in return, that when scores of John's music became available, he could have copies for his library.

There were differences in the backgrounds of these two men. Mr. Ives grew up in the New England countryside. John grew up in an ugly railroad town, a suburb of Evansville, Indiana. He enjoyed the city more than he did the country. He liked any city. In that I think he was different than Charlie. And Mr. Ives was surrounded by music from the time he was born, while John had no music in his early life. But there were qualities and shared interests which brought these two men together. Both were interested in literature, and they admired that trait in each other. John Kirkpatrick said in one of his letters to me, when we were sending the Ives correspondence back and forth, that sometimes Ives would break into Latin when writing to John, but that this never happened in any of his other correspondence. And John and Mr. Ives were both family men. Their letters were about intimate things concerning the children, their activities, the cute things they said and did. Mr. Ives wrote about their daughter Edie, about their own health problems and the problems of their brothers and sisters. Later on when our son John was old enough to be in the service, Charlie and Harmony had nephews in the service and they would write about how disturbed they were about these things. And then later, they were very thrilled over Edie's marriage and the birth of Kit [Charles Ives Tyler, born 1946]. I think that both men had great respect for each other first as men and then as composers. John wrote to Ives: "I'm so appreciative of your kindness and friendship. My loyalty to you as a man and artist will in the passing years prove it all. I want to dedicate my most important work to you, if you will accept the dedication." This was his multimedia work, *Marriage with Space,* that was written in 1933 and has never yet been performed, though it was one of the first multimedia works in America.

Another way in which the men were alike was that neither one of them was interested in writing music just for the public. They wrote what they wanted to write. They were very independent and uninhibited. As John said: "I've never written with my hand on a conductor's shoulder." All the way through, Ives recognized John's courage, especially in the matter of getting these concerts in the West, when he had no one to help share the criticism that he knew would certainly arise. As far as the men were concerned, it was a two-way friendship arrangement. They just thought so much of each other that each one would do whatever he could to help the other.

John and Mr. Ives both had had to earn a living for their families. Mr. Ives made the decision to go into business, and he worked on his music late into the night. John taught for a while and was able to work at music until he became director of the Federal Music Project. Then this was a full-time job, and sometimes he was away evenings on public relations things or going to concerts, so he had to work far into the night on his music at the time when he had his greatest creative urge. The thing that resulted was that he had a break in his health later in life, just as Charlie Ives did.

The two men did not influence each other's music—they met after their ideas had been well formed. Ives's music was much more programmatic than John's. John always felt that when Ives wrote pure music with no outside material that he was at his strongest. For example, he felt that the title of *Washington's Birthday* would be better if it were not quite so programmatic, and Ives felt that possibly he was right and that if he used it (which he did not) and wanted to change it, he could call it *A Winter's Holiday.* John preferred abstract music. However, he was very anxious to point out to all his musical friends all of the new innovations of Ives, and how Ives had done things before Schoenberg, and that he was always amazed at the fecundity of Ives's themes and material. As far as John was concerned, it was Ives, Schoenberg, and Varèse.

Ives supported all of the organizations that were furthering the cause of new music. And he also helped many of the composers who were helping him get his works in order so that they could be legible for performances.

And John was one of these. He had worked on the *Chorales*, the *Fourth Symphony,* and *General William Booth Enters Into Heaven.* And of course Ives insisted that the works be paid for and would send checks to the composers who were doing works for him. And I've always felt that he was more generous to John, because he realized that John was here in the Midwest giving these concerts on his own, and also that he had the responsibility of a large family, and that it would be difficult to manage with a teacher's salary. Ives worked very hard to try to get lectures for John and to try to see if there weren't better positions available for him. He really exhausted all of his contacts in this respect, and it was especially appreciated because he was not in good health and it meant extra effort on his part, as well as somewhat of an emotional strain too when he became involved in the problems of other people.

I met Mrs. Ives, but I did not meet Mr. Ives. When John and I were in New York together for the first time in the forties, we were invited to tea at the Ives home. John saw Mr. Ives, but I was not permitted to see him, because he wasn't feeling well enough to meet anyone new. I found Mrs. Ives a charming person. She and I had many things in common. She had gone to Chicago in 1900 to do social work. For anyone to come from the East to wild and woolly Chicago to do social work in 1900 was certainly just as courageous as any of the music that Charles Ives was writing. She worked in the same area of Chicago that I did social work in later on. And I also found out that she liked to fish. I had always loved to fish. In one of her letters Mrs. Ives said, "I understand from John that you like to fish," and she wrote that in her younger days she very often went trout-fishing with a rod and reel.

John and Edie had quite a close relationship to each other, and I think this is possibly because Edie and Mary Cecilia, our daughter, were approximately the same age, and Edie was very interested in writing stories and Mary Cecilia had been writing poetry. At Christmastime, Mr. Ives and Harmony would always send specially well-chosen gifts for the children. The one time when he included the whole family, it was a wonderful box of Washington apples. And at other times, indestructible toys or books. But they never failed to do this, and considering that they had health problems, it meant a great deal of effort on their part. And then in return, the children would write them letters thanking them for the gifts, so that Mr. and Mrs. Ives were living people to them.

John's last visit with Mr. Ives was in February of 1953 when we were in New York while John was on sabbatical leave. I saw Mrs. Ives, but I was again unable to meet Charlie. John never said very much about that visit with Mr. Ives. I think that he felt very deeply that Mr. Ives was possibly nearing the end, and he just didn't want to talk about it.

Most composers include their revisions in their own final scores. In the case of Ives, however, scores by editors and copyists are often more important because they often contain revisions not to be found elsewhere. Sometimes, patches used by copyists were lost, leaving only the copyist's score surviving. Musicians who were interested in Ives's music often worked on editions. These included: John J. Becker, E. Power Biggs, Henry Cowell, Lou Harrison, Bernard Herrmann, John Kirkpatrick, and Nicolas Slonimsky. In John Kirkpatrick's Ives Catalogue are listed twenty copyists who are to this date unidentified by name. In addition, there are six others who did a great deal of work for Ives: Greinert and Reis (first names not available); Emil Hanke, Carl Pagano, George Price, George F. Roberts. Two other names appear—Victor van de Molen, who worked for George Roberts on a few scores, and Walter Lachowski, who worked only on General William Booth Enters Into Heaven. Of these copyists, only GEORGE F. ROBERTS has been located. He was interviewed, together with Mrs. Roberts who also knew the Iveses, at their home in Northport, New York, on June 16, 1969.

In the early thirties, I worked at NBC with the copyist that Ives had, Emil Hanke. Hanke decided that he was going to give it all up and become a Jehovah's Witness. He was the most remarkable copyist I ever knew, and he made a beautiful manuscript. It looked like print. But his hand shook so, you'd wonder where he was going to land on the paper. He always did land in exactly the right place. At NBC they had four arrangers and twelve copyists on salary at that time. After Hanke went out, I found myself the head of the department. I was there for quite a few years. Then when Dr. Frank Black became the music director for NBC, I went to work for him. I took care of his collection of music manuscripts of famous composers, and I did all his copying. I showed Dr. Black one of the Ives scores one time. All he said was, "Take it away."

Through Hanke I was invited up to Ives's 74th Street house one day. Ives said he had been to school in New Haven, and I said I came from there. We discovered that my aunt Margaret Roberts was one of the few people who had tried to help and encourage Ives with his music when he was at

A page of manuscript from Washington's Birthday *by Ives's copyist, Emil Hanke.*

Yale. She sang in the quartet at Center Church in New Haven, where Ives played the organ. As soon as Ives heard the name Madge Roberts—he called her Madge—he said, "What memories that brings up." And I was *in,* right away. Another coincidence was that we both had studied with Professor Horatio Parker. I played violin with the New Haven Symphony as a young man, and I got acquainted with Parker. For some reason he took an interest in me and said he would like to help me. I told him that I wanted to learn how to compose, and he gave me lessons and never charged me anything. Ives and I used to talk about Parker sometimes, and about how Ives had to change the *First Symphony* ending so that he could get his degree at Yale. Ives said that the original ending was much better.

Even before Hanke took me to meet Ives, I had heard of Ives when the *Sun* published something that said if anyone would write in, Ives would give them a copy of the *114 Songs.** When he made the book of *50 Songs,* I got them. I had never sent for anything like that before. I couldn't sleep when I started to study them. I didn't know what to make of some of them, but I enjoyed them very much. That was my first introduction to Ives's music. So when Hanke spoke about him and told me that he worked for him, I was very much interested. Later on I did get the *114 Songs.* I told Ives that I had bought it somewhere in a secondhand store, and he got mad because he was giving the volume away and then somebody would charge for it.

On 74th Street we'd go to the top floor, Ives creeping up on all fours. It took him a long time to make those stairs. Once there, he'd always offer me a cigar. He had them there for Carl Ruggles, and I don't know how many years he had them, but they were dust. He had them up in Connecticut, too. I think he carried them with him, in case this man would show up. He had a piano in the studio on 74th Street and he'd play, sometimes for a couple of hours, if he got started on something. He played many things—parts of the *Concord* and those chromatic piano studies that he wrote. He'd go over that piano with tremendous speed. It was the most peculiar sensation when you heard these things, because it wasn't a chromatic scale really. It sounded like something else. They're chromatic studies, but the notes are spread an octave apart—C and then C sharp, a ninth up, you know.

Ives had his music photostated and blown up so the notes were about that

---

*Ives sent a copy of *114 Songs* to the *Sun* in thanks for their permission to use poetic texts previously printed in the *Sun*. They misunderstood Ives's intention and printed a notice of the volume and Ives's offer to send complimentary copies to interested parties which was in the back of the book of songs. Ives sent a letter to the *Sun* complaining about unwanted publicity, but he did send complimentary copies of the *50 Songs* to those who wrote to him. For Ives's letter to the *Sun,* see Boatwright, *Essays,* pp. 132–33.

big around. Then he could see them. He'd have to put them down on the floor. I don't know if they ever kept any of those.* I prepared some of the things that were done by *New Music* and many other things that he wanted to have in clear copies, because no printer could set up the music from *his* manuscript. I got a young man to help me with this because I hadn't the time. I had a full-time job at NBC and a lot of work to do, so I would make a pencil copy quickly, but clear. And then the young man made the ink copy for me. He didn't know anything about music; he was a draftsman. Mr. Ives was very much interested in the fact that he didn't know anything about music. He couldn't understand how he could do it.

I'd send Ives a bill when I completed something. He wrote me a letter once telling me I was a fine musician but a poor businessman. He didn't think I charged enough. He always had to add a little to whatever bill I gave him. In fact, I would have been glad to do it for nothing. That's the way I felt about it.

I did some of the *Concord Sonata.* Every time I went there it was new. The printers were on his neck all the time. He used to laugh about it. He didn't care; he was in no hurry, and he always had something new to put in. His handwriting wasn't any too good and his hand was shaky too, later on. The earlier scores were all right, but when he made those additions! If he wanted to add something, he'd put a little mark on the spot and say, "See page twenty-five." This would be on page two, and he'd have the change on the back of page twenty-five. Sometimes we couldn't find where he had put the change.

Some of the things I did for Ives were: the three *Harvest Home Chorales; Central Park in the Dark;* the *Trio for Violin, Cello, and Piano;* the *Second String Quartet;* the *Thanksgiving* section from *The Holidays;* the *Emerson* [first] movement of the *Concord.* The string quartet was one of the most difficult ones to do. One of the last pieces I worked on was the song called *They Are There!*†

Ives gave away a lot of scores to people he thought might use them. He told me about sending Walter Damrosch the score for the *Second Symphony.* Damrosch wanted to correct it for him. He thought it was just carelessly written. This wasn't true, because Ives knew what he was doing. Price [the copyist] used to try to correct his scores, too. On one of the scores

---

*Ives's MS score for *He Is There!* survives in large photostat size. The positives are enlarged from the negative photostats in a ratio of about four to five. The pages measure 12¼″ by 18″.

†*They Are There!*, a song for voice and two pianos, was adapted from *He Is There!*, which was composed in 1917 and arranged for chorus and orchestra that same year. In 1942 the name was changed by Ives to *They Are There!* and the words updated to World War II.

A page of manuscript from Central Park in the Dark *by Ives's copyist, George F. Roberts.*

[*The Fourth of July*] Mr. Ives has written, "Mr. Price, Please don't try to make things nice! All the wrong notes are *right*. Just copy as I have. I want it that way."*

The *Universe Symphony,* the unfinished one, he didn't intend to finish. He told me that anybody else could add to it if they felt like it. It was going to be something. Maybe someday they'll do it, with orchestras here and there on the hills, and different choruses all around the countryside.

We did not have a strictly business relationship with the Iveses. My wife and two girls went up to his home in Connecticut with me every summer. We knew Edie, of course, and after she was married I met her husband. Edie once bought a record player for her father. I remember that he played it for me once. He got so excited and so mad because they had left off the introduction on the recording. It was a barn dance.†

I used to walk with him in Redding. He had a pine forest up at the back of the house, and it was quite a thing. He called it the Schwarzwald. He had all the limbs cut off so you could walk under the trees. And he had a natural stone seat up there. He'd walk up that far and then he'd sit down and rest. He had to take it very easy and always carried his cane. And when he got excited, that cane would fly around.

My daughter Janet took a picture of Mr. Ives on one of our Redding visits and she focused so long, trying to make sure that she got it right, that Mrs. Ives said, "Mr. Roberts, she'd better hurry up. He's not going to last much longer." We got such a fine picture. I gave them a copy. They wanted to know if they could have the negative to make some more copies for the family, and they would return it. But I never did get it back. I have a print somewhere.

---

*See MS, p. 40.
†The *Barn Dance* from *Washington's Birthday,* Columbia Concert Orchestra, Bernard Herrmann, conductor, recorded from broadcast of WABC, New York City, March 31, 1943.

Photograph of Ives taken by Janet Roberts at West Redding, ca. 1940.

The Iveses' trip to Europe in 1932 began with two months in England, after which they spent about a month each in Germany, France, and Switzerland. In Berlin, the Iveses stayed at the pension of Frau Elsa Schmolke—Henry Cowell had recommended it and was there, and they met MARY BELL, a soprano, who subsequently sang some of Ives's songs.

Most of the early performers of Ives's music are deceased; others had no personal meetings with Ives. Radiana Pazmor answered a request for an interview with a letter giving details of some early song recitals, and she sent memorabilia relating to them—a signed photograph of Ives, a few letters, and her working score of General William Booth Enters Into Heaven. *Miss Pazmor, a contralto, never met Ives personally, nor did Mina Hager, mezzo-soprano, who was interviewed about her performances of contemporary music in the thirties. Mary Bell was the only one of the early performers found who had actually worked with Ives. "Marybell," as she likes to be called, lives in New York City where she was interviewed on December 10, 1970.*

It's possible that Adolph Weiss told me about Ives. I wrote to him, and he sent me a letter in return and a book that was a little bit mutilated. He wrote, "I'm sorry I can find no more complete copies of the large book of songs but hope to later and will take pleasure in sending it to you. In the meantime, I am mailing you copies of a collection of fifty songs which I ask you to accept with my compliments."

I can hardly think of his music without being moved, particularly the songs which I know the best. I love many of them. *The Indians* and *Evening* and the ones that bring in his feeling about America—*The Things Our Fathers Loved*—old things, you know. He had such humor about the old-fashioned things and the endearing people, most of the time in a nice way—in a jesting, gentle way. I guess he thought of himself as a Sunday composer, but with that great talent there couldn't have been any doubt in his mind what he was.

Ives played a few things for me. I recall vividly *Mists* and *A Christmas Carol*, and he talked a good deal about the rhythm of these songs. He played *Mists* the way it should be played, and it was a revelation. It was most important to him to have those high right-hand chords in measures 2, 3, 4, 5, and 16, 17, 18, played with a very, very soft stress, giving a special atmosphere. Thank goodness I heard him, because I have been able to tell accompanists with whom I have worked since then.

Concert of March 15, 1940, by Mary Bell at Carnegie Chamber Music Hall.

Hamburg concert of 1932 with Henry Cowell and Mary Bell.

That was during the only time I spent with him. It was in Berlin in the summer of 1932 at the pension of Frau Elsa Schmolke. Schmolke was a great friend of Henry Cowell. She was a born hostess, a German lady Cowell had known for years. I saw Slonimsky there and many other musicians. It was a unique sort of place, artists of all kinds, and many psychiatrists. Wherever you looked was a psychiatrist. It was 1932 and Freud was king, you know. Schmolke's pension was on Nurembergstrasse right at the zoo in the center of everything. The three Iveses came there. He seemed pretty well and was stimulated and interested in being in Germany. Ives liked things there, but he couldn't stand Wagner. He couldn't even talk about Wagner, and you just didn't. I saw once (I didn't bring up the subject, but it was brought up somehow) his attitude. You just didn't do it again. I don't remember anything else that he felt so strongly about at the time.

We were in Berlin together for about a month. Henry Cowell was there also. I remember that we took some walks around in the great Tiergarten, a wonderful park, and a lusty band would be playing. Mr. Ives got a big kick out of that. And then there was an evening at somebody's house—I think it was the house of a conductor named Adler [F. Charles Adler]. I sang the *Seven Songs* by Adolph Weiss and Mr. Ives said that he loved one song so greatly. It was called *Cemetery,* and Mr. Ives said that of all modern literature that was the most beautiful song to his way of thinking. I wrote this to Mr. Weiss, who was then on a Guggenheim scholarship in Lago di Garda in Italy. They invited me to Italy, but there I sat in Berlin hoping for an operatic engagement. Nothing happened. Hitler came instead. It was a good time to get out. Before I left Germany, I did a concert with Henry Cowell in Hamburg [December 1932] of contemporary songs. It included the Weiss songs and three by Ives.

The longest program I ever did of Ives was at the New School. The other times I have sung three or four songs on programs with works of other modern composers—Riegger, Weiss, Copland, Rudhyar. I knew Wallingford Riegger quite well. He gave me a few songs. One of them is very modern, with a text by Dylan Thomas. I met Varèse in '33 in Paris and later worked with him at the New School. We did some Bartók, and being an actress, I would do some of the reading of the verses. Every September when Weiss came from the West Coast this group met—Cowell, Varèse, Otto Luening, Riegger. I felt privileged to be included with these creative people. I think of them often and of Ives and the beautiful time we had together.

In the thirties, after the Iveses returned from Europe, performances of Ives's music did not increase very much, but a few new names were added to the handful of early enthusiasts. These included: Lehman Engel, John Kirkpatrick, Lou Harrison, and Goddard Lieberson.

LEHMAN ENGEL is a composer, conductor, and writer, especially on the subject of the American musical theater. One of Mr. Engel's many activities was the Madrigal Singers which he founded and directed for many years. His most recent book, Words with Music, *was published in 1972. The interview with Mr. Engel took place in New York, on October 12, 1969.*

I knew about Ives earlier, but it was in 1937 that I first wrote asking him for copies of his *Sixty-Seventh Psalm.* I wanted to perform this work with the Madrigal Singers which I had founded and was conducting for the WPA Federal Music Project. Mr. Ives sent me copies, and we did perform the *Sixty-Seventh Psalm* a number of times. We recorded it for Columbia Records [March 22, 1939], and Mr. Ives was very pleased that I had done

Listen in ......

THE MADRIGAL SINGERS

LEHMAN ENGEL, Conductor

Sunday Evening, August 29th, 1937, 10.30 to 11 E.D.S.T.

Columbia Broadcasting System Coast-to-Coast Hookup
over Station WABC, New York

PROGRAM

CHARLES IVES' SIXTY-SEVENTH PSALM
LE CHANT DES OYSEAUX BY CLEMENT JANEQUIN
FRENCH, GERMAN and ENGLISH, and RENAISSANCE MUSIC

Postcard announcing Lehman Engel and his Madrigal Singers performing Ives's
Sixty-Seventh Psalm *for a radio broadcast in 1937.*

Harmony Ives, 1948. Photo Clara Sipprell.

it, because insofar as I know it had not had any public performances, except perhaps in the Danbury Church, shortly after he wrote it many, many, many years before. I remember his making jokes about the fact that the Danbury choir always sounded to him as though it were singing in two keys simultaneously, and the *Sixty-Seventh Psalm* is written in two keys. Ives eventually sent copies of the two printed volumes of songs, various symphonies, string quartets, and sonatas.

I remember very well my impressions of him and his wife Harmony and their house on East 74th Street. It was a painfully plain house, so plain that you knew the people who lived in it must be wealthy, because poor people would have decorated it with something. There was absolutely no decoration. I'm sure that nothing new had been brought in; there'd been no reupholstering at any time ever. And I remember that Mrs. Ives always sat in a rocking chair and always was knitting. When I would call, ring the bell downstairs, a servant would let me in, and I'd walk up one flight of stairs to the living room, usually find Mr. Ives with his gray goatee, peeping over the side of the railing, and usually making jokes to me as I came in. He'd shake my hand very warmly and get close to me and stare with squinting eyes—I believe he had cataracts at the time—and smile. He showed in no uncertain terms that he was always extremely enthusiastic to see me, and I felt extremely pleased, because I knew many, many people of distinction at that time who had tried in vain to see him, and he just, for one reason or another, refused to see most people. But I would come in and Ives would take me by the hand warmly. I'd go into the living room, which was in the front of the house, and meet Mrs. Ives, and then Mr. Ives would start talking to me at great length and heatedly about something that happened to him in his early life when the sissies wouldn't perform his music. He had nothing but contempt for people like Walter Damrosch who had conducted the New York Symphony in the earlier days, and of course Ives had literally lived with no performances of any sort for almost all his life, in utter loneliness. He'd get so carried away and so excited that he would have to throw himself down on a couch and pant for breath, which terrified me. Mrs. Ives never looked up from her knitting, never looked concerned, never frowned. She'd make some remark, such as, "Well, Charlie, if you're going to carry on that way, you know this is going to happen." And she'd say to me, "Don't worry." And he'd catch his breath and be up and going about the same thing again.

Some few months after I'd first met him, I had an idea that we should have a music press that would publish serious contemporary music. And at that time the need was acute, because no established publisher would touch any of it. There were two things that preceded it—one was the Cos Cob Press, which was financed and run by Alma Morgenthau Wertheim Wiener. Aaron Copland was her entire adviser, and she published things by Sessions, Piston, and Thomson, and a variety of other people—not a great deal of music, but a thousand times more than anybody else had ever done. And then there was Henry Cowell's publication, *New Music*. This also went along in a very limited way. But I thought that we should have a regular publishing house, and Aaron got Mrs. Wiener to deed over the Cos Cob catalog to us, because it had been defunct for some time, so that we'd have something to begin with. We called ourselves the Arrow Music Press. I was president and Aaron Copland was secretary and treasurer, and two vice presidents were Virgil Thomson and Marc Blitzstein. At this time we were all of us concerned with going around among our friends to get any kind of contribution toward publishing music. We could only function, really, if we invited a composer to pay for his work to be published, and we gave him something like 90 percent of everything that came in and kept the too little 10 percent, so that we were constantly in trouble, having to raise extra money just to keep going. As I recall, the American Music Center was being formed about that time, and we made a deal with them to handle our stock for quite a while. I went to Ives during this time and told him the whole business about the publication idea, that composers had to pay for their own music and so forth, and would he be interested. He was really marvelous. He said, of course we were at liberty to publish any of his music that we wanted, and he would pay the bills, and the first thing we contracted for was the *Concord Sonata* for piano, which had been played often by John Kirkpatrick, and was recorded, and has been played by many people since. We also published the *Sixty-Seventh Psalm* and a few other pieces. Ives not only paid for these works, but told us that we could keep all money that came in from them, so that we would have some money to run the press with, and perhaps publish some worthy composer's work who was in no position to raise the money himself.

I remember particularly one very emotional afternoon I had with Ives, because his attitude when I arrived, from the very beginning, was very unusual in that he seemed to want something and he was playing footsy with me. He was being a little coy and unable to bring himself to say what was on his mind, and it really didn't become him, because I thought of him as a great man and a very rugged individualist, which of course he was. Finally he came to the point. He spoke of a composer, and I tell you honestly I don't remember his name right now. Ives said, "This is a very good friend of mine. He's very sincere. He's very honest. And he's written a symphony and I would like to have you publish it and I will pay for it." And I felt that this was a very serious situation, because I knew that my colleagues would not want to publish this work. I didn't want to leave saying, "Well, let me discuss it with my colleagues and then see you the next time." So instead of that, I took the bull by the horns and I must say I was terrified. I must have been all of about twenty-seven at the time, and I said, "Mr. Ives, I think it's wonderful that you want to do this for your friend, but I think it's misguided. This is going to be very expensive, and I'm sure it would be better if you could make him a gift of the money that he could use in his way. To my utter amazement, instead of rising to white fury, which I would have thought he would have done, he burst into tears, and it was very hard for him to get in control again. And finally when he did, wiping his eyes, with the backs of his hands, he said, "It's so terrible that God should create a man who's as good as he is, who works so hard at his music, and that he can't get anything performed or published." It's a very moving story as I recall it. It hits me in the solar plexus, and it had an ending which I never would have thought he was capable of. I thought he would have fought me and ordered me out of the house, rather than to have agreed to something like this.

I have a few other fragmentary bits that I can tell you about him. He always talked about Pa and Lincoln as though they were two people that one met every day on the street. He constantly was talking about what Lincoln said to Pa and what Pa said to Lincoln. And none of it, unfortunately, do I remember. It had to do with parades and marches and celebrations, and of course he was so imbued with this love of American folk music and hymnology and all that.

On many of the music manuscripts there are notes that Mr. Ives had written, usually about politics or about philosophy of some sort. He was an avid critic of society as it was. I have a feeling that if he were alive today, he would fit in admirably with the youngest possible generation.

He also was constantly throwing out venom about the musical establishment of his day. He hadn't approved of it, probably largely because they hadn't approved of him, hadn't accepted him in any possible way. He told many little anecdotes about Danbury and the choir and the church. Everything about him was so apple-pie American. It was Connecticut; it was New England; it was picnics and get-togethers and the old songs, *Shall We Gather at the River*—all this. He frequently burst into singing one of those old songs here and there. And he would shake his fist in my face when he wanted to make a point. Not at me, but as though he were shaking his fist at somebody else. He would clench his fist and come stand bent over right in my face, and I thought frequently he was going to really hit me, but none of this was directed to me. It was about somebody else or about something else. He got terribly wrought up. Once he played the piano, and noisily— something of his own, very noisily and with his fist sometimes. I never was there that Mrs. Ives was not in the room, and sometimes his daughter Edith was there, but never anybody else. I knew Ives liked me and liked to have me around. I don't understand how or why. I really don't. I'm not being modest or anything else. It was my fault that I didn't see more of him than I did. I was very busy, but he always encouraged me to come and see him, and I never did call that he wasn't eager to make an engagement for me to be there again. I would usually go for an hour, and I had the feeling that I could come every day and spend all day had I wanted to. I just couldn't.

Wherever Henry Cowell went, word of Ives's music followed. Cowell came originally from San Francisco. He often returned to the West Coast to live and work, and he spread his enthusiasm for Ives to musicians wher- ever he went. A most willing subject, who soon developed his own over- whelming enthusiasm for Ives, was LOU HARRISON, the composer, who lives and works in his native California, where he was interviewed on March 24, 1970, at his home in Aptos.

Henry Cowell was the first living composer that I got acquainted with. This was mid-thirties. He was teaching an extension course in composition at night school at the University of California in San Francisco. I went there, took the course, and then began to study with him privately. I learned a very great deal. I'd studied material from *New Music* from the San Fran- cisco Public Library, and I expressed an interest in the work of Mr. Ives. Henry Cowell suggested that I write to Mr. Ives, which I did [March 25, 1936], and he began sending me things. He sent me the *Scherzo* [second movement] from the *New Music* printing of the *Fourth Symphony,* and he sent a photostat of the *Third Symphony* from which I conducted for the premiere performance in 1946 [April 5]. Then he sent me a curious edition of the *Concord,* in which he had changed the *Emerson* and combined it with the other three movements torn out from the first edition. Finally there arrived a large crate which included all eleven volumes of chamber music in photostat. Later Ives asked me to give those to the New Music Edition Library for the West Coast. I lived with all of this music for a number of years and carted it around with me, first to Los Angeles, then to New York.

I began playing excerpts from the *Concord Sonata.* I did *Emerson* several times in 1936 or '37 at San Francisco State College. These were during student noon concerts. I also played a Chavez sonata, and Henry Cowell's piano music, which by this time I had begun to learn from Henry. When I look back at it, the reaction was polite, and mostly mystified. Nothing was said, but there was a tone of startlement. I don't remember hearing much other modern music on those noon programs.

Out here, in California, our cognizance was only of Cos Cob Press and *New Music,* so we were very eager to get their records and publications, and then we made what performances we could among ourselves. I remember getting private readings here of the Ives *First Quartet,* the *Third Violin Sonata,* and I think the *Fourth Violin Sonata.*

I grew up with Mr. Ives's music. I think one of the things that was so very exciting to me as a young man about the scores of Ives was their proclamation of freedom. It was clear that if Mr. Ives did those things, it was possible for others to do them, and other things too. Ives, combined with the stimulus of working with Henry Cowell in very detailed melodic germinal motives, set a way of thinking that I've never entirely gotten rid of. I still think in terms of very small germ motives flowing out. There are times when Mr. Ives's music gives me goose pimples all over, you know. Still. I spent bewitched, fascinated years in the scores. I don't know that many people had the number of Ives scores around that I did.

Schoenberg was a very great influence on me, too—in some ways more of an influence, because in addition to the expressive powers in Mr. Ives and the sense of freedom, there is the need for method. It is to me the friction of the polarity between the free and the controlled that is very stimulating. You have to have both. Naturally, Schoenberg in a completely chromatic event represents the more fundamental control. Let's face it, Mr. Ives's methods are personal, and they are for the solution of particular artistic problems, whereas Mr. Schoenberg's solutions of a generally chaotic tonal situation were in the grand manner, for all species. And it was this sense of order that I needed from Schoenberg. I love systems and methods. No sooner had I encountered the twelve-tone system than I invented a method of my own, which is still perfectly usable. I remember when I was writing a twelve-tone piece, Henry Cowell was very upset about it. He said, "Make up your own system. Make it an eleven-tone piece or a seven-tone piece, or make up a whole new system." Mr. Ives, of course, was very stimulating in that regard. He thought up an awful lot of things, as everybody now knows.

San Francisco, where I grew up, is the city of my heritage. It consisted of Henry Cowell, Charles Ives, Arnold Schoenberg, Chinese opera and Indian music and dance, Balinese records, plus reading Blake, Whitman, Emerson, and Thoreau. I got enough of that tradition to be able to know not just objectively way out here in California what those notes sounded like, but also to have some sense of the tradition that Mr. Ives's social life represented and his intellectual currents coming from Emerson.

I got the idea intellectually from Mr. Ives of inclusivity—that you don't do exclusively one kind of thing. I really like what Henry Brant calls the "grand universal circus," and I think that Charles Ives was the great creator musically of this, just as Whitman was poetically. After all, not one thing is everything. I loved Carl Ruggles's music and quickly learned, of course, from the books and from Henry Cowell that Mr. Ives and Mr. Ruggles were friends, and I could see why. But I also saw in Carl's music something else than in Mr. Ives's, and that's the principle of exclusivity. It's a "nothing but" thing, rather than an "also with" thing. Carl Ruggles would be chiseling off a bit here, off something there, and then balance it way over somewhere else. It was a kind of static thing and a very exclusive procedure. It seems to me that the Ives achievement is total. It's complete, it's grand, it's world-scale, and it's there forever. I think Carl's claims are not quite so universal, but within their range they are of course of the highest perfection.

In New York, whenever Cowell gave a concert I was there. He gave me a lesson every week [before 1937], and this was all for free. He was altogether extraordinary. He was the general information booth for all of American music for so long. At that time, he was not composing a great deal, because he was so busy being a general information booth. He introduced me to so many things. I heard Leo Ornstein's music, and then he introduced me to Radiana Pazmor. She was a majestic woman, very tall. A friend of mine and I, after one of her concerts, invited her to a reception at our house. We had lots of people, but there was never a moment that you couldn't spot her because she was taller than anyone else. She was really quite beautiful, in a grand and glamorous way. She had a wonderful contralto voice and a delightful stage mannerism. Every concert she forgot something. She'd be singing along and then she'd stop in the middle of a phrase and she'd look at you with great big eyes and say, "Oh, I've forgotten." You were fifty times as acute a listener after that. Whether trick or not, it worked, because her concerts were very much loved. I think that recording she made for *New Music* records, with Genevieve Pitot accompanying her, of *General William Booth Enters Into Heaven* is the grandest of all performances of that Ives song. She performed a number of times for the New Music Society concerts, and it was there that I heard Henry Cowell's marvelous idea of repeating the first half of the concert. There was never scheduled a full concert for the New Music Society. They were always one-half concerts, fairly large, and repeated. When I did the premiere of the Ives *Third Symphony,* I took that idea and offered after the full concert a repeat of the entire *Third Symphony.* I strongly believe, in the presentation of new music, that it should be performed twice in the same evening.

As a music reporter for the New York *Herald Tribune,* I encountered a performance by Joseph Barone with the New York Little Symphony, in which there were, as I pointed out in a review, wrong notes in a very simple piece by Handel, and I scolded them quite thoroughly about it. I was young and intemperate in my reviews sometimes, and Mr. Barone got in touch with me. He invited me to do a little guest conducting and since you're not invited all the time to conduct, I promptly accepted. I decided to try the *Third Symphony,* which, after all, I had lived with since 1936, nearly ten years or more. I knew it at least in part, so then I really made a study of it, and as I explained to Mr. Ives in a letter, it did fit the bill, since it could be done by a chamber group. Barone confirmed right away that I could do Mr. Ives's symphony and Carl Ruggles's *Portals,* and a little piece of my own which I was writing at the time. I copied all the parts. I still have right here all the original parts to the *Third Symphony* which I copied from the photostat of the original score. It was exactly the same one he had given me years before, and being somewhat of a fetishist, I conducted from it although it's a very dim photostat.

I did have a little trouble with the orchestra at first because they were a trifle hostile about modern music. They were playful in testing a young conductor, especially in this kind of music. I don't think they too much enjoyed playing Carl's piece. And they were dubious about the Ives too at first. I was having a little trouble, and then fortunately Mr. Ives's music came to the rescue, because there's that passage (I think it's at the end of the first movement) where it's quite slow and the woodwinds are in three and strings in four, or vice versa. I stopped the orchestra and I said, "Gentlemen, there's now a question of conducting. Please tell me which hand you would like the three conducted in, and which the four?" And so they chose, and I did it as they asked. That settled the matter, and I got no further testing. In fact, I got a very great deal of cooperation. There were mistakes, probably in my copying as well, but nonetheless we did get it across as a piece, and in the repeat it was just as impressive. We had a very enthusiastic audience, and very good reviews, and it resulted in a fine Sunday piece by Olin Downes. And then later, of course, the Pulitzer Prize for Mr. Ives.

A letter from Ives to Lou Harrison.

The morning after the concert, I went up to the American Music Center, where all hell had been going on all morning. There had been phone calls and telegrams from all over the eastern seaboard, and Koussevitzky was demanding the score. I said, when they told me about the conductors wanting it, "But there are three other symphonies. Why don't they get busy on those?" They all wanted the *Third*. There wasn't a conductor in that whole group who asked for any one of the other symphonies. Bernstein did the *Second* in 1951, and Henry Cowell and I helped get it together for him. And then of course much later [1965] Stokowski did the *Fourth*.

Mrs. Ives came to the concert, so lovely in her brown silk and so warm backstage to me. Mr. Ives was very greatly pleased when he read the reviews. At about that time I broke down, and when I was recuperating, Ives sent half of the Pulitzer Award to me. He was a wonderfully generous man. He assigned to me quite a large number of royalties. Beginning about five years ago, the checks got to be quite large. I am under the impression that Mr. Ives told me that these were meant to help in my own music, or for general musical purposes. I don't know how many people are recipients of the assigned royalties, but I know that I'm not the only one. I devote the money to musical purposes in every instance, and not entirely for my own music, either.

One evening in 1948 in New York, Billy Masselos said he was going to give a concert and I said, "Why don't you do the Ives *First Sonata?* I will get it out for you." I called, and Harmony asked Mr. Ives if we could have permission to do it on the concert. The date had already been settled. [February 17, 1949]. Mr. Ives said yes, and so Billy and I set to work. And we worked day and night for a long time. He came over almost every night while I worked at the score proper and we discussed problems that arose. These were not just transcriptions or editions. They were excavations! There were movements in the *First Sonata* that were literally excavations. Apparently I did mostly right, because Mr. Ives did approve the manuscript, and Bill played it.

Off and on, over the years, I did a fair amount of work with Mr. Ives's scores for him, at his request or at Henry's request. Sometimes Henry would be asked to do something that he didn't have time for. The biggest project of all was the completion of *They Are There!* It was commissioned by the League of Composers during the war. That was a fairly serious job of orchestration and completion and even a certain amount of internal recomposition, which I did in several of his works. I always asked him about these things, and he initialed a number of places to show his approval. In helping to get out the *Second Quartet,* I had to fill in a few measures. I did

A manuscript page from the First Piano Sonata.

write a few measures in that. I was hesitant, but his reaction usually was to do whatever I thought best. I do recall his making a defense of some accidentals. You must remember that my relations with him were profoundly reverent. It's an old-fashioned word, but it is that. There's no doubt of it.

I only met Mr. Ives once in person. Needless to say, it was a very intense experience, after absorbing him and his music for so many years. I was told by Henry Cowell about his health, and so I had never really had the idea that I would meet him. When the invitation came from Mrs. Ives, it was like the parting of the clouds, a divine hand or something. When I went to meet him, the only image I could think of was that he looked like God the Father as done by William Blake. I felt a kind of reverence which came partly from Henry Cowell's book [*American Composers on American Music*] and from Henry's own beliefs and feelings about Ives. It was a cumulative feeling of great reverence, so that the meeting was very exciting and also very funny.

The invitation from Mrs. Ives for luncheon was around the time when I did the *Third Symphony,* in February '47. Did you know the house? It was a brownstone, and you came in underneath and up a flight of stairs to a kind of loggia. The first thing I encountered was Mr. Ives waving a cane so vigorously in a whirling fashion that I was quite frightened. He was shouting, "My old friend! My old friend!" and I had never seen the man before in my life! Then he greeted me, so grandly, so enthusiastically. I almost expected to find him incapacitated, and was quite taken aback to discover myself ducking from a cane. He literally danced, he got so excited. We had a very pleasant conversation at luncheon. I don't remember what it was about, but it was very intense conversation, and Harmony was very calm and polite. Then we retired to the living room, and Mr. Ives brought out some scores, and I remember he said, "I want you to be my eyes," and he proposed for me to go through his works to get them into edited form and to help him make his works complete and public. I don't know what I answered, but at any rate we started. He brought out the organ work [*Variations on America*], and he was already unable to see, and this is why he said, "I want you to be my eyes." But he actually directed me to a certain measure in the bass clef and said, "That should be an E flat." And I realized that the man had memory of every page he'd ever written. I believe that he knew every note he'd ever written no matter what a mess it was or where it was.

I always wish Mr. Ives had lived in a time and place when opera would have been possible for him. The tradition wasn't there for him in his social background. Wouldn't he have written the grandest opera ever, with the range of expressivity of the orchestral works and the characterization that his songs show? And his command of emotional excitement! He could have done it in the grand, transcendental manner about war and peace. It would have been something for all time.

GODDARD LIEBERSON, composer and critic, became one of the most important figures in the recording industry. He is a senior vice-president of CBS, Inc., and president of the CBS/Records Group. Mr. Lieberson has always maintained a vigorous interest in American composers and a dedication to American cultural history. He has been among the most active and helpful enthusiasts in American music, giving support to causes which might otherwise have failed. In 1945, Goddard Lieberson produced the first commercial recording of the music of Ives for Columbia Records. This was of John Kirkpatrick performing the Concord Sonata.

An interview with Mr. Lieberson in New York City on October 23, 1969, revealed that Ives had given a great deal of printed and photostated music to Lieberson. In preparation for the publication of the following interview, a search through the music which Ives had given to Lieberson revealed a startling discovery: the long-lost orchestral score in Ives's own hand for the first movement (St. Gaudens in Boston Common) *of* Three Places in New England. *The appearance of this score is a major event for Ives scholars, and the excitement of its discovery was intensified by the timing—this particular work was in the final stages of a new edition, performed for the first time in New Haven in February 1974. Goddard Lieberson has deposited the score in the Yale Ives Collection.*

It must have been the year before I wrote the article for *Musical America** that I met Ives. That was 1939. So the years that I met with him were '38 and '39. I had just come to New York and I went to see him three or four times. He was not so old, but he seemed ancient to me. That's a common fault of youth, of course, but he really seemed ancient, I think, for other reasons. He was both sick and sickly.

I went to see him because I admired him and wanted to meet him. Around that time I was involved with the founding of the American Composers Alliance, with Aaron Copland, Virgil Thomson, Bill Schuman, and others.

*Goddard Lieberson, "An American Innovator," *Musical America* 59, no. 3 (February 1939): 22, 322–23.

Meanwhile, here was Charles Ives, not wanting to have his music copyrighted because he wished it to be available to everybody—a point of view not quite amenable to a collecting society, but typical of him. I wanted to do an article about him. There weren't very many articles about Ives in the popular press at that time. The piece I wrote in *Musical America,* which was a very square magazine, may have been one of the first of the articles to reach a wider public. That was my objective. I was then a composer, and my work on *Musical America* was just a job, so I tried to enliven it by doing something for my own psyche. I went to see Ives and was deeply impressed with him. He gave me a lot of his music. Anything I didn't have that he had around, he gave me, generously—even the autograph ink score with many additional pencil markings by Ives of the first movement of *Three Places in New England.* Much later he gave me a signed photograph, which, I think, is one of the few signed photos of Charles Ives. You know, he liked my article very much. I think what he really liked about it was that

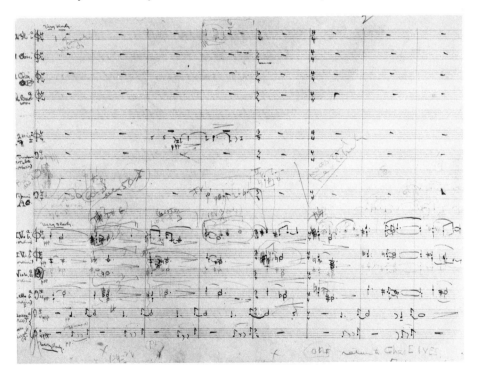

Page one of Ives's manuscript of St. Gaudens in Boston Common, *first movement of* Three Places in New England. *The full orchestral score was given to Goddard Lieberson in 1940. Mr. Lieberson has deposited the score in the Yale Music Library, Ives Collection.*

it appeared in something other than the small magazines or insurance news. The fact that it was in *Musical America,* as horrifyingly conventional as that magazine was, meant something to him.

What was really strange about Ives was his curious development out of his own limitations, if I can put it that way. What I'm trying to say is that he doesn't show any influence, he doesn't talk about any influence, he was isolated. He knew about Stravinsky and Schoenberg. I know those weren't strange names to him, but he wasn't interested in discussing them. Or Hindemith, let's say, who was current. And what he did was not out of a sense of modernism or out of a sense of avant-gardeism, or out of a sense of adventure, but out of a kind of necessity. Maybe I'm wrong, but he seemed to me a musical isolationist. I didn't feel any connective tissue with other contemporary music at all. And even in talking to him I had that feeling with him. It was as if you had gone into the north woods, and somebody said to you, "Hey, there's a fellow up there who composes." That aspect of him interested me very much. In general, I think it is true that he had very little influence on others, and the reason was that he himself was a disorganized genius. Perhaps it's all part of a similar phenomenon. He's unedited. He put everything down. He seldom, as far as I know, took things out which perhaps should have been taken out.

It's very hard to know with Ives. I think we have to face this situation of appraising how much was done out of a real desire to achieve a specific sound, or how much of it was done by an inexpert hand, particularly in his orchestrating. I know this won't be a very popular point of view, but it seems to me that very often things that he achieved were accidental. That's all right, because we live in a period of aleatory art, and if it was the accident of a cultured man at work, that, too, is OK. But a great deal of it is indigestible for that reason, because one is suffocated by it. I tried to mention something like that to him. I, of course, didn't say it this way. But we did talk about editing and it really passed over very quickly. It just didn't register.

The songs are more successful because he couldn't do any more with them. I mean, there's only one voice line and only ten fingers (although you wouldn't think so sometimes from the way he writes), so there were some limitations. At the same time, you have a feeling that in some songs there are quirks which are not just unconventional; there is something else—eccentricity.

I never could get from Ives what he really was thinking about, or what the thought was behind the kind of music he wrote. And I don't think he really revealed it to anybody. He created so many things within a short time and he compressed all of it into a music which has a kind of madness to it. He was an extremely complicated man, a genuine eccentric in the best sense of the word—the kind that we don't meet up with enough any more.

MARY SHIPMAN HOWARD had a recording studio for many years in New York, known as Mary Howard Recordings, where she recorded Charles Ives and many of the great composers, conductors, and musical lights of the day. Those recordings which she made in 1943 of Ives playing the piano and occasionally singing, were known only to the Ives family and a few others close to the Ives scene. After two years of searching for Mary Howard, she was finally discovered close by, alive and well. As a result of an interview with her in Washington, Connecticut, on September 24, 1969, not only the master discs of these recordings were found in her collection, but also, a previously unknown recording of The Alcotts *(third movement) from the* Concord, *played by Ives. These recordings are scheduled for release by CBS Records in spring 1974.*

I played the viola, but I got arthritis at an early age, and since I always loved acoustic mechanical things—the process of translating a sound wave into an electrical impulse and back into sound—I got into recording. It was unusual for a woman to be a recording engineer, particularly as far as the union was concerned. When I went to work for NBC in the early forties, they wouldn't let me in the union. But when the war came on and they got short of manpower, the union decided to let women in. I was the only gal around the NBC studios for about six months and then others came in. They were all terribly good, but I got to do the studio things.

I don't know quite how it came about, but I was assigned first to Glenn Miller, whose music I loved, and then to the recording sessions for Toscanini at RCA downtown. They had to have an NBC studio engineer at RCA Victor. It was a union deal between NBC and RCA. So I was the lucky one who got sent down there, and I didn't do anything except sit with my eyes falling out of my head, and my ears dropping off. It was fascinating. I worked for eight years while Toscanini was recording. Then I left NBC after the war, because it was an awfully tough session. I ran a small studio on 49th Street where I lived, which was only three blocks away from NBC.

When I left NBC, I suddenly found that people came flooding in. I had all the best Ampex equipment, and I was the first private person ever to own a Scully lathe. Nobody else could afford it. I couldn't afford it either, but I got a loan from the bank. It was wonderful fun while it lasted, and the most fun were the people who suddenly, by word of mouth only, came to have me make recordings for them.

Among them, Mr. Ives. I know that Mrs. Ives's father married my mother and father, but this had nothing to do with it. Mrs. Ives just called me on the telephone, just as Mr. Toscanini called me one day and said, "I want you to do all my recordings of the rehearsals and the broadcasts"—and I thought it was a friend of mine making fun of me. It must have been '42 or '43 when Mrs. Ives called. As I recall, Ives came two or three times. The reason he came was that he got letters from conductors and performers who were going to play something asking how they should interpret the music. He would come storming in the studio—"Interpret, interpret! What are they talking about? If they don't know anything about music—well, all right, I'll tell them." So he'd sit down at the piano and play very loudly, and sing and make a running commentary while he was doing it. "This is how you do it. Now you're stupid. Don't you know, this is how you do it. I'll play it over again in case you didn't get it the first time."

I had a very erratic elevator in my building. I'd hear a great crash and then a great shout, and I'd know that Ives was out of it. Then he'd sit down and talk about the elevator in no uncertain terms for about three minutes. The Iveses would come down and spend the entire day. He'd store things up that he had to do, and come in at ten in the morning. They'd go out for lunch for an hour and a half and then they'd come back for the rest of the day. Ives was absolutely full of beans and it wasn't bad temper. It was just excitement. I remember that he sang one phrase from the *Concord Sonata* over and over. "Now do you get that?"—and he'd pound and pound and Mrs. Ives would say, "Now, please take a rest." He drank quantities of iced tea, and he'd calm down and then go back at it again, saying, "I've got to make them understand."

Ives was a perfect charmer—not just as a musician, but as a fascinating man with many facets. He was interested in the mechanics of recording, and he was crazy about my boxer. And of course, Mrs. Ives was most concerned about his health, and his getting excited and his eating. Harmony was a marvelous name for his wife. She sat and read a book, but her whole interest was on the recording and on the music and once in a while she would correct him. She'd say, "That's not what you said this morning." Then I'd have to dig through the recordings and find out what he'd said that morning. I'd make notes as I went along. He'd say, "Didn't do that right the first time, didn't do that right the second time. The third time was best." So I'd edit them, but I never threw anything away because you never know when people are going to change their minds. He knew exactly what he wanted and he got it. He couldn't play the big sixteen-inch records, so I'd supply him with the excerpts that he wanted to send people. He'd say, "I don't want them. I can remember." And he could. But he'd give me a list of people to send them to. I remember Ormandy was on the list, and several other conductors. It wasn't a long list because in those days there weren't that many people who played his music.

LOUIS UNTERMEYER, poet-anthologist, visited with Ives only once in 1943 or 1944. Ives had used the text of a poem by Untermeyer, "Swimmers," and so poet and composer met to discuss the wedding of text and music in songwriting. Mr. Untermeyer was interviewed at his home in Newtown, Connecticut, on October 13, 1971.

Ives and I exchanged a couple of letters, and he asked me to stop by the house in West Redding. He was close to seventy and I was close to sixty. He had put my poem "Swimmers" to music and he talked about another one, "Landscapes," which I don't think he ever did.

We talked quite a lot. At least I talked quite a lot and Ives listened very well. I expected a very quiet person, very reticent, and at first he was. But I kept on talking and he finally had to talk, and he talked very well. What did we talk about? Mostly about Emerson. I was working on a book on Emerson then which appeared a year or two after. Ives admired Emerson, Thoreau, and that whole New England school of writers to such a degree that he shut out the earlier and the later school of New England writers. I mentioned Frost, and it evinced no response from Ives whatsoever, which was very curious because it was somewhat like the poetry he himself was writing but on a somewhat higher level.

I wonder why he didn't compose songs to more contemporary poetry. There was good poetry being written all around him at this time. He loved the past more. There's no question about it. His early reminiscences of Danbury, of his father and his grandfather, and a kind of homely homespun was what he loved. And it seemed to me he cared little for what was being done around him, or was completely ignorant of it. I don't know which. He told me that he wasn't interested. He didn't want to say outright that the New England poets of the past did a damned sight better than these people of the present. But I think if he had read Frost, he wouldn't have liked him very much. He needed the thing that Emerson gave him, the thing which was both beautiful to listen to, beautiful to think about, and a kind of moral lesson. He liked tremendously the fact that there was a moral import to it. With the poetry of his day that had ceased. You didn't do a maxim or say "Thanks for the heavenly message brought by thee, Child of the wandering sea," as Oliver Wendell Holmes wrote in "The Chambered Nautilus." But I think Ives liked that. Writing a war song, for instance, he took "In Flanders Field"—a rather static thing but it had a deep meaning to Ives, a deep patriotic feeling of what these boys were giving their lives for. He put Milton to music, and Kipling. It was often of the past. Or he could take a scrap, a headline from a newspaper and somehow dignify it with music that surged over it. It could be a triviality, but somehow or other it fired his imagination and the music came spontaneously. I liked what he did with "Swimmers" because it got immediately from the very first notes of the piano, the surge of the sea, the welling up of the waves and a great sense of movement. He took just part of the poem. All that I tried to do in words he was doing in sound. He did it again and again. He took only part of a Kipling poem, part of Milton, too. Just a phrase would fire his imagination. It was extraordinary what he accomplished.

Maybe the great thing about his songs, many of which he himself says are unsingable or shouldn't be sung, is their terrific spontaneity. When I first saw them I disliked them. I had been brought up to be a composer, too, in a very minor way. I was a pianist, and my mother was a singer. I was wedded to the romantic music, mostly of the German lied type—Schumann, Schubert, Hugo Wolf, and that sort of thing. The Ives songs seemed like an outrage, like an affront. Was he doing it on purpose? Was he just pulling one's leg? It took me some time to get used to the fact that there was no particular melodic line except every once in a while and then a very commonplace melodic line, almost plebeian like pop music. Gradually it came to me that it was on purpose. He could write melody. Something had happened, and he was as much a pioneer, a breaker of new ground, an innovator, as Frost was in his poetry, as Stevens in his poetry, as Ezra Pound, as any of these people. Little by little, although I never loved the melodies for melody's sake. I loved the fact that there was this spontaneity, and to me much of it very dramatic and just right. And so I have learned, first to stand it and then to understand him.

I had much less difficulty with the orchestral work. In song I was accustomed to the simple melodic line, the romantic line. In orchestral things I was used to Wagner, Strauss, and beyond, even to some of the modern, atonal things. I had heard Schoenberg and the twelve-tone scale had come in. No, I found very little difficulty. The fact that there could be part of the orchestra playing one theme and part playing another didn't bother me. I did a great deal of translating from the German, particularly with Heine lyrics which have of course been put to music by Schumann, Schubert, and the rest of them. It was that that I had grown up with, and so the departure from that was a shock, whereas in the orchestra, no. I did quite a bit of composing in my late teens and early twenties, but before I began to write much poetry I listened to what I had been writing and found that I had been rewriting Schumann and Schubert and all the people I had loved. I was composing dead men's music. I was not composing, I was decomposing. So I stopped.

What I have seen of Ives's prose writing has the same flow, the same verve, the same spontaneity as the songs—a talk kind of prose, not an effort to stun you with his erudition. It is not a stylistic, fancy kind of writing. But it is both ingenious and ingenuous, with tremendous vitality, and a kind of shirtsleeve, man-to-man prose.

I remember one other thing—his presence impressed me. There are a few people who have presence per se, not because they're handsome or because they're powerful-looking, but because they have a quiet dignity, a kind of self-assurance. He knew what he had done. He knew what he was, and that was that. He took it for granted and I took it for granted. He didn't have to boast. He didn't have to talk about his published work. I spoke a little about it, and he sort of waved it away. It was taken for granted that I knew who he was and that he knew, and that was that. I have had that with a few people only. Robert Frost was one. He had that quality too. Few people had it. I felt it immediately with Ives.

"Music by an unexampled creative artist of our day, probably the most original and extraordinary of American composers, yielded the outstanding experience of Mr. John Kirkpatrick's piano recital last evening at Town Hall." These words by Lawrence Gilman in the New York Herald Tribune, *following John Kirkpatrick's performance of the* Concord Sonata *by Charles Ives, finally woke America to the fact that here was a major work by a great American composer. After studying the sonata for ten years, and performing individual movements of it, John Kirkpatrick gave his electrifying*

performance in 1939. Since that time, the name most closely associated with Ives has been that of John Kirkpatrick, in terms of performance and in regard to the complicated and extraordinarily difficult cataloging and editing of the manuscripts. He has continued to work with Ives's music through the years, with indescribable care and devotion.

John Kirkpatrick is Professor Emeritus of Music and Curator of the Ives Collection at Yale University. Previously, he taught at Cornell University for twenty-two years. He is a noted pianist and has performed and edited many works by Ives, Ruggles, Gottschalk, MacDowell, and others. JOHN KIRKPATRICK was interviewed in New Haven, on February 6, 1970.

In the spring of 1927, I saw *Concord* on Kitty Heyman's piano in Paris. She was an American pianist—I knew her very well. It looked as if there was something real there, and it intrigued me. I was sort of a young, enthusiastic chauvinist for American music. I think I probably borrowed Kitty's copy for a while, and the little bit that I got into it then was the beginning of a very gradual penetration. Kitty said that if I wrote Ives he'd send me *Concord* and the *Essays.* So I did, and he did.

For about six years I had no further contact with Ives. By '32 I was playing *The Alcotts,* and it must have been in connection with this that I wrote him again in '33, and from then on we had a fairly continuous correspondence. Later there were a good many questions about *Emerson* and about *Concord* in general. In '35 I sent Ives a questionnaire—there was a long reply in Mrs. Ives's hand. It was only after Ives died, and I started sorting his papers, that I found four different sketches for that letter. That's just a gauge of how conscientious he was about things like that—just to make sure that he'd said exactly what he wanted to say and accounted for all the points he wanted to account for.

My work with *Concord* was very gradual . It was in '34 that I determined to learn the whole thing, but I knew I couldn't do that in a hurry. Other pianists had already played parts of *Concord.* Anton Rovinsky played *The Celestial Railroad* in '28, and Keith Corelli played *Emerson* in a good many recitals around '29. I played some of *Emerson* for George Antheil at his apartment in July '34 when I was learning it, and in public for the first time in March '35 at Princeton. It had a mixed reception—one lady muttered "absolutely inexcusable!"; while a gentleman told me he felt as if he was looking at times straight into Emerson's soul, and at times straight into Ives's soul. When I played *Emerson* in New York in January '36, Griffes, Copland, Harris, and Gottschalk were also on the program. Mrs. Perkins*

*Mrs. James H. Perkins (later Mrs. William Arthur).

underwrote the recital, God bless her. For most people Ives was the big surprise, because not too many people had heard Slonimsky's Ives performances, and there was a limited audience at Yaddo for the performance of seven songs by Hubert Linscott and Aaron Copland. By '38 I was playing the whole sonata. I did a performance of it in a private series in Cos Cob—that's in Greenwich, Connecticut. Paul Rosenfeld came out to hear it. He was very charming that evening with everybody, and he wrote it up in *New Music*.

As far as I can make out, the sonata was mostly composed in 1911 and 1912, but from prototypes. The *Orchard House Overture*—that is, the prototype of *The Alcotts*—was apparently started in 1902 and shaped up in 1904. Unfortunately, it's lost. The *Emerson Overture* was apparently from 1907, perhaps as far back as 1905 in its beginnings. The *Hawthorne* sketches toward a concerto are perhaps from 1910, and *Thoreau* was apparently original with the composing of the *Concord Sonata*. Ives had planned an overture series that he was going to call "Men of Literature." The only one that does exist all finished up is *Browning*.

I'd gotten so fond of the first printed version of *Concord* that when Ives sent me the *Emerson* transcriptions, I couldn't see any rhyme or reason to what he was doing with it. I still think the first version is the best, though with some of the revisions I gradually could see what he was driving at, and I could recognize that there were real touches of genius. In playing it I use some of the old and some of the new in varying degrees. Practically every time I take it up again, I see some of these choices in different lights, and everything changes slightly.

In order to learn *Concord*, I copied out the whole thing and made a kind of metrical interpretation of it, just as an aid to memory. I don't have the kind of musical intelligence that could swim around in this kind of prose rhythm with no bar lines at all. I had to explain to myself very clearly just where all the main first beats were—not that I was going to emphasize them like a ton of bricks—but so that I could act freely in respect to them. Ives was very nonplussed one time when I told him about my working copy of *Concord*, and having to make a metrical analysis of the whole thing in order to memorize it. I told him that, in regard to that aspect of the work, I was really Rollo.* He didn't say anything—he looked puzzled.

Concord takes a limber piano. You can't do *Hawthorne* on a piano that has much resistance. It should sort of fly through the air with no effort

---

*Rollo was the main character in a series of children's books which were popular in mid-nineteenth-century America. Rollo was a nice boy with a literal mind and little imagination. Ives often applied the name "Rollo" to those he wanted to criticize.

The first manuscript page of Emerson, *first movement of Ives's* Concord Sonata.

I. "Emerson"

The first manuscript page of the Emerson *transcriptions.*

whatever. When I started out playing *Concord,* it used to take something like forty-seven minutes, and then several years later it was down to about thirty-eight. I think it's now about thirty-six.

You play it with all kinds of memories, all working together—the aural memory of the way you know it sounds; the tactile memory or the tactile sense of interval with the fingers sort of doing their dance into the keyboard in a kind of massage of each slur; the dramatic memory of the way it unfolds; the synthetic memory of the way it coheres or the way it makes sense; and (if you're lucky) a kind of spiritual memory of just the precise approach to life in general. But that's nothing you can aim at very consciously—that's a kind of reward. But all those memories, they work together.

Part of Ives's point of view toward performance was derived from Emerson. He wanted to make music that would be good for the players' souls. It was a little bit as if he said to them, "This may hurt, but it will be good for you." Ordinarily his performers had practically carte blanche to do anything they wanted. His supposition was that if your heart was in the right place, and if you were really devoted in an idealistic way to the music itself, anything you did would have a certain validity, comparable to the validity of what he himself would do in the situation.

I once asked Mrs. Ives whether he'd consciously modeled his life on Emerson's. She thought a moment and said that she didn't think he would have thought of it that way, because he would have thought that he was a little unworthy to set out to model his life on Emerson's—he had such an exalted idea of Emerson. But of course he was very intimately and very deeply influenced by him.

Emerson came to Danbury sometime in the 1850s, and Ives's grandmother heard him lecture. The family tradition is that he stayed at the Ives house, because Ives's Uncle Joe [Joseph Moss Ives], his father's older brother, had made Emerson's acquaintance when he was in Boston in business. Emerson lectured on *The New England Reformers,* an essay that Grandmother Ives knew almost by heart. She was shocked, and somewhat put out, to find that the essay was only a point of departure in his lecture, and that the whole thing was improvised all over again on a similar outline. Ives aimed at the same spontaneity, the same freedom. Emerson was a Yankee independent—he didn't give a damn for the reactions of anybody. He said what he thought just as clearly and as well as he could. Ives set out to present his music in a somewhat similar manner. In one way Ives even went beyond Emerson, because Ives always invited his performers to take some part in the actual formulation of the music as it went along. He would imagine a performer improvising certain aspects of the texture, just as he would himself. And he was just naïve enough, in that department of his being, to presume that other people had the same talents as he had, and could do this kind of thing. Now of course for ordinary mortals it's a little beyond them. And I explained to him, that for me the only kind of freedom I could imagine in connection with a work like the *Concord Sonata* was a freedom in choosing between the various ways that had occurred to him at various times. I told him that I was the kind of pianist who had to play what he'd practiced.

Ives's adventurousness in philosophic thought went even beyond Emerson, but one of the many paradoxes in Ives was the contrast between his radically adventurous self and his churchgoing self. His churchgoing self was conservative almost to the point of what's called Fundamentalist. He was almost in a state of "Give me that old-time religion, it's good enough for me."

The more I think of it, the more I suspect that I'd probably known him before, in another life. I have no psychic memory that way, but people do come back in bunches, either somewhat analogous or somewhat opposite to the relationships that they had some time in the past. I think that any such thought would have shocked Ives rather deeply because his churchgoing self was so accepting of the position of the Christian church. I remember Edie telling me that at one time she got interested in reading some occult stuff, and when her father found out about it, he was very upset. That wasn't the kind of thing he felt a young lady should be reading.

Ives's prose writing is so much like his music, particularly the Emerson essay and the *Emerson* composition—the way his sentences spin out and are a little bit reluctant to close. They qualify the thoughts and even counterqualify them. The ideas tumble in on one another, and they make a kind of magnificent soaring ascent. But in another way, the gestures that his music makes, and the gestures that his talking made, were just like a throw or a hit in baseball. All the clauses sort of focus onto their key words, as if the syllable before the key word is like a windup, and the syllables after the key word are like a follow-through.

My first meeting with Mr. Ives was in 1937, ten years after our first correspondence. Mrs. Ives phoned to invite me for lunch. When I arrived, she met me downstairs, and I asked her if there were certain subjects I ought to keep off of, because I had heard that Mr. Ives was so easily excitable, and she said, "No. Just be yourself. Be perfectly natural, and if he gets excited, don't mind." Of course now I'm kicking myself that I didn't go each time with an agenda, and then immediately afterward write down every single word I could remember. Now I can't remember just which time was which, or even how many times there were. I saw him about three or four times each year.

He seemed inwardly very energetic. But this terrific energeticness that hounded him would leave him exhausted very soon, and then he'd have to lie down. He was rather an awesome creature, because of this very high dome of a skull and this fairly narrow long face with a kind of a Van Dyck beard, and this very intent walk, sort of like an old man meaning a great deal with each step. And then the peculiar, the energetic inflections of his talking—he talked fast and emphatically.

One time, it might have been in '38 or perhaps '39, I was saying good-bye and he was on the landing. I had gone a few steps down the stairs and was looking up at him. Suddenly he burst out with something like, "Well, maybe you think I like this kind of idleness, this doing nothing," and it went on for about three or four minutes, all about how awful it was to be consigned to this inactivity—those weren't the words he used, they would have been more direct.

Another time, he played for me—that must have been sometime in '38. I was hoping to get his critique of the way I was doing *Emerson* and I started it. And then he sort of brushed me off the piano stool and started to show me *The Anti-Abolitionist Riots*. That's so characteristic of his mind—he wasn't the least bit interested in trying to criticize my treatment of any concept of his that had been of the past. All he was interested in was showing me *further* developments of the *Concord* material, the *Emerson* derivatives—that is, *The Anti-Abolitionist Riots* and the other cadenzas from the concerto—and also some of *Hawthorne,* and some of *The Celestial Railroad,* and some of the quirks that the material had taken on since he had composed *Concord.* It was the only time I played for him or he played for me. It was a deft, flitting kind of playing, often seeming to be all over the keyboard all at once.

Some pieces, like *Concord,* Ives never did twice the same way, and he almost always resented the thought or the fancied obligation that he should put it down precisely, because he loved to improvise it. But, of course, some of the songs are very exquisitely crystallized, and they're perfectly definite. And some of the chamber music pieces are very definite. I did a lot of work on the songs for both recordings that I made with Helen Boatwright,* trying to get the notations as helpful to the performance as I could.

I got Ives very annoyed one time by supposing that his spelling didn't make all that much difference. For instance, in the song *Maple Leaves* he

---

*Recorded by Overtone Company, no. 7, 1954; CBS recording to be released in 1974.

has a descending fourth for the words "The most are gone now:" A sharp, A sharp, G sharp, F natural, F natural. Acoustically, and in the conduct of the melody, that A sharp to F natural acts as a perfect fourth, and it serves as the core of the harmonic effect as a perfect fourth. So I tried to explain to Ives that as far as I could perceive the musical beauty of that song, I thought my admiration for it was largely based on the beauty of that perfect fourth, and why didn't he spell it as a perfect fourth? He exploded, and that went on and on, largely about, "Why the hell, when something looks as if it might be 'la soh me'—why do you have to spell it 'la soh me'?"* He finally ended up with, "I'd rather DIE than change a note of that!"

But much later, after he died, it finally dawned on me that what he had in mind was a suggestion of an interval that wasn't really a perfect fourth. The A sharp would be a little higher than a B flat would be, and the F natural would be a little lower than an E sharp would be. So it was really slightly more than a perfect fourth, and for the words "The most are gone now," "gone" would be a little under what you'd expect as the interval of a fourth, and would be correspondingly expressive in that way.

Ives could be like a volcano. After I'd done the first performance of *Concord* and after Gilman's review, Gilman insisted that I do it over again. I asked Mina Hager [mezzo-soprano] if she would do a program with me, and do some of the songs, and I'd do *Concord,* and she was delighted. So I told Ives what I'd dreamed up, and he was very annoyed because if he'd had his way, practically anybody that had ever done anything for his music would have been on that program and the whole thing would have been sunk—it would have been so generous and complicated and fulsome. In that concert we were going to do the song called *The Indians.* It's originally for a small orchestra—Ives made an arrangement for piano, but he didn't include the Indian drum that's one of the central bits of the texture in the orchestra. So we arranged for the boy who was turning pages for me to play that Indian drum part, while I played the rest of the orchestra part on the piano. So I went down to a shop where they had Indian artifacts and got a beautiful drum with a thunderbird on one side, and I took it up to Ives to show him. He was delighted, and ran his fingers over it, and he found out all the different things he could do. So he kept up a kind of improvisation on this drum for about two minutes, just all sorts of jazzy rhythms— though he would have called them ragtime rhythms.

I have heard from other people, perhaps from Henry Cowell, that Ives always maintained he could play anything he'd written, and that he could

---

*Ives's spelling used here.

JOHN KIRKPATRICK

Piano Recital

TOWN HALL
113 West 43rd Street

FRIDAY EVENING AT 8:30
JANUARY 20th

Sonata in C major, Op. 53 · BEETHOVEN

I. allegro con brio
II. Introduzione, adagio molto
Rondo, allegretto moderato—prestissimo

Concord, Mass., 1840-60 CHARLES E. IVES

SECOND PIANOFORTE SONATA (1911-15)
("an attempt to present one person's impression of the spirit of transcendentalism that is associated in the minds of many with Concord, Mass., of over a half century ago")

I. **Emerson** ("a composite picture or impression")

II. **Hawthorne** (an "extended fragment" reflecting "some of his wilder, fantastical adventures into the half-childlike, half-fairylike phantasmal realms")

III. **The Alcotts** ("a sketch")

IV. **Thoreau** ("an autumn day of Indian summer at Walden")

FIRST PERFORMANCE

STEINWAY PIANO

Tickets: Box seats $2.75, Orchestra $2.20, $1.65, $1.10, Balcony $.83
Tax included   At Box Office

Management RICHARD COPLEY, Steinway Bldg., 113 West 57th St., New York, N. Y.

The program from John Kirkpatrick's first complete performance of the Concord Sonata,
Town Hall, January 20, 1939.

MUSIC

By LAWRENCE GILMAN

A Masterpiece of American Music Heard Here for the First Time

John Kirkpatrick

Player of Charles E. Ives's "Concord Sonata"

Piano recital by John Kirkpatrick, at Town Hall, Friday evening, January 20.

PROGRAM

1. Sonata in C major, Op. 53...Beethoven
   I. Allegro con brio
   II. Introduzione, adagio molto
      Rondo, allegretto moderato—prestissimo
2. "Concord, Mass., 1840-'60"
   Charles E. Ives
   (First complete performance in New York City)

MUSIC by an unexampled creative artist of our day, probably the most original and extraordinary of American composers, yielded the outstanding experience of Mr. John Kirkpatrick's piano recital last evening at Town Hall.

The music in question was written by Charles E. Ives, a New Englander, now dwelling in New York, whose name means nothing whatever to most music-lovers and musicians—although that fact is almost certainly of small interest to the individual in question. For Mr. Ives is one of those exceptional artists whose indifference to réclame is as genuine as it is fantastic and unbelievable.

* * *

Charles Ives is sixty-four years old, and for nearly half a century he has been experimenting with musical sounds, and writing them down on Shuffle'; or something else in the Wonderbook—not something that happens, but the way some-

The review of Kirkpatrick's performance by Lawrence Gilman, January 21, 1939.

hear everything he wrote in his imagination, and I think that's true. He had that kind of all-encompassing mind that could be aware of a whole multiplicity of things, all spread around in apparent disorder, but he could be aware of them in exactly the kind of relations they had, spatially and logically, without having them grouped into convenient groupings.

He was such a paradoxical person in many ways, and one of the most amazing paradoxes was the extent to which he was a pacifist and the extent to which he was temperamentally an old fighter. He would get sort of fighting-furious about pacifism. Another paradox was the kind of gregariousness that made him a successful insurance man, and the kind of pathological shyness that kept him so relatively solitary as a musician. He really could be pathologically shy. I suppose those inner pulls must have been just as devastating as anything to the cohesion of his health.

Ives's first heart attack was in 1918, and he didn't actually retire from business until 1930. He'd been living this double life ever since '98. Harmony told me that shortly after they moved into the 74th Street house, he came downstairs one day and with tears in his eyes said that he couldn't seem to compose any more—nothing would go well, nothing sounded right. This was in '26. From '98 to '26 would be twenty-eight years of that double life. And even before that, I suppose, when he was in college, he probably skimped on sleep to write things down at night. His ill health was a combination of heart condition, diabetes, extreme nervous excitability, and some kind of palsy. His hand didn't shake constantly, but you can see from his snaketracks how hard it must have been to write. He had cataracts which gradually accumulated and they were operated on in '37, successfully.

One picture I have of him is the growing into a kind of jiggity old age, because his sense of humor always remained very much as it was at Yale— that is, turn of the century puns. I remember when we first brought my son David to see him, when David was just a little shaver, about two and a half. We brought him to the house at West Redding, and Charlie came out and he looked at David and said, "Well, how's Arthur?—Our thermometer." Of course David was completely nonplussed and actually a little frightened. But then Charlie sort of got his confidence, and took him down to show him the little pond. Hope* and I still vividly remember that picture of David with his little hand reaching up to Charlie's, and Charlie walking with his slightly jaunty gait, and these two little paddling feet going along beside him.

There are puns in the music too. But more often his musical sense of

---

*Hope Miller Kirkpatrick collaborated with John Kirkpatrick in performing some Ives songs early in their married life, between 1940 and 1944.

humor is like an awareness of rhythmic incongruity—of two things going on at the same time, each of which would throw the other into a funny incongruous light. There are lots of musical jokes in the take-offs, and in pieces like *The See'r* and *1, 2, 3*. It's too bad that some of the take-offs are lost—like the *Mike Donlin-Johnny Evers* of which we have only one of the two pages.

I never called him Charlie. I didn't get to know him quite that well, and I wasn't an old friend of the family. Henry Cowell apparently got calling him Charlie, at one time. It was very subtly let be known to Henry that Charlie was a little uncertain about whether he liked it or not. After Ives died, I did call his wife Harmony, and I got the impression after a few years that she wasn't sure that she liked it. They were very, very old-fashioned.

Mrs. Ives was a very beautiful woman, who had the reputation of being the most beautiful girl in Hartford. When Lawrence Gilman wrote and asked Ives if he could borrow a copy of *Concord*, when he was going to review the performance, Mrs. Ives wrote him back as Harmony Twichell Ives. When I met Gilman afterwards, he said it was such a surprise—"So that was what became of Harmony Twichell!"—because he'd had quite a crush on her when he was a boy in Hartford at school.

And Edie was such a nice person. There was something a little elfin about her—she had that kind of an imagination. It was a tragedy to me, her going when she did, because I'd been hoping to ask her a lot more about Charlie. She was forty-two.

Ives talked about his father as a personality. He lived, or that side of him lived, almost in a state of Chinese ancestor worship. He talked of his father as if he were still living, as if he were still a member of the household—it was that immediate. He spoke with great reverence and with great intellectual interest in his father's curiosity about everything. As he says in the *Memos*, "Parker was a famous musician and a composer and Father wasn't a famous musician nor a composer, but I would say, of the two, Father was by far the greater man." When Harmony was telling me all kinds of things about the older generations, she suddenly stopped and said, "Now you must remember, I never knew any of these people. But the amount I can tell you about them is just a gauge of how much he talked about them."

Ives died in May 1954. In June, as soon as we got down from Ithaca, I asked Harmony if it would be a help if I started sorting and listing the manuscripts. She was most grateful, and told me that she had dreaded going into that room—she knew the disorder. When Ives was alive, I had wanted to list them. And I wasn't alone—Benny Herrmann asked him, Nicolas Slonimsky asked him, John Becker asked him, Henry Cowell asked him—and I think to all of us he probably said the same thing that he said to me: "Well, when I feel better I'll get around to it." Of course, he never did—and if he had gotten around to it, that wouldn't have been at all up his alley. It was my privilege to sort those manuscripts after he had gone, and after he was no longer there to ask questions to—and my only consolation is that, if I had started it while he was alive, he probably would have torn up a great deal of it, particularly the things of his boyhood.

While I was sorting, every now and then Harmony would come out to the barn with some little fragment in her hand that had shown up somewhere in the house, but it was mostly all in the barn, in no kind of order at all. In each drawer (and there were ten) was a pile of manuscripts lying flat. There was every evidence that he'd rummaged for things in an unsystematic way, pulling out a batch from below and leafing through it and then that became the top layer—and then pulling out another batch from below and that would become the top again, and the whole thing had been shuffled and reshuffled many times, so that different leaves of manuscripts would show up at different levels of different drawers.

There's every evidence that he couldn't find some of his music sketches. For instance, he told me of a patch that was an improvement of a certain measure in the *Second Violin Sonata,* but he never could find it. After he died, when a whole trunk of manuscripts came up from New York, I went through them and sorted them—and then I found a big piece of wrapping paper on the bottom of the trunk. And just to be thorough, I picked up the piece of wrapping paper, and under it was a little fragment of music paper. That was the patch.

At first I made a rough classification just as quickly as I could, because Helen Boatwright and I were going to make that record for Dick Burns for *Overtone,* and I wanted desperately to see if there wasn't some manuscript source for *Evening.* There's one bass note in *Evening* that could be either a low E or a low G, and both of them sound perfectly plausible. The E sounds more natural, the G sounds more interesting. No manuscript turned up, and probably no one will ever know the truth.

One can't have known Charlie without being influenced. It's the most interesting music that I know of in the twentieth century, and the most stimulating to one's own thoughts. One thing that I tell my piano students in reference to people like Beethoven, for instance, is that you trace the steps of greatness and your own soul grows. I've always felt that way with my own acquaintance with Ives's music. Ives is like a reminder of values that are eternal. He completely transcends his period, and more, he brings those who are acquainted with his music back to a reverence for the awareness of that which is eternal.

INDEX

(Interviews are indicated by italicized page numbers.)